LIFE OF
DAVID LLOYD GEORGE

VOL. II

Photograph by Thomason

Mᵣˢ D. Lloyd George
and her daughter Megan.

LIFE OF
DAVID LLOYD GEORGE

BY

HERBERT DU PARCQ, M.A., B.C.L.

OF THE MIDDLE TEMPLE, BARRISTER-AT-LAW.

VOLUME II

LONDON

CAXTON PUBLISHING COMPANY, LIMITED

CLUN HOUSE, SURREY STREET, W.C.

PREFATORY NOTE TO THE SECOND VOLUME

THE author desires to acknowledge the courtesy of the editors of " The Manchester Guardian," " The Daily Mail," " The Lincolnshire Leader," and " The Oxford Chronicle," who have assisted him by granting permission to quote from articles and reports in their papers. He is similarly indebted to Messrs. Hodder & Stoughton and to the publishers of " Hansard's Parliamentary Debates."

H. DU P.

CONTENTS

CHAPTER I

I

II

III

IV

CHAPTER II

I

CHAPTER V

I

II

III

CHAPTER VI

I

II

III

CHAPTER VII

I

II

III

CHAPTER VIII

I

II

III

APPENDIX

I

II

III

LIST OF ILLUSTRATIONS

CHRONOLOGICAL TABLE

VOL. II

1899.

May 1.—Mr. Lloyd George appointed a member of Select Committee on Old Age Pensions.

September.—Mr. Lloyd George returns from Canada.

October 11.—War with Transvaal begins.

October 27.—Speech on South Africa, House of Commons.

November 27.—Speech at Carmarthen.

1900.

January 29.—Speech on the war at Oxford.

February 6.—On Lord Edmond Fitzmaurice's amendment to the Address.

March 6.—Peace meeting at Glasgow (with Mr. Cronwright-Schreiner).

March 26–29.—N.L.F. meetings at Nottingham.

April 11.—Mobbed at Bangor.

April 28.—Speech at Carnarvon.

May 8.—On " breach of privilege " motion (House of Commons).

July 5.—Liskeard meeting broken up.

July 25.—On Mr. Chamberlain (House of Commons).

September 15.—At Nevin.

September 25.—Dissolution of Parliament.

September 26.—At Conway.

October 6.—Polling day, Carnarvon Boroughs.

Mr. Lloyd George's majority over Colonel Platt, 296

November.—Defends Penrhyn strikers, Bangor Petty Sessions.

December 10.—Speech in debate on Address.

1901.

February 18.—Speech on the War, House of Commons.

June 17.—Moves adjournment of the House to call attention to the condition of the Concentration Camps.

June 19.—" Pro-Boer " meeting at the Queen's Hall.

July 4.—Speech on War Loan Bill.

July 9.—Party meeting at Reform Club.

October–November.—Peace meetings in Wales (see p. 264).

October 23.—At Pwllheli on the war.

October 31.—Speech at Edinburgh.

November 7.—At Leigh (Lancs.).

December 4.—N.L.F. at Derby.

December 16.—Lord Rosebery at Chesterfield.

December 18.—Meeting at Birmingham broken up.

Rioting in the streets.

1902.

January 6.—Peace meeting at Bristol.

January 13.—London Liberal Federation meeting.

January 21.—Speech on Mr. Cawley's amendment to the Address.

February 14–15.—N.L.F. at Leicester.

March 20.—Speech in the House on the war.

March 24.—Education Bill introduced.

April 22.—Birth of Megan Arvon George.

May 8.—Speech on Second Reading of Education Bill (See App. I.).

June 10.—Queen's Hall meeting to condemn the Education Bill.

July 9.—Speech in the House on Passive Resistance.

October 13.—Letter to the " Times " on Education compromise.

November 11.—On Mr. Chamberlain in the House of Commons.

November 20.—End of Committee stage, Education Bill.

December 2.—Third Reading of the Education Bill.

December 12.—Speech on Education at Lincoln (See App. II.).

1903.

January 17.—Address to the people of Wales (See App. III.).

January.—Convention at Cardiff.

February 20.—Interview in the "Echo."

May.—Negotiations for " Concordat " on Education.

July 25.—At Altrincham on Roman Catholicism.

September 24.—Welsh Liberal Conference at Bangor.

1904.

January 5.—Speech at Carnarvon.

March.—Welsh County Council Elections.

March 14.—Speech on Education Act, House of Commons.

April 5.—Conference of Welsh Education authorities.

April 26.—Education (Local Authority Default) Bill introduced.

July 15.—Second Reading of Education (Local Authority Default) Bill.

August 5.—Committee stage.
Mr. Asquith leads the Opposition out of the House.

September 14.—Conference of Welsh County Councils at Shrewsbury.

October 6.—Second National Convention at Cardiff.

October 18.—Mr. Lloyd George and Mr. Winston Churchill at Carnarvon.

LIFE OF
DAVID LLOYD GEORGE

CHAPTER I

I

Conservatives in Khaki—Imperialists and " Little Englanders "—" A difference in tempera
ment "—The Old Age Pensions Committee—End of the Canadian holiday—" C.-B,"—
Mr. Chamberlain and Sir Edward Clarke—Speeches in the House and at Carmarthen—
The bias of Nationalism.

NOTHING is more difficult than to take a really long-
sighted view of contemporary politics, just as nothing
is more easy than to be wise after the event. When,
in 1900, Mr. Chamberlain asked the nation for a vote
of confidence in the middle of a great war, nobody, I think, doubted
his sagacity, although many questioned his motives. The very
ground on which the plan was attacked was a tribute, the cynical
might say, to its wisdom. It was alleged against the Colonial
Secretary that he wantonly seized an opportunity for a wholly
unnecessary General Election at a time when it was certain that
the Government would be returned with an undiminished majority.
And yet that Khaki Election was the first real step towards the
Liberal triumph of 1906. The nation, flushed though it was with
the excitement of the war, was no less tired of the Tory Government. Men voted for an expeditious ending of the war who
expressly abstained from supporting Tory measures. The carrying out of the mandate did not raise the War Office in the popular
estimation. But it was not disgust at the incompetence, real
or imagined, of individual Ministers, or hatred of later developments of the Ministry's South African policy, or even a conservative distrust of the economic new Jerusalem with which Mr.

Chamberlain tried to allure the populace, that brought the Unionist Administration to an ignominious end. These things were all factors, no doubt, in the great rout of 1906. But its main cause was the obstinate determination of the Government to act as if it were the idol of a people which in fact only tolerated it. The General Election of 1906 was in the truest and most literal sense a Nemesis, and Mr. Chamberlain's coup in 1900 made such a Nemesis almost a certainty.

For the present, however, we must consider facts as they appeared in 1899 and the following years of the war, and Liberal politicians had little enough time then to indulge in speculations, of whatever kind, as to the future, and still less encouragement to take a hopeful view for their party. The war seemed to come like a devastating flood in which publicists who would have sought to avert it were soon impotently struggling. The nation set forth upon its martial enterprise rather in the spirit in which some of its units start out upon a Bank Holiday excursion, with noisy and hilarious confidence. Its most widely read papers had proclaimed first that there would be no war if England stood firm, then that the war would be speedily over : " A two months' limit from the time the first shot is fired in open conflict," was one of the sanguine prophecies.[1] The South African adventure was to be a short triumphal march, in the course of which an audacious foeman would be taught a sharp lesson at the cost of hardly any bloodshed. Men talked almost as if the annual Army manœuvres were going to be carried out, more realistically and on a somewhat more expensive scale than is usual, in the Transvaal instead of at home.

It is unnecessary to discuss here the problem of the rights and wrongs of the war. Readers whom the subject attracts will find it dealt with ably and from varying aspects by writers, some of whom have marshalled the evidence. The books upon the subject by Sir E. T. Cook and Mr. J. A. Hobson, for instance, are good statements, written from the opposite poles of opinion, of a case about which honourable men have been content honestly to differ. The late Justin McCarthy has treated the subject dispassionately, if not with complete neutrality, in the last volume of his " History of our own Times." This much may be said here, that no reasonably unbiassed person can study the question and not see that there was a strong case to be pleaded, before the outbreak of the war, against both its necessity and its desirability, and that, strong as the case for war may have been, many of the arguments, and

---

[1] " Rhodesia," quoted in the " Daily Mail," September 25, 1899.

almost all the prophecies, of its supporters were falsified by time and experience.

This other obvious reflection may be made—that nobody who took it upon himself to advocate the cause of peace at a moment when the nation was eager for arms, or to criticise the conduct and the aims of the war when it was being waged with a long sequence of "regrettable incidents," can have been actuated by a desire for popularity. The prescience of those who had prophesied a long and arduous campaign was not counted to them for a virtue. From the days of Cassandra, nobody has ever gained popularity by being able truthfully to say " I told you so."

It was certainly no desire of popularity that brought the member for the Carnarvon Boroughs into the field as an active and aggressive critic of the Government's South African policy. I have suggested earlier in this history that it is impossible, with any regard to this chapter in his life, to believe that his instincts are those of the demagogue, who, though he may sometimes champion an unpopular cause, drops it fast enough when the knowledge of its unpopularity is forced upon him. Some of those who at a later stage in Mr. Lloyd George's career attacked him for inflaming popular prejudices would have had a better title to do so if they had ever made an attempt to restrain the angry mobs of respectable citizens whom a martial intoxication had temporarily disqualified for the functions of citizenship, for, while there was a strong case for the war, it is very certain that those who thirsted for the blood of Mr. Lloyd George and the " pro-Boers " did not know what that case was. It seems, however, to have been adopted as a rule by some politicians that when their opponent is popular, he is a demagogue, and that when he is unpopular, he is the convicted enemy of his country.

The taunt that some critics of British enterprise or aggression are " friends of every country but their own," or, to use the politer phrase, are swayed by a " bias of anti-patriotism," is not perhaps devoid of truth. There are men who will condone in strangers faults which shock them in their own kin. The modern scoffer has suggested that the tables of consanguinity are based upon a natural aversion, and the tie of country, like that of family, may sometimes be an irksome bond. Mr. Lloyd George never had the acidity of temperament which afflicts this soured school. Nor was he by temperament a " little Englander " according to any intelligible construction of the term. At a time when the war had not yet made decision necessary upon a concrete set of facts, he had not taken the line of opposing all expansion of territory and all war in the abstract. A speech which he de-

livered in January 1899 at Ardwick, East Manchester, shows how
he regarded the differences among Liberal politicians upon questions of foreign policy.   Its allusions to the growing differences
between the imperially minded section of the Liberal party and
that represented by Sir William Harcourt and Mr. Morley show
that he was at any rate not a bigoted adherent of the latter.

Unfortunately [he said], Sir William Harcourt has thought it necessary
to resign the leadership of the party in the House of Commons,[1] and Mr.
Morley has followed him.   We must all regret it.   No party ever had finer
leaders. . . . It must be admitted that they are men of deep convictions,
even although they have allowed their convictions to run into oversensitive-
ness, as I think they have.   It is true that there are differences of opinion
among Liberals. . . . What is true of the Liberal party is equally true of
the Tory party.   I must say, after reading Mr. Morley's speech, that I
agree with what he said about Fashoda.[2]   It is a great misfortune that we
should have indulged in so much offensive bluster in our attitude towards
France—the only really democratic country on the continent of Europe.
It would have been a calamity to civilisation and to human progress if we
had fought France, and particularly at this moment, when she is engaged
in a deadly struggle with the worst and most corrupt and most reactionary
force that ever assailed a democratic community.   France is engaged in
a very noble struggle, and at the present moment there seems to me to be
every symptom that she will emerge from it in a way that will do credit
to that great nation, and will be a material advancement of the cause of
human progress.   It seems to me to be cruel to select that particular moment
to reinforce all the worst elements in the French community, by taking
France by the throat, and, by blustering and browbeating her, to encourage
all the forces of militarism in that country.   It might have ended in a great
disaster to France, to this country, and to the cause of humanity.

He went on to say that, while he agreed, and believed that
the majority of Liberals agreed, with Mr. Morley, he could not
accept it as a logical conclusion from those premises that Mr.
Morley should "resign his trust as one of the Liberal leaders."
Mr. Morley had assumed in his speech that France must surrender
Fashoda, and that was exactly the assumption made by Lord
Rosebery, Sir Edward Grey, Mr. Asquith, and other Liberal
leaders.   All were agreed that England could not surrender the
Soudan, where so much blood and treasure had been expended,
and a rotten despotism overthrown.

[1] The correspondence between Sir William Harcourt and Mr. Morley which
announced the former's resignation will be found in the London newspapers of
December 14, 1898.
[2] The Fashoda incident terminated in October 1898.   See, for a discussion of it,
McCarthy's " History of our own Times," Vol. VI., Ch. vi.

The real difference is a difference in temperament and disposition, in the way questions are approached. . . . Mr. Morley would not surrender any portion of our Empire : he would make the best of what we have got, and he would defend our rights at all costs. That is what all the other Liberal leaders would do. He admitted that under certain conditions expansion is inevitable. Some men are more combative in their disposition : others are more cautious or probably more timid. No one can go to the extent of saying that all pugnacious men must be driven out of the Liberal party, or that all the timid men must resign. We must have men of every disposition in the party if we are going to make it a strong party.

The real test of Liberalism, he said, was not its readiness to fight, but the object for which it fought. If it was desired that this country should enter upon a course of militarism and of fighting our neighbours for our own aggrandisement and for theft and plunder, that was a course of action which the Liberal party at all costs should fight, either in or out of its own ranks.

If, on the other hand, it is simply a question of defending such possessions as we have already got, and which, I believe, we administer well, or if it is some great question of principle, some question of the protection of the weak and oppressed, then we should all unite in regard to it. Mr. Morley said he did not quite believe in a party that comes down to the House in the broad-brimmed hat of a Quaker one day, and the next in the panoply of a Crusader. But Mr. Morley must know that we never had better fighters in England than the old broad-brimmed Puritans. In the days of Elizabeth, the Puritans were the best fighters, but they fought for a noble and a just cause—the cause of religious and civil freedom, whether in England or abroad. And as long as there is some great cause of that kind to fight for, we ought to be as ready to fight for it now as we were three hundred years ago.

Enough has been quoted to show that Mr. Lloyd George did not face the problem of the Transvaal war with the prejudices of a " peace at any price " man. I find this fact recognised after the war had begun by a paper which was certainly not predisposed in his favour.

" It is generally assumed," said the " Western Mail " on April 6, 1900, " that Mr. Lloyd George is not only a pro-Boer but a pronounced Little Englander. This is far from being the case. As a matter of fact, Mr. Lloyd George is of the school of Lord Rosebery on all other topics except the South African one. Even on this subject he is at one with the objects of the Government, believing that the peace and prosperity of South Africa depend upon British rule being supreme in that part of the world. This object he believes would have been attained by pacific methods. The fact that the Government are attaining it by more forcible methods has impelled him for the time being to go into the camp of the enemy."

This paragraph must not be regarded as verbally inspired, but it was accurate at any rate to this extent, that Mr. Lloyd George has never been among those who think that war is never justified or that Great Britain can afford to abdicate her position among the nations.

Honesty demanded that he should apply to the war against the Transvaal the test which he had formulated in the speech already quoted. Were we fighting to defend our possessions, or for some great question of principle, or to protect the weak and oppressed ? He could not bring himself to believe that, judged by this criterion, the war was either inevitable or just. He had no love for the reactionary policy of President Kruger, but he believed that the progressive forces among the burghers of the Transvaal would, if left to themselves, give effect within a reasonable time to the legitimate aspirations of the Uitlanders. He and those who thought with him never admitted that the war was "inevitable." Most of them thought, as Mr. Lloyd George told an interviewer at the beginning of 1902,[1] that Kruger was "a pig-headed, stubborn old Tory." Their sympathies were with "the young Liberal Party of the Transvaal"—with Botha and Joubert, with Schalk-Burger and Delarey. They viewed with suspicion the eagerness of our Government, which showed no zeal for reform at home, to hasten by an appeal to the sword the extension of the franchise in a distant continent.

Two other considerations, as will be seen, weighed heavily with him. The first was the cause of nationality. The man who rejoiced at every sign of the new birth of a national spirit in Wales was not likely to welcome the extinction of another small nation. The second was the knowledge that war exhausts the resources even of a conquering Empire, and exhausts them at the cost of the poorest of her own subjects.

" If we go to war with the Transvaal there will be no pensions. They are fools to quarrel with the Boers. It will ultimately be unpopular, as it is not only essentially an unjust quarrel, but, what is more from the point of view of the man in the street, an unprofitable one. There is neither gain nor glory in it at all adequate to the sacrifices."

These words, taken from a letter he wrote to his brother in the summer of 1899, show with what apprehension he heard the first rumours of a possible war in the Transvaal. The letter was written just after he had been appointed a member of the Select Committee to report upon the question of Old Age Pensions. The

See the " Pall Mall Gazette," January 3, 1902.

Committee was appointed on May 1.[1] Mr. Lloyd George recognised from the first, at a time when he was almost alone in his opinion, that a war in South Africa would be a long and costly undertaking, and that if once the nation embarked upon it, discussion of any scheme for pensioning the aged poor would become a mockery for many years to come. This fear did not prevent him from throwing himself wholeheartedly into the work of the Committee. In June he had a long interview on the subject with Mr. Chamberlain, who treated him with great friendliness and amiability, was much struck by a suggestion he made to meet one of the difficulties of the problem, and invited him to come and talk over the subject whenever he liked. That interview seems to have laid the foundation of a belief in Mr. Chamberlain's sincerity as a social reformer which even the sharp animosities engendered by the war never shook.

The Committee reported in favour of the grant of a pension to every British subject with an income of less than ten shillings a week (with certain exceptions in the case of those who had been convicted or had received poor relief) who " had endeavoured to the best of his ability, by his industry, or by the exercise of reasonable providence, to make provision for himself and those immediately dependent on him," on his attaining the age of sixty-five. A committee of the Guardians was to act as the pension authority in each district, and the amount of the pensions was to vary between 5s. and 7s. a week, according to the cost of living in the district. The Committee had not the time nor the means at its disposal to arrive at any estimate of the cost of such a scheme, which they left for the consideration of experts. This much at least was achieved—that a Committee in which Unionists and Conservatives were of course in a majority had put on record its approval of a fairly advanced scheme of pensions. In the final division upon the report Mr. Lloyd George voted with the majority. Only four members (two Liberals, a Conservative, and a Liberal Unionist) voted against it.

But men's eyes were by then turning away from the empty cupboards of the poor to the voteless miners (and the rich mines) of the Transvaal. Mr. Lloyd George, as we have seen, was travelling in Canada in the early autumn, and it was there that the bad news of impending hostilities reached him. He hastened to

[1] It was constituted as follows : Mr. Anstruther, Mr. Chaplin, Mr. Cripps, Mr. Davitt, Lord Edmond Fitzmaurice. Sir Fortescue Flannery, Sir Walter Foster, Mr. Hedderwick, Mr. Samuel Hoare, Mr. Lionel Holland, Mr. Lecky, Mr. Llewellyn, Mr. Lloyd George, Mr. A. K. Loyd, Sir James Rankin, Mr. William Redmond, and Mr. Woods.

return, leaving abruptly a country whose vast resources and marvellous scenery clearly made a great impression upon him. I quote two of his letters :

September 18, 1899. Passed yesterday through scenery that defies description for grandeur and sublimity. Such scenes as you only see in dreams are witnessed—at least the last five hours of it—by brilliant moonlight, which added to its impressiveness and weirdness. Uncanny is the word for a good deal of it. Fancy crossing a bridge and looking down into a ravine seven hundred feet below you—winding along ledges of rock with a dark valley a thousand feet beneath you, and a river meandering along like a silver thread. Think of passing beneath two mountains—one of them a sheer precipice shooting up a mile and a half from the railway, and the other no less precipitous and almost as high. Gorges—valleys—ravines —snow-cloaked mountains—glaciers.

British Columbia, September 18, 1899.—The news from the Transvaal threatens to alter my arrangements. War means the summoning of Parliament : the former now seems inevitable. The prospect oppresses me with a deep sense of horror. If I have the courage, I shall protest with all the vehemence at my command against the outrage which is perpetrated in the name of human freedom. I may be able to decide, after seeing tonight's bulletins when they arrive, what to do. I am rather anxious to be on the spot, and as far as the holiday is concerned, I feel I have had enough. I am set up as I have not been for years, and now I want to get to work.
Bulletins to hand. Transvaal bad.

He hurried back to England. On October 11 a state of war began with the Transvaal, and on the 16th he wrote as follows in a hurried note to his brother :

Not seen any one as to Transvaal. A letter awaiting me from the new Editor of the " Speaker." He has been staying with Morley at Hawarden, and at his request wrote me for my opinion what should be done on opening of Parliament. Shall not reply until I have time to reflect deeply over new situation created by Boer advance. At present am rather inclined to agree with " Chronicle " than with Labby over that. Boers have invaded our territories, and until they are driven back, Government entitled to money to equip forces to defend our possessions. In my opinion the way these poor hunted burghers have been driven in self-defence to forestall us aggravates our crime—there is something diabolical in its malignity.

On the 17th Parliament was opened. Sir Henry Campbell-Bannerman made a speech in which, while promising that he would place no obstacle in the way of the granting of supplies, he condemned the manner in which the apostle of the new diplomacy had conducted negotiations. Here is Mr. Lloyd George's comment upon it :

Bannerman did very well under most trying conditions. Our party is divided on the question, and his *métier* as leader is to keep us together. That is what he was elected for. You can see that he is opposed to the policy of the Government that made war inevitable.

On the 19th Mr. Chamberlain delivered himself of a long apologia. He was unfortunate in having to face a criticism delivered from his own side of the House by the greatest lawyer in the House of Commons. " Been listening to Chamberlain and Sir Edward Clarke," Mr. Lloyd George writes. " Former an inadequate performance, latter a powerful attack on position of Government."

He expressed his own views on the war for the first time in the House on the 27th. His speech was the last delivered before the prorogation, and he had not intended to speak " until next Session, when all would be sick of the war." But many of the Radicals insisted on his saying a final word. Two sentences from his speech will show the line of his attack :

The fact is that the war has been forced on us by a Government which has divided three millions of money amongst its own supporters by a measure carried by a Chamber composed of landlords, who benefit to the tune of hundreds of thousands of pounds a year—a Chamber for which no native-born British subject has the right to vote. That is the Government and the Chamber which is spending millions of money in order to enforce a pure and honest administration in the Transvaal.

The hitherto unreported comment of a Tory M.P. to a Press representative may perhaps serve to show how the speech was regarded on the Ministerial benches : " I don't agree with him, but he is a clever little devil, and he will be heard of in the future. But," added this honourable member, " it was very mischievous." The Radical members, on their side, were delighted at the success of a speech which, it was said, had " made Joe visibly writhe."

Indications were very soon forthcoming from the Carnarvon Boroughs that the line their member was taking was not popular there. In a letter dated November 1, 1899, Mr. Lloyd George refers to an interview with a prominent local supporter :

—— has been here. Had a long conversation. He is quite sound on the Transvaal question, but he says he is alone amongst Pwllheli people. This is a pity. I must go down there and say a word to them, but do as they will, I shall continue to protest, even if they turn me out.

Later in the month he made his first public speech in Wales after the outbreak of hostilities, at the Guildhall, Carmarthen, before an audience which was far from being wholly friendly. He had come to the conclusion, he told his hearers, that he would be recreant before God and man if at this first opportunity he did not enter a protest against what he considered to be an infamy. " And here I do it to-night," he said, " even if I leave Carmarthen to-morrow without a friend."

One may find in this speech, as in the letters already quoted, an echo of a note in his diary written nearly fifteen years before, when he had welcomed the certainty of peace, because " war would put an end to Local Option, Disestablishment, and the like for another six years." [1] He quoted Milton's saying that " war breeds war," and predicted that when the war was over men would not sit down to begin again the work of social reform which it had interrupted, but would raise an outcry for a bigger army, more modern artillery, and speedier transports. Those present would be old men before they saw the battle resumed for human liberty.

There was not a lyddite shell which burst on the African hills that did not carry away an Old Age Pension. What is the satisfaction ? Oh, it killed two hundred Boers—fathers of families, sons of mothers, who wept for them. Are you satisfied to give your old age pensions for that ? We have lost, killed and wounded and prisoners, five times as many men as Sir George Colley lost at Majuba. That is the revenge of Majuba. Providence works in curious ways.

He described Mr. Chamberlain's diplomacy in the negotiations which had preceded the war, and said that Kruger had been treated unfairly.

And yet the Government goes with a smug face to the Conference at the Hague, and says, "It is time to inaugurate the blessed reign of arbitration." Oh, yes. As far as Russia, Germany, and France are concerned, with their huge armaments—Russia especially—the Government want arbitration; but they want to fight a little country, the total of whose population is less than that of Carmarthenshire. The British Empire against Carmarthenshire !

Perhaps the last sentence reveals the deepest source of the hostility which the war aroused in him. His country, far from " protecting the weak and the oppressed," seemed to him to be using her giant's strength in order to stifle a small nation in the interests of her own aggrandisement. Could he have been convinced that we indeed " sought no territory and sought no gold-fields " and that the " helots " of the Rand were a weak and

[1] See Vol. I., p. 45.

much-wronged body of men, his verdict upon the war would have been very different. Believing as he did that the spectacle provided by South Africa was that of a small nation cherishing its freedom and struggling for its independence, he could take no other course than to oppose the war. From his earliest days he had exalted nationalism into a supreme ideal. The sentiment of patriotism is never more intense than when the object of its devotion is small and overshadowed by rivals, and no intensely patriotic man can despise in others sentiments which are most sacred to himself. A patriotic Welshman could sympathise to the full with the aspirations of the patriotic Transvaal burgher: it was less easy for him to feel any delight in a conquest which was to extend his country's territory at the cost of blotting out the word " Free " upon the map of South Africa.

II

A speech at Oxford—Lord Edmond Fitzmaurice's amendment—Mr. Cronwright-Schreiner—
Glasgow : a noisy meeting—Mr. Lloyd George mobbed at Bangor.

Perhaps his finest statement of his position upon the war is contained in a speech which he delivered to the members of the Palmerston Club at Oxford at the end of January 1900. By this time Mr. Chamberlain had done much to remove the reproach of the Carmarthen speech that the Government, relentless in its dealings with a little country, was subservient to the greater Powers. He had, in May, made the notorious speech in which he quoted with regard to Russia the proverb that " who sups with the devil must have a long spoon," and at the end of November he founded upon the scurrility of some French comic artists a general exhortation to the French nation to " mend their manners." It is interesting, in view of later developments of Imperialism, to observe that in the same speech he made definite advances, not only to the United States, but to Germany.

The Palmerston Club which Mr. Lloyd George now addressed upon the new diplomacy and the new Imperialism is, with its friendly rival the Russell Club, joint custodian of Liberalism among the undergraduates of the University. It may be noted as one of the minor coincidences of history that, twenty-two years before almost to a day (on January 30, 1878), Mr. Gladstone had been the guest of the same club, and had made a special allusion in his speeches to the remarks of a Liberal undergraduate, Mr. Milner, who had come to play a sufficiently prominent part in Imperial expansion. Sir E. T. Cook has quoted in his book on the war Mr. Gladstone's acquiescence in the sentiments of Mr. Milner, "who argued that it was unwise to proclaim to the world that on no occasion were they disposed to draw the sword." [1] That was a sentiment with which, had it been quoted to Mr. Lloyd George after the lapse of twenty-two years, he would certainly not have disagreed. But his immediate purpose was to combat the "Disraelian Imperialism" which Lord Rosebery and other Liberals had been preaching.

The country is suffering [he said] from an overdose of Imperialism, and the greatest service the Liberal party can render to it is to inculcate the sound, healthy ideas of Fox, Cobden, Bright, and Gladstone. The situation is undoubtedly grave, although in my opinion the immediate danger is exaggerated. There are some leading Unionist statesmen who seem to think that the existence of the Empire is at stake in this war. I do not take so gloomy a view of the prospect. The new Imperialist seems to be a somewhat hysterical person, alternating between the neurotic exaltation of Fashoda and Omdurman on the one hand, and the equally morbid depression of the "Black Week" on the other. The life of the Empire is no more at stake in this war than it was in the conflict with our American colonies. One of Mr. Chamberlain's speeches does more to jeopardise the Empire than a score of Nicholson's Neks, and this war will do us an infinitude of good if it teaches us to realise the fatuity of such utterances and the policy which they proclaim.

We are rather fortunate in one respect—that the follies of aggressive Imperialism, which has dominated our statesmanship for the last few years, have been brought home to us in a war with a small community in South Africa, rather than in a struggle with a great European empire. George Meredith said in one of his books : "The fates are Jews with us when they delay the punishment." That shrewd observation ought to afford us some consolation in the present crisis. There is much to be said for Lord Rosebery's theory that this war may be a blessing in disguise.

The fate of the Empire depends not so much on the war, as on the way we profit by its real lessons. It is the function of the Liberal party to see that while none of those lessons are lost, due weight shall be given to the more important of them. Still, the situation at the best is undoubtedly a serious one, and the slightest reflection upon the set of circumstances which led up to it will convince any man that it was all the outcome of aggressive Imperialism. We have heard a good deal of the inevitableness of the war and of the reverses which followed. I agree that the war and its disasters were both the inevitable consequences of our policy. The military position of the war I need not dwell upon. Every detail of it must be painfully in the mind of every man present. But unfortunately that does not represent all our difficulties. We have the whole of the civilised world banded in hostility to us. Lord Rosebery said the other day that Europe was unanimous in its opposition to us. He might have made

[1] "Rights and Wrongs of the Transvaal War," p. 287.

an exception in the case of Turkey, which is sympathetic. As to America, four-fifths of the American Press are opposed to us, and opinion there is growing very rapidly in favour of the Boers. They made an honest effort at the first to find some excuse for us, but the facts were too strong for them. How do you account for the unanimity of this hostility? It is due unquestionably to the aggressiveness, the arrogance, and the rapacity which characterise the demeanour of the new Imperialism. Take one of the speeches of Mr. Chamberlain, who is Lord Rosebery's rival for the position of stage manager of the new Imperialism. He first of all insulted Germany and America with that most offensive form of patronage, which assumes you are flattered by a profession of regard and friendship from the person who addresses you. As for France, it is difficult to characterise the insolence of his tone. Here is a country with a population of forty millions, with an army at the very least three or four times the size of ours, and comparing favourably, to say the least, in efficiency with it, and a country with a historical record of which any nation might be proud. This powerful and renowned State Mr. Chamberlain presumed to address in language which no proctor would dare address to an erring undergraduate. After that, one could not be surprised at anything he said about the Transvaal. Mark the superciliousness of his tone in referring to it as " the country we created." The new Imperialists will have to procure a revised version of their Scriptures—a Birmingham edition, commencing " In the beginning Joseph Chamberlain created heaven and earth."

But our misconduct is more fundamental than that. One need not go outside South Africa to find abundant illustration of it, and it is such instances that have produced the suspicion, the mistrust, and the bitterness which have resulted in the most disastrous war which we have ever waged. Take the case of Kimberley. I take the facts from Froude, the Conservative historian. There was the Orange Free State, which had always been a quiet, peaceable, and inoffensive neighbour. The land was poor on the whole. Suddenly, owing to the discovery of the diamond mines, it was found that one corner of the wilderness was valuable. We suddenly pounced upon it and annexed it to our own dominions by a series of transactions which no decent commercial community would ever have tolerated in one of its own members. Then, again, there was the Jameson Raid. The facts are too fresh in your memory to need recapitulation ; but to my mind the worst feature of the whole squalid business was the deception practised by those who, while they were steeped to the lips in complicity with the Raid, disavowed it and its authors in the face of Europe after its failure, and while they punished the poor instruments of the conspiracy, who had at any rate risked their lives in carrying it out, at the same time glorified the arch-plotter in the high court of this kingdom. Whom can we expect to trust us after a series of disreputable transactions of that character ? And yet we say that the animosity of foreign nations is all attributable to envy of our greatness and goodness. It is true that good fortune makes men the target for the jealousy of the meaner sort among their fellow-creatures, even though they use their prosperity for the common good of all but it will be found invariably that such men win the warm regard and admiration of the majority of their neighbours. What country is there to-day that either admires or respects Britain in this last action of hers ? The most deplorable feature of the situation is the way the Liberals of Europe have given us up. There was a time when they looked to Britain for lead and succour. Now they have turned away in sorrow and sadness of heart from the country which was once for them an exemplar of freedom. One of these papers this week lamented with evident sincerity the change which had taken place in the statesmanship of Britain—" the old champion of liberty." There was no envy there. The land that has protected Portugal against the rapacity of Continental despots, the land that has been the refuge of persecuted patriots from every clime—that land is now straining her resources to the utmost to accomplish by force what she has failed to effect by fraud, the destruction of the independence of two small Republics in South Africa. What is there in that for Continental Liberals to envy ? If they speak in tones of aggravated anger, it is because their indignation is accentuated by a sense of disappointment that their idol should have proved false. Lord Rosebery has summed up our losses in this war, but the greatest loss of all is not comprised in his enumeration. It is true that at the end of this war we shall miss millions from our coffers. We shall lose much of that deference which is always paid to the masters of many successful legions. We shall miss many a gallant name from the roll-call of our warriors. But there is something infinitely more precious to every true lover of Britain that we shall miss, and that is the distinction of being the hope and shield of the weak and oppressed in all lands, which was once the brightest gem in Britain's glory. No Liberal at least would have bartered that for all the gold in the Rand. I have read carefully through Lord Rosebery's speech, and failed to discover in it any single note that would indicate any appreciation of this loss. Lord Rosebery would set himself to restore the damage done to our prestige. But what are the materials he would use for this purpose ? He supplied us with a list of them. He waxed eloquent over the mere category. What were they ? We had transport arrangements that no country in the world could emulate. We had an incomparable Navy. We had more capital than any other nation could command, and—though he spoke with some reluctance on this point—we had a fine national character. This he seemed to treat as a more doubtful asset. But these sentiments of Lord Rosebery have not even the merit of originality. I recollect that the great poet of the new Imperialism uttered the same ideas in those immortal lines :

> We've got the ships, we've got the men,
> We've got the money too !

You do not convert music-hall rant into high-class statesmanship by the simple process of substituting the word " capital " for " money " and " transport " for " ships." In Lord Rosebery's schedule of materials for the restoration of the impaired temple of Britain's prestige he has omitted the most important item of all, and that is the " righteousness that exalteth a nation." Lord Rosebery would sharpen England's sword in order to make it more deadly. Let him rather purge the Empire's conscience, so as to make its statesmanship more upright. He will find that pay even as a military resource. That is one of the lessons of the war that Lord Rosebery has overlooked. Its greatest surprise is not the Boer military preparations, their artillery, their weapons, their numbers, or even their strategy. You will find that even all those had been anticipated. But what we had not expected was the courage, the tenacity, the devotion, the wholeheartedness of the Boers themselves—the way in which each Boer has put the whole of his intelligence, strength, and soul into the struggle. That has been our greatest difficulty. That is going to be the greatest barrier in the path of our success. It proves that the most formidable weapon with which a nation can arm itself is a righteous cause—" Thrice is he armed that hath his quarrel just." That is where the Boers' armaments have outclassed ours. I am not begging the question when I assume the superiority of their cause. It may be said, in the words of Lord Rosebery, that the Boer Government was a " corrupt oligarchy," although such a statement comes with a bad grace from a peer who sits in an assembly adorned by the presence of Hooley's directors, and whose members voted to themselves out of the public funds millions of money under the pretence of relieving agricultural distress. But, at any rate, it can be said of the Boer farmer who lined the trenches that the hand that grasped the Mauser was never soiled with a bribe. He fought for the freedom and independence of his native land, and there is no more sacred cause for which a man can die.

Two days after this speech at Oxford the member for the Carnarvon Boroughs was interviewed by a representative of the "Morning Herald." "We cannot of course go cap in hand to Kruger," he said, "and say, 'We have sinned against Heaven and thee,' but there are many ways of stopping the war. We have only to give the word to McKinley, and the thing could be done. But the Liberal Party, whatever happens, must stand clear of the whole business. The Government have made their bed ; let them lie on it."

His letters at this time were full of the war. He followed the campaign closely, and in his nightly letters to his uncle and his brother recorded and commented on the latest bulletins. He was anxious that criticism of the war should be focussed upon the essential question of its justice or injustice. " Wyndham," he wrote on February 1, 1900, " made a very fine defence of the Government from the military point of view. Very glad of it, as I don't want the argument against the Government to be a military one."

A few days later (on February 6), he made a long speech on Lord Edmond Fitzmaurice's amendment to the Address. The amendment, which, with a somewhat transparent ingenuity, had been so framed as to unite in one lobby Liberals of the most discordant opinions, censured the Government for "the want of knowledge, foresight, and judgment " they had displayed "alike in their conduct of South African affairs since 1895 and in their preparations for the war."

This speech must have been one of the most successful of his career. It won from Sir William Harcourt a notable tribute: it was, he said, worthy of Grattan in his best days. Mr. Balfour was said by a Conservative paper [1] to have told a friend that, much as he disagreed with it, it was the best speech he had ever heard in the House of Commons, and according to one Press correspondent,[2] Sir Henry Campbell-Bannerman, in offering his own congratulations to Mr. Lloyd George, told him that "a talented London actress had begged her escort to bring her again whenever the member for Carnarvon was likely to speak."

In March he had, I think, his first experience of the rioting which began to be associated with "peace" meetings. Mr. Cronwright-Schreiner, a South African of unmixed British blood (his name was originally Cronwright and he adopted his wife's surname upon his marriage), and a member of the Legislative Assembly of Cape Colony, had come to England to tell such audiences as he could gather what he conceived to be the truth about the war. His views were on the face of it worthy of attention, for he had been a professed opponent of the Conservative policy of President Kruger before the Jameson Raid. A quotation from the book ironically entitled "The Land of Free Speech," which he wrote after his experiences in England, may serve to show his opinions after the Raid and during the negotiations between Mr. Chamberlain and the President :

I did all I could with many other people who love this country and its peoples, and wished to avoid war, to induce political concessions ; not because I thought England had any right to demand them, for I repudiate that right as strongly as Oom Paul himself ; nor because I thought the Republic on the whole was badly governed, because I have never thought this ; but because I thought it was the best policy to checkmate the capitalists in the long run ; because, not being a Tory, it consorts more with my ideas of government ; and because I did not want war, which, apart from its horrors, meant that we should be handed over bound to the capitalist-speculators, whose rule I knew would be corrupt and selfish and subversive of all true freedom, both for white and black.[3]

On March 6 Mr. Cronwright-Schreiner was one of the speakers at a meeting of " citizens opposed to the war policy of the Government " which had been announced to take place at the Glasgow

---

[1] " Western Mail."   [2] The correspondent of the " South Wales Daily News."
[3] From the Introduction of " The Land of Free Speech," published 1906.

City Hall. The names of his principal supporters were Mr. Lloyd George, M.P., and Mr. H. J. Wilson, M.P. It is a mild description of the meeting to say that it was stormy. Some of the University students saw in it an opportunity for an exceptionally uproarious evening, and it is alleged by Mr. Cronwright-Schreiner that their amateur efforts were supplemented by subsidised disorder. An army of students marched upon the hall, but by the time they got there it was completely filled, and they could only join another hostile mob which was clamouring and fighting on the staircase. Meanwhile a crowd of some thousands had gathered in the streets outside.

Inside the hall the supporters of the peace party were in a majority. At the head of the defending forces was the rising Socialist and Labour leader, Mr. Keir Hardie, and the stewards who assisted him seem to have been fairly warlike keepers of the peace. Resolutions were carried condemning the war and declaring for the independence of the Republics, and after a last wild fight with the stewards in the hall, the dissentients apparently quieted down, discouraged by the fact that the police had been called in to clear the stairs, and that all hope of reinforcement from outside had therefore vanished.

It was in this relatively calm atmosphere that Mr. Lloyd George rose to speak. Perhaps I cannot do better than quote a few lines from Mr. Cronwright-Schreiner's book to show the impression he made.

Mr. Lloyd George then arose to speak, but had to stand for many minutes before the noise quieted down. But the self-restraint of the peace men, and the cutting off of the outside mob, and Mr. Lloyd George's good-humoured patience at last secured comparative quiet, and he got in a few sentences. Once started, he behaved in the most skilful way. Humouring the rowdies, parrying smartly, and speaking eloquently, he at last got complete control, which he held for about forty-five minutes, making a fine speech which was concluded amidst thunders of applause.

After the meeting Mr. Keir Hardie and three ladies of his family were roughly handled by the crowd, and had to be rescued by the police. Mr. Lloyd George left the meeting in a cab. Its windows were broken, but he escaped without injury.

It might have been easier to face angry crowds in England and Scotland if there had been any certainty that in his own constituency the course he had marked for himself was approved. He did not, however, get much encouragement from that quarter. It was his desire to hold a meeting in his constituency—at Bangor —in April. The leading Liberals did their best to dissuade him from the idea. Such counsels were little to his taste. Again an echo of his old diaries comes back to one's mind. In 1885 he was "awfully annoyed" when some "weak-kneed Liberals" decided not to hold a meeting for fear of rioters.[1] On March 22, 1900, he wrote the following letter to his brother:

I *am going* to Bangor. I mean to insist upon it. I hear the bulk of the leading Liberals are strongly opposed to a meeting at this juncture, and they entreat me not to go. I will not listen to them. Here are my reasons:
(*a*) There may be a general election soon.
(*b*) You may rely upon Chamberlain forcing dissolution in the height of the war fever.
(*c*) If the policy of abstaining from meetings to instruct the people is adhered to, judgment will go by default against us and we will be hopelessly beaten—and we deserve to.
(*d*) If the Association still deprecate meetings I resign my candidature, as I cannot hope to succeed if I am shut up.

Preparations for the meeting were continued, although the trustees of the hall in which the meeting was to be held insisted upon being secured against damage.

March 30, 1900.—Just had a wire from Bangor, that trustees of Penrhyn Hall won't let it without substantial guarantee against damages. . . . And we are fighting for free speech and equal rights in the Transvaal. First-rate object lesson. I mean to get there.

The required guarantee was secured, and the meeting held. Before he left London Mr. Lloyd George received a letter from his agent with the comforting news that nothing worse was to be expected than the throwing of missiles at the audience as they arrived and left. A large force of police had been brought into the town, and a strong body of stewards had been organised to keep order within the building. As the time of the meeting approached an unfriendly crowd gathered round the front entrance of the Penrhyn Hall. It was unusual for speakers to use this entrance, as the platform is commonly approached by a back door. Instead of following custom, however, Mr. Lloyd George drove up to the front entrance. When he stepped out of the carriage, smiling and bowing to the crowd, there were howls and shouts of "Pro-Boer," and some one threw a clod of earth at him. In the hall, where a few supporters of the war among the audience had beguiled the time of waiting by singing that stirring ballad of Empire, "The Soldiers of the Queen," he had an uproarious reception. He spoke for an hour, to the accompaniment

[1] See Vol. I., p. 49.

of cheers, interruptions, and the smashing of windows at the back and front of the hall. Twice the chairman, Mr. Henry Lewis, appealed to the stewards to call upon the police to guard the hall, and on the second occasion he added that they could not get on with the meeting if the noise continued. "We can get on with it right enough," said Mr. Lloyd George, who went on with his speech, dealing good-humouredly with the opposition, and intervening to protect his interrupters against those who threatened expulsion. His speech ended with a passionate appeal to his countrymen not to countenance an attempt to crush two small nationalities. A resolution condemning the war and protesting against "any settlement which would involve the suppression of the existence of the Republics" was carried by a large majority.

Outside the hall a great crowd awaited the speakers, hooting indiscriminately all who came out—"even the reporters," as a Conservative newspaper pathetically observed. Mr. Lloyd George's friends were anxious that he should hurry away in a cab, but he refused to recognise any danger and preferred to walk home. Mrs. Lloyd George, perhaps fortunately as it turned out, was separated from him in the crowd and drove home with friends. As Mr. Lloyd George was entering the High Street some zealous patriot struck him a heavy blow on the head with a bludgeon. His hat was crushed, and for a few moments he was stunned, but he managed to make his way into a café close by, where he remained for some time under police protection. Till midnight a great crowd remained outside the café, singing, with a misplaced loyalty, "God save the Queen," and intending, as it appeared, to complete the work which one individual had so vigorously begun. Before the mob separated, Mr. Lloyd George had made an easy escape by a back entrance which it had not occurred to the besieging force to guard.

Such an experience did not weaken his hostility to the war or lessen the force with which he expressed it in his constituency or elsewhere. He knew that there was a great body of Liberal opinion against him, and it cannot have seemed very likely that he would keep the seat. These were only reasons for prosecuting with greater vigour the campaign for what he believed to be justice.

A speech he delivered at Carnarvon in April[1] must be noticed on two grounds. First, it deals with the charge freely made against him, in common with other critics of the war, that he had attacked the British soldier. That accusation has appeared, vaguely stated, at intervals ever since the Boer War, and an

[1] April 28, 1900.

impression seems to remain upon the public mind that Mr. Lloyd
George has some need of forgiveness for his strictures upon our
troops.   Unless it be treason to English soldiers to refuse to belittle or traduce their foemen, I do not find in his speeches the
faintest ground for such a charge.   The views that critics form
of his attacks upon the policy and conduct of the war must be
coloured by their opinions, and those who did not go the whole
way or who went none of the way with him will find excessive
violence of expression where others will applaud his plain-spoken
vigour.   But the object of the vigour or the violence was never
the fighting soldier.

The second point of importance in the speech is his defence
of his refusal to vote supplies.   That question, as has been seen,
had given him much anxious thought, and he had decided upon
what was obviously an extreme course.   Only deep feeling could
justify it.   Critics who are not content to accept that as his
motive may look for another, but one fancies they will look in vain.
The motive was certainly not expediency, or a craving for popular
applause.   This too may be said, that there were notable precedents, as he points out in the speech from which I am about to
quote, for the course taken by Mr. Lloyd George.

The charge that he had insulted the British soldier, he said,
was an absolute and unmitigated falsehood.   He had never
spoken of British soldiers without expressing admiration of their
tenacity and heroism.   The men who went about howling, breaking up meetings, and smashing windows were very tender of the
soldiers, but did not mind sending them to be killed and maimed.
All this was cant and hypocrisy.   Those who loved the soldiers
were the men who thought their lives too precious to be squandered
upon a miserable squabble like this.

He made a further answer to the charge by reminding his
audience that he had opposed in the House of Commons a system
by which the regular soldier was paid 1s. 3d. a day when the
Colonial volunteer received 5s.   He had claimed, he said, for the
Welsh and English soldiers a payment equivalent to that paid
to the Colonial soldier.   As a Welshman, he added, he was proud
of the Welsh Fusiliers, proud of the gallant charge they had made,
and proud of the fact that the Welsh national regiments were the
only national regiments in South Africa not as yet represented as
prisoners of war in Pretoria.

It was in reply to a heckler that he made the vindication of
his attitude in refusing to vote supplies to which I have referred.
He had taken that course, he said, because he did not believe in
half measures, and thought it was logically consistent with the

position he had taken up. He and Mr. Bryn Roberts, who voted with him, had been denounced as traitors. If they were traitors, they were in very good company, for Lord Chatham and John Bright had refused to vote supplies for a war of which they disapproved, and Mr. Chamberlain, the noblest example of all, had refused supplies. Quite apart from these reasons, the voting of large sums of money to a Government meant an expression of confidence in it. He had no such confidence. The Government asked for twenty millions, and he would not give the money because he did not believe the present Government were the right people to use it. Even if he were in favour of the war, the present Ministers were the last people in the world he would trust with the money. He condemned the lack of preparation which had kept Lord Roberts helpless at Bloemfontein for the lack of an adequate supply of horses, and attacked the bungle of the Spion Kop dispatches, which had kept a general in the field while undermining the confidence of his men in him. To the charge that he had given a vote which would have prevented the sending of food and clothing to the troops, he replied that the provisions were already in the ships, and if every member of the House of Commons had given the same vote, not one suit of khaki or case of bully beef the less would have been sent out. From the first he had believed that the Government wanted territory, and he would not vote money to acquire territory. To drive the Boers out of Natal or to gain equal rights he might have voted money, but he would not vote money to be spent upon a war of aggression.

In the same speech a fresh illustration may be found of the insistence with which the national aspirations of the Boers appealed to the nationalist of Wales :

They say we are fighting for equal rights for white men in South Africa. We could have had that without going to war, had it not been for the cruel blundering of Mr. Chamberlain. We could now, without firing another shot, get equal rights. We could get disarmament. We could even get a war indemnity. But that is not enough. We have now got beyond all that, and nothing short of annexation will suffice us. Now annexation of an unwilling nation is not a light task to undertake, especially when it is remembered that we are talking of annexing a race which for a hundred years withstood all the power of Spain, when she was at the height of her military glory. The Dutch, though defeated in every pitched battle, managed to exhaust the power of Spain, and the decay of Spain dates from that very time. It is true the Dutch in the war with Spain were fighting on a religious issue, while now they are fighting for a racial issue. But race is deeper than religion. Even in Ireland, wherever a racial issue has been involved, the people have repudiated their religious masters.

III

At Carnarvon some of his old supporters told him frankly that they would not vote for him because of the opinions he had expressed upon the war. His reply was prompt and effective. He would, if they wished, stand aside and let them choose another candidate. To that offer only one answer was possible. No other candidate was as likely as he to preserve unity in the Liberal ranks, and no practical opposition was forthcoming, although a weakening of the support hitherto accorded seemed inevitable.

Meanwhile he was busy in the House of Commons. He was more and more impressed by the leadership of Sir Henry Campbell-Bannerman, but it was not long before he found himself in conflict with him over a minor point. On May 8 a curious incident arose in the House. At the time it made a great stir ; its only importance for us is that it brought Mr. Lloyd George to some extent into collision with the leader of the Opposition, Sir Henry Campbell-Bannerman. The incident to which I refer was one of those discussions over an alleged breach of privilege in which the House is seldom seen at its best. A firm of solicitors had written a letter which made reflections upon a member of the House who was also a member of the Select Committee on Government contracts which had been appointed to inquire into the impartiality of War Office contracting. The member made a statement to the House, and in the absence of Mr. Balfour a motion was carried, against which most of the Liberal Opposition voted, declaring the letter to be a breach of privilege. Mr. Balfour arrived in the House to find this pious declaration made, and advised that it should not be followed up by any attempt at punishing the offenders. He has indeed been fairly consistent in the view that the less the House says about affronts of this description the better. The result was a little ludicrous. The House, after a very solemn verdict of "Guilty," refused to pass any sentence. Sir Henry Campbell-Bannerman was content to point the moral with some caustic criticism, and concurred with Mr. Balfour's advice that the matter should be allowed to drop. Mr. Lloyd George wished the solicitors to be brought to the Bar of the House, to defend or excuse their letter : he knew, he said, that they would be glad of the opportunity. " I confess I am rather disappointed," he said, "with the advice given to the House by the

Leader of the House and the Leader of the Opposition." Mr. Lloyd George's speech had its effect on the Opposition, the majority of whom followed him in the division lobby.

On May 14 Mr. Lloyd George is advising his brother to "read carefully" Mr. Chamberlain's speech on the Australian Bill. He was, it is clear, profoundly impressed by a passage in the speech which, while it assorted ill with some of the current theories of the new Imperialism, was an admission, or more correctly a recognition, of what Liberalism sees to be the strength rather than the weakness of the nexus between the various parts of our Empire. The passage to which he particularly referred is so important that I transcribe it, but it is right to say that it should be read with its context before it is accepted as a statement of the political philosophy of its author.

We have got to a point in our relations with our self-governing Colonies [Mr. Chamberlain said] at which I think we recognise, once for all, that these relations depend entirely on their free will and absolute consent. The links between us and them at the present time are very slender. Almost a touch might snap them. But, slender as they are, although we wish, although I hope, that they will become stronger, still if they are felt irksome by any one of our great colonies, we shall not attempt to force them to wear them.

These were months when the news from South Africa had made the hopes of a swift triumph ludicrous, and had transformed premature exultation into a sullen determination. On May 4 there was a debate in the House of Commons on the military administration of the war, and in particular the reverse of Spion Kop :

Government badly damaged by the Spion Kop debate [he wrote]. Asquith has never done better—but the speech of the debate was delivered by Acland-Hood,[1] a Tory Guardsman. The Tories are bursting with indignation at the conduct of the Government.

The letter goes on :

Roberts captured Brandfort. The Boers offered no real opposition. People are getting sick of these easy victories which simply lead to the next kopje.

Later in the month the country was enabled to indulge in triumphal orgies by making the most of an incident which, in a

[1] Sir A. Acland-Hood's speech strongly censured the Government for its conduct in publishing the "Spion Kop Dispatches." "A general officer," he said, "commanding 30,000 men, has been censured in face of his whole army and in face of the whole world." See "Hansard," May 4, 1900

more successful war, might have been received with calm. The defence of Mafeking was a great piece of work, the defenders are entitled to all the glory which historians of the war can grant them. Of the scenes which greeted the news of the relief of Mafeking in our cities perhaps the less said the better. When Mr. Lloyd George reached his office in the morning he was amused to find all his clerks adorned with the red, white, and blue ribbon popularly, and erroneously, supposed to be emblematic of England. A penny Union Jack surmounted the typewriter. The clerks clamoured for, and got, a day off.

Whatever may be thought of Mr. Lloyd George's opinions and speeches upon the war, he was demonstrably correct in his estimate of its duration, at a time when public and expert opinion was united in a wrong view. From the first he believed, and acted on the belief, that the campaign would be long and costly in money and in life. In June, when the tide had turned in our favour, his forecast was that " Christmas would find the war still on," although even Mr. Cronwright-Schreiner thought it would be over in another six weeks or two months. A month later he writes to his brother :

People are beginning to grumble against Roberts for the delay. It will be time enough April next to growl. The war will be going strong then.

In July he was the chief speaker at a peace meeting at Liskeard, Cornwall, in the constituency of Mr. Courtney, as he then was. The chairman was the distinguished writer Mr. A. T. Quiller Couch, afterwards a knight, later a Professor, and known to fame best of all as " Q." Local enthusiasm for the war did not permit the meeting to be held. I transcribe a brief note in which Mr. Lloyd George describes what occurred :

July 6, 1900.—I have returned from the Liskeard meeting—a very stormy one. No time to send details. Stormed platform—wouldn't listen to anybody. Simply 100 or 150 young hobbledehoys. The bulk of the meeting was with us. Assured it will do good. Courtney was very pleased.

In the same month [1] the Colonial Office vote gave the Opposition an opportunity of declaring their views upon the conduct of the war, which was now being pursued with the avowed object of annexation. It revealed differences of opinion upon the Liberal benches which were the more serious because by now every one knew that Mr. Lloyd George's prophecy that Mr. Cham-

[1] July 25.

berlain would force a dissolution was to be fulfilled. Sir Wilfrid Lawson, who moved a reduction of the vote by £100, attacked the theory which found much favour, as he said, in the street, the pulpit, the newspaper office, and the House of Commons, that it was a man's duty to support "his country, right or wrong." He declared our policy in South Africa to be that of "the free-booter, the filibuster, the burglar, and the Boxer." Sir Robert Reid [1] urged a not dissimilar view in language of greater moderation. Mr. Chamberlain spoke next, and repudiated, with the indignation which he knew so well how to display effectively in debate, the sinister suspicions which had gathered about his person :

I am quite aware there are many suspicions about the Colonial Secretary. Whom have I to thank for that ? The suspicions are all derived from the speeches of hon. gentlemen opposite ; they are not derived from fact. They are not derived in the least from fact, they are not derived from anything I have said, from anything I have written, from anything I have done ; but they are derived from ignoble motives which hon. gentlemen have imputed to me, from articles in the Press, from Conciliation Committees, and Stop-the-war Committees, and from their literature, which I do not read, but which I see when it comes back to me from South Africa as having been quoted and repeated by some of the leaders, I will not say of the rebellion, but I will say some of those who are hostile to the British position in South Africa.

Sir Wilfrid Lawson had been able to quote against Mr. Chamberlain words of grave import which the latter himself had used only four years before in the House of Commons.[2]

A war in South Africa would be one of the most serious wars that could possibly be waged. It would be in the nature of a civil war. It would be a long war, a bitter war, and a costly war, and, as I have pointed out already, it would leave behind it the embers of a strife which I believe generations would not be long enough to extinguish. To go to war with President Kruger in order to force upon him reforms in the internal affairs of his State, in which Secretaries of State have repudiated all right of interference —that would be a course of action as immoral as unwise.

Mr. Chamberlain's answer to this timely quotation was that he had been unduly pessimistic.

In the speech to which the hon. Baronet referred, I did no doubt say four years ago that a war in South Africa would create feeling which might take generations to allay. Well, that was a prophecy. I should like to say now that, with greater knowledge, I am more hopeful. I do not

---

[1] Lord Loreburn.   [2] May 8, 1896. Hansard [4th Ser.], Vol. XL., p. 914.

conceal from myself the terrible divisions among families, among peoples, among races, among religions, which exist at the present time in South Africa. But it seems to me that those who know most of the country are of opinion that hitherto those divisions have been based upon a misunderstanding on the part of the Boers of the English character and the English power, and that now that that misunderstanding has been removed by the war, the probability is that after a short time they will settle down to a condition of things in which certainly they will not have anything to complain of.

Race feeling in South Africa had not been created by any policy of his : its appearance synchronised with the activity of the Afrikander Bond. With regard to the settlement of the war, he explained that it was the Government's intention to supersede military government as soon as possible by a Crown Colony government, which would not, however, necessarily last for long. The question of its length would depend chiefly on the behaviour of the Boers under Crown Colony government.

Mr. Lloyd George rose immediately after the Colonial Secretary. The opening words of his speech show that at this date he still adhered to the view that independence should be restored to the Boers. This was, however, hardly more than a pious aspiration or counsel of perfection : it was, as we shall see, soon forced upon him that the question of annexation was no longer an issue of practical politics. He began by declaring that he was cordially in agreement with a portion of the Colonial Secretary's speech in which he had said that he could not conceive it possible for a man who conscientiously believed that the war was unjust to do otherwise than think that the annexation of the Republics was wrong and their independence ought to be restored. To Mr. Chamberlain's claim that his conduct had given rise to no suspicion, he replied in a spirited passage :

For my part I rather admired his speech for what I would call its audacity. The right hon. gentleman held up his hands in holy horror, and exclaimed that he could not imagine how anybody could regard his conduct with regard to South Africa with suspicion. He could not conceive how it was possible that his attitude should be so misconceived. " Suspicion ! " he said. " On what basis of fact is this suspicion built ? " Surely the right hon. gentleman cannot have forgotten the Hawksley letters, the concealment of facts in the South African committee. He cannot have forgotten the promotion of one of the men implicated in the Raid, and the reinstatement of another of the conspirators. Indeed, the history of the last four or five years in South Africa is simply one record of facts, each and every one of them affording good, solid, substantial ground for suspecting the attitude of the right hon. gentleman in everything he does in South Africa.

He next dealt with Mr. Chamberlain's prophecy of 1896, and with the defence that he had altered his view in deference to the advice of men who knew the country :

Four or five years ago he considered that a war in South Africa would be a protracted war, a costly war, and would create endless bitterness and strife there ; and he came to the conclusion that it would be an immoral proceeding. To-day, recanting these, among a good many other opinions formed in the course of his life, he declares that he has changed his mind, that he has had further knowledge since then. He has seen men who know the country. That is perfectly true ; but he had seen these men " who know the country " then, and it is rather curious that these men, " who know the country " perfectly, thought that they could take Pretoria, the capital of the Transvaal, with 600 men ! These were the men who had been living in the country all their lives, who were the sources of information to the Imperial Government, upon which information the Imperial Government based their whole policy. These were the men who knew so much about the country that they thought they could do with 600 amateur soldiers that which it has taken an army of 250,000 men eight or nine months to do. These were the men who informed the Imperial Government that President Kruger would climb down. Why, there are people in this country who have never seen South Africa, who have shown greater knowledge about South Africa than these other men who have lived in it all their lives, but who are blinded by local and racial feeling, and who could not be trusted in a matter of this kind.

His reply to Mr. Chamberlain's accusations against the Afrikander Bond was ingeniously contrived to lead up to one of those personal gibes which, differentiated by their delicacy from personal attacks, do not fail to amuse the House :

The right hon. gentleman has just been denouncing the Afrikander Bond practically as a treasonable conspiracy. He said, " I have evidence." There has been too much so-called evidence which is kept back. Why should the right hon. gentleman be the sole depository of all these confidences ? This is, after all, nominally a democratic country. What has become of the right hon. gentleman's rooted policy of taking the people into his confidence ? Here is evidence which, according to him, is sufficient to ground an indictment against the people of South Africa, and yet he withholds it from Parliament. I have looked carefully into the Blue Books, and so far from finding any evidence of conspiracy, I only find that Sir Alfred Milner has filled them with the shavings and sawdust of the South African League workshop—chippings from newspapers and society gossip in South Africa. As a serious bit of evidence, there is a conversation with a gentleman called Schreiner, seventeen years ago, at a dinner party. Gentlemen who reveal the confidences of a dinner party are the men on whose evidence you are going to indict a whole nation ! This gentleman met a Mr. Wright at this dinner party. I have read the whole conversation, and Mr. Wright said nothing whatever to Mr. Schreiner about a conspiracy. But it was said that his countenance was stern with self-confidence, and that he wore a self-satisfied smile. Therefore that means that he wanted to expel the British flag from South Africa. If a self-satisfied smile and a countenance stern with self-confidence are sufficient to expel the British flag from South Africa, I cannot understand why there should be a Union Jack left within a hundred miles of Birmingham.

He went on to enforce the point which made so strong an appeal to his own mind, that the outbreak of the war had compelled the abandonment of domestic reform. On the other side of the account we could, he argued, set no gain in prestige. He refused to accept the proposition that it was irrelevant, in considering the rights and wrongs of the war, to look at the loss and suffering it had entailed. Was not the price to be paid a matter to be taken into account when the desirability of a war was being considered? Lord Salisbury at least thought that it was.

We had a perfectly good case for war against France in regard to Madagascar, but Lord Salisbury came to the conclusion that British trade in Madagascar was not worth the immense suffering and sacrifice of life that would be produced by a war with France.

The Government had set out to gain equal rights for all. Now its policy was Crown Colony government, which meant not votes for all, but votes for none. So he passed to a peroration which may be quoted as an epitome of his views at this stage of the struggle :

He has led us into two blunders. The first was the war. But worse than the war is the change that has been effected in the purpose for which we are prosecuting the war. We went into the war for equal rights ; we are prosecuting it for annexation. That is a most serious change in the tactics of the Government from any point of view. There may be something to be said for a war so long as it is entered upon for an unselfish purpose. The influence of a war must always be brutalising, at best ; but still, if you enter upon it for an unselfish purpose, there is something which almost consecrates the sacrifices, bloodshed, and suffering endured. But when you enter upon a war purely and simply for the purposes of plunder, I know of nothing which is more degrading to the country or more hideous in its effects on the mind and character of the people engaged in it. Any one who looks at the illustrated papers must see the horrible presentment given of incidents which were formerly relegated to prints like the " Police Gazette "—details which I cannot give to the House without a gross breach of good taste. Incidents of that kind are not given for the purpose of producing any disgust in the minds of the people, but with every circumstance of indication that they are there to invoke admiration. And all these are circulated broadcast in every household throughout the country. The right hon. gentleman the Colonial Secretary, in a speech quoted by the hon. member for Cockermouth, said that a war in order to impose internal reforms upon President Kruger would be an immoral war. If that be so, I ask the right hon. gentleman or any of his friends to find an adjective sufficiently expressive of the character of a war entered upon for the purposes of annexation. The right hon. gentleman admitted that we had no right to meddle in the affairs of the Transvaal, and that there was only one possible justification for it—that our motive was an unselfish one. We have thrown that justification away now. It is exactly as if you had entered into a man's house to protect the children, and started to steal his plate. You entered into these two Republics for philanthropic purposes and remained to commit burglary. In changing the purpose of the war you have made a bad change. That is the impression you are creating abroad. Our critics say you are not going to war for equal rights and to establish fair play, but to get hold of the goldfields ; and you have justified that criticism of our enemies by that change. But, worst of all, a change has been effected in the character of the war. Up to a certain point it was conducted with considerable chivalry, with apparent good temper on both sides. A war of annexation, however, against a proud people, must be a war of extermination, and that is unfortunately what it seems we are now committing ourselves to—burning homesteads and turning men and women out of their homes. The telegram received from Pretoria, which had passed the military censor, stated that fact, and I do not think he would have let it come unless it was true. It is also confirmed from Lourenço Marques by information that 600 women and children have been turned out and sent to the hills. There has been the burning of the homesteads of the rebels, and this war will brutalise the people, and the savagery which must necessarily follow will stain the name of this country. It seems to me that in this war we have gradually followed the policy of Spain in Cuba. The action of the Spaniards in Cuba produced such a feeling in America that they could not tolerate it, and we know how that war degraded the name of Spain. This is the state of things into which the right hon. gentleman has brought us. During nine or ten months' warfare we have lost between 40,000 and 50,000 men, there has been enormous expense, and the end is not yet in sight. And this Government, the advent of which we were told would terrorise all other Governments abroad, has been reduced to the necessity of appealing to Japan to protect its own Ministers in China. The right hon. gentleman has made up his mind that this war shall produce electioneering capital to his own side. He is in a great hurry to go to the country before the facts are known. He wants to have the judgment of the people in the very height and excitement of the fever. He wants a verdict before the pleadings are closed and before "discovery" has been obtained. He does not want the documents to come, but he wants to have the judgment of the country upon censured news, suppressed dispatches, and unpaid bills. The right hon. gentleman may not be a statesman, but he is an expert electioneer, and in his desire to go to the country before the country realises what the war means he is the one man who pronounces the deepest condemnation upon his own proceedings.

Sir Wilfrid Lawson's motion was rejected by a majority of 156. It did not receive official support : Sir Henry Campbell-Bannerman, unable to go so far as the mover of the resolution, and unwilling to express confidence in the Colonial Secretary, absented himself from the division and recorded no vote, while the Liberal Imperialists voted with the Government.

IV

The General Election—Colonel Platt his opponent—A meeting at Nevin—An audience " who came to curse "—The conversion of Bangor—The scene after the election—Another triumph.

The General Election came in the autumn. The Government was offered the certainty of a new lease of life, and it was hardly in human nature to refuse it. The Liberal party went into the contest without hope. At the meetings of the National Liberal Federation [1] in March, the party had contrived to pass unanimously a resolution upon the subject of the war, but the discussion had revealed a deep and real cleavage. Mr. Lloyd George had taken part in its debates, and it may be thought characteristic of him that he intervened in them not only as a strong and fearless partisan, but also as a peace-maker. By the use of the powers of suasion which have never deserted him he procured the withdrawal of a motion which would have split the party ranks. The delegates, who attended in almost unprecedentedly large numbers (" there is nothing like a crisis to bring a party together," as a distinguished statesman once observed), were said by impartial observers to be pretty evenly divided. So the election found Liberal candidates.

From the point of view of expediency there was only this to be said for the attitude of a strong anti-war man, that Liberals who supported the war escaped charges of treachery and disloyalty none the more for that. There was nothing to encourage Mr. Lloyd George to take a sanguine view of his own prospects, but his letters show no depression on that account. " I can promise them that they won't beat me easily," he says, and he plans a hard campaign in his constituency.

In the election campaign of 1900 Mr. Lloyd George had as his opponent a retired military officer, Colonel Platt, who made the most of such capital—and it must not be belittled—as the member's opposition to the war provided. In the election address which the Conservative candidate published, it was alleged that Mr.

[1] Held at Nottingham, March 26-29, 1900.

Lloyd George had "scoffed at our Army as 'hired troops,' and spoken in discreditable terms of our brave generals."

"I am entitled to ask Colonel Platt," the member replied in a speech at Conway,[1] "when and where I have scoffed at the soldiers or attacked our brave generals. I challenge him to-night to prove it, and when he comes to Conway, I hope that one of my friends will ask Colonel Platt to prove it. If not, I vow to attend one of his meetings myself for that purpose, even if I am bludgeoned again."

In the same speech he turned his enemy's flank by recalling what had happened in the House of Commons in May upon Mr. M'Kenna's motion to extend the benefits of the Workmen's Compensation Act to the families of the soldiers serving in the war :

At Manchester the other night Mr. Balfour stated that it had always been his intention to do something for the families of the soldiers who fell in the war. In the House of Commons two Welsh members brought the matter forward. Mr. M'Kenna proposed that the families of the soldiers who fell should be compensated just as if they had met with an accident at a factory. The Government contributed £1,600,000 to the landlords and the parsons, while the families of our own soldiers were starving. It was I who had the honour of seconding Mr. M'Kenna's motion. What did the Government do ? Mr. Balfour put up two front-bench Ministers to speak against the motion. Not a single Tory spoke in favour of it. Many of the Tories were absent at a race meeting, and the Whips found that the Government could not defeat the motion. When the Speaker called for the Ayes, all the Liberals responded, and when the Noes were asked to speak out, every Tory—Mr. Balfour among them—called No. You can see, therefore, that it was against the will of the Government that the motion was carried.

Visits to his constituency at this time were not quite the triumphal marches of the past. There were always dour faces to be seen among the audience at any of his meetings : leading local Liberals, who resented his policy and the vehemence of his speeches, kept off the platform and took their seats in the body of the hall with a grim determination not to be over-persuaded. Such occasions were much more exhilarating to him even than the vociferous acclamations of unanimous admirers. I once discussed his attitude upon the South African war with one who had worked with and under him in the difficult early days of the working of the Insurance Act. What had been the essential motive of the course he took ? Why had he jeopardised his career for an unpopular cause ? An answer came readily, and it

[1] September 26, 1900.

probably contains more than a germ of truth. "He is never happy unless he is up against a brick wall."

It is hazardous to impute motives, and it need not be supposed that he was consciously influenced by any less noble passion than the love of Nationalism, or that detestation of powerful alien forces which is its corollary. But one may discern at this, as at other stages of his career, the influence upon his mind of an unfailing pugnacity. To the mere advocate—the man to whom advocacy is an end in itself—the supreme joy of his art is the moulding of the stubborn stuff of others' minds to his own will, and the honest politician, although with him advocacy must always subserve the truth, is not thereby rendered insensible to its delights. If, besides being fervently sincere, the politician happens also to be a born advocate, his enjoyment of a difficult and almost hopeless task takes on a double character. To the joy of the successful evangelist he adds the zest of the player bent on the accomplishment of an incredible feat. A speaker may well be happy when his words find acceptance with his listeners, but when those remain to bless who have come that they may curse, he may be forgiven if he feels not only the spiritual joy of winning souls, but a certain more human pleasure at having won a game.

His meetings at the 1900 election gave him plenty of opportunities for the conversion of a stiff-necked generation. A striking and rather amusing instance of his success at this congenial task is afforded by the story of a meeting at Nevin.[1] Nevin was supposed to be, from his point of view, the weakest spot in the constituency. He had been warned that he could hardly expect a vote of confidence. There was no sign of enthusiasm when he began his speech. The audience was suspicious and undemonstrative. Mr. Lloyd George, speaking in Welsh, began with a few words about the war, which were rather of a nature to disarm criticism.

It is difficult to judge the merits of any war while it lasts. Every war is popular while it lasts : few have been so after they were over, and the country has had leisure to count the cost. I admit that I may possibly have taken a mistaken view of affairs in South Africa, but in any case I am perfectly honest in that view.

Having said so much upon the war, he directed the attention of his audience to the Government's record of legislation, where he was on safer ground. Under the spell of his eloquence the meeting gradually became enthusiastic. Soon he was in the old

[1] September 15, 1900.

DAVID LLOYD GEORGE
At the age of sixteen.

(From a photograph kindly lent by Mr. William George.)

friendly atmosphere : hearing him dilate upon the delinquencies of the Tories and the familiar watchwords of Liberalism, his listeners forgot their suspicions. They began to applaud. By the time he had finished dealing with the Agricultural Rates Bill and the unredeemed pledge of Old Age Pensions he had them cheering wildly.

Then came a reference to the contracts of Kynochs Limited, a Birmingham firm to which the Admiralty had shown great consideration in the matter of contracts. From this he passed to his peroration :

Five years ago the electors of the Carnarvon Boroughs handed me a strip of blue paper, the certificate of my election, to hand to the Speaker as their accredited representative. If I never again represent the Carnarvon Boroughs in the House of Commons, I shall at least have the satisfaction of handing back to them that blue paper with no stain of human blood upon it.

That out-spoken utterance, which, had it come at the beginning of his speech, most certainly would have been resented, now brought the audience to their feet with a storm of cheering. Perhaps the Welsh temperament deserves some of the credit for this episode, but a great deal must be allowed to the skill of the advocate.

He was not less fortunate in the change which came over the opinions of Bangor, where a few months before he had been mobbed and bludgeoned in the streets. Here sympathy and indignation were doubtless factors as well as the genius of the orator and the plasticity of the Welsh temper. We have seen what happened in April. At the meeting which Mr. Lloyd George held at Bangor, in the same Penrhyn Hall, in the thick of his election fight, wildly enthusiastic crowds filled the hall and clamoured for admission at the doors. The truth was that the change of feeling which came over the English mind when the hot fit of the war had died away was reproduced in the Carnarvon Boroughs with greater intensity and rapidity. The fever of war died and a reaction in its turn almost as feverish followed within the space of a few months. We must not look to the Saxon temperament for such speedy transitions. Let me quote a few lines from an impression of the scene at the Bangor meeting which Mr. Harold Spender contributed to the "Manchester Guardian" :

The devotion shown by these people to Mr. Lloyd George was pathetic in its intensity. At Bangor the whole meeting rose to its feet as he entered and met him with acclamation. I often hear Mr. Lloyd George in the House of Commons, but never do we see him there as he is before his own people, laughing with them and then, in swift passage from laughter to tears, moving them to pathos and pity. He is among his own family; the laugh is the laugh of love, and their very eyes are full of affection as they watch him. And so he moves from Welsh to English, and English back to Welsh, just as the audience wishes.

He did not put any policy before his constituents which did not involve a recognition of the altered circumstances in South Africa :

The war is nearly over, and the territories of the Transvaal and the Orange Free State have ceased to exist as independent Republics. I am not so indiscreet as to think that this can be undone. It cannot be undone ; no, not even by the Tories. Lord Roberts is in South Africa and he will settle the question. . . . Some of you do not agree with me on the South African question : but are you, on a question which has been settled, going to forsake the principles of Liberalism ? [1]

It was rumoured in Conservative circles that Mr. Chamberlain himself was coming to Carnarvon to oppose the member, though there seems to have been no foundation for the rumour excepting that there was a determined effort made to persuade him to do so. Colonel Platt had no such illustrious aid, and in the midst of the Liberal depression of the Khaki Election Mr. Lloyd George was again returned by the largest majority he had yet achieved—296. The polling day was Saturday, October 6. We are fortunate in having an able and glowing description by Mr. Harold Spender of the election and of the scene after the declaration of the poll, and I take leave to quote it from the columns of the " Manchester Guardian " [2] :

I am but a Saxon, and words fail me to describe the scenes of delirious enthusiasm which I have just witnessed in this little borough of Carnarvon —the welcome of a people to their triumphant champion, the expression of a great relief, the reaction from a great fear. For when, after a long day of working and suspense, the figures revealed an increase of over 100 on the previous poll, then came recoil from dread to exultant triumph. Great joy sometimes kills, and the delirium of the people became a positive peril to their hero, who was almost sacrificed to the frenzied worship of his followers. Never do I remember such a scene of ecstasy. It had been a long, anxious day for all the Liberals in the boroughs, who had alternate fits of hope and fear, sanguine assurance and perilous despondency. These feelings varied very much with the districts ; for while in Bangor and Carnarvon the Liberals were perhaps too anxious, the little townships of Criccieth, Nevin, and Pwllheli already simmered with satisfaction. " Wales

[1] Pwllheli, September 17, 1900.　　　　[2] October 8, 1900.

expects Nevin to do its duty," wired Mr. Lloyd George at midday, finding himself unable to get as far as the remote little township, which lies on the northern coast of the peninsula, and faces the Atlantic with an open courage that should breed the finest politician. Nevin stoutly replied, and from Pwllheli came the same note of cheerful confidence. More than half the town had polled before midday. When we arrived at Criccieth in the afternoon every face was wreathed with smiles—"All polled but fifty, and they sure." But Bangor openly gave warning of an increased majority against us, and the Carnarvon people shook their heads. It all seemed to depend on which was stronger—the eastern boroughs or the western. Such are the doubts and anxieties of a fight which extends over six small townships, perhaps the most difficult electoral battle that any man can wage.

But now work was over, and the issue lay within the Carnarvon Town Hall, whither the ballot-boxes have been brought by the evening trains to be counted the same evening. And then great throngs of people began to come from the neighbouring districts into Carnarvon. Processions began to parade the streets, singing election songs ; and shouting for their favourite candidate. There was no mistake as to the voice of these crowds. In the afternoon I had seen some flag-waving processions, especially one of boys escorting the embarrassed Colonel Platt. But now all the "Mafficking" seemed on the other side. "Lloyd George for ever !" "Lloyd George for ever !" "Lloyd George for ever !"—that was the cry of these multitudes, and their only wear was yellow. I had the good fortune to be with Mr. George in his journey from Criccieth to Carnarvon, and it was one continuous ovation to him all the way. Perhaps the most touching tribute was that of his own native town, where the people turned out in hundreds and accompanied him to the station with a deafening uproar of cheers and shouting— "Mr. Lloyd George for ever ! For ever !" So it went on until, with a few parting words from his carriage window, he bade them be of good cheer. Then to Carnarvon, a procession at the station to take him to the Town Hall, and then, while the counting proceeded, a gradually swelling crowd filling the whole street in front, stretching as far as eye could reach, wild with excitement and expectation. From the crowd came a combat of songs —first from one side "Rule Britannia," then from the other that great Welsh anthem "Land of Our Fathers," swelling up in greater and greater volume until the song of menace and aggression was drowned in the song of freedom and home-love, as the Venus music in the "Tannhäuser" is drowned by the Pilgrims' March. Then as the time went on rumours began to ooze from the counting-room, as they always will ooze, in spite of all regulation of concealment—first "George in," then "George in by 300," then "George in by 200," then "George in between 200 and 300." The rumours flew up and down the town, invading whole streets, setting processions moving, adding van-loads and windows-full of citizens to the loud-voiced triumph. But the more prudent held back, waiting for the official figures.

It was close upon midnight when the suspense ended, and the Mayor stepped out on the balcony of the Town Hall. "Lloyd George," he cried, but he could say no more. One mighty shout rose from the multitude beneath. No future word could be heard. Then came delirium. It began with the usual appearance on the balcony, but it did not reach fever-pitch until Mr. Lloyd George, finding that no carriage came through the crowd, essayed to reach the Liberal Club under the escort of six constables. He might just as well have relied on a set of corks to face the rapids of Niagara. The love of those people was almost terrible ; it was certainly dangerous. They closed upon their hero, they wrung his hand till it almost came off, they patted his back until it almost broke, they drowned his protests in their shouts. Manfully the constables fought their way forward, but from above Mr. George's white hat looked like a little paper boat in a raging sea. And so they brought him to the door of the club, a helpless hero, a conqueror almost slain by his own conquest. We well knew how dangerous these jokes may be. Mr. Cowen was once nearly killed thus. And so there we closed around him and carried him up the stairs through the throngs on to the balcony outside. Mr. William Jones, M.P., who has played a yeoman's part in this contest, at last obtained silence, and then Mr. Lloyd George spoke a few of those brief, pregnant sentences which he knows well how to coin. "While England and Scotland are drunk with blood, the brain of Wales remains clear, and she advances with a steady step on the road of progress and liberty." A mighty shout rose up, such as rose when, in 1895, he cried from the same window that the wave of reaction had broken on the rocks of Snowdon. Then occurred the noblest scene of all. Descending from the balcony, we mounted into a brake, where Mr. Lloyd George could be seen of all and yet saved from their too perilous attentions. This brake was filled with the untiring lieutenants who have brought Mr. Lloyd George safely through the fight. They advanced slowly down the main street, the crowd with one consent formed up behind in marching column, and as they marched they sang. Ah ! how these Welshmen sang the old election song of Carnarvon Boroughs :

> Hurrah ! hurrah ! We're ready for the fray !
> Hurrah ! hurrah ! We'll drive Sir John away !
> The grand young man will triumph ; Lloyd George will win the day :
> Fight for the freedom of Cambria !

They sang it to "Marching through Georgia," the song to which a continent has fought two wars and will yet fight another. It is one of the best marching songs in the world, and looking back on that great multitude you saw its tread become perfectly rhythmic ; its confusion become order ; delirium pass under the magic of a song ; the mob became an army. And so they marched through the whole town, while every window and doorstep was filled with waving hats and handkerchiefs. It was like the welcome of a king returning from his wars. The darkness seemed to matter nothing, all seemed lightness to-night. The enemy, so strong at midday, had disappeared. Seized by a sudden inspiration, Mr. Lloyd George stood upright in the carriage, and so with lifted hat met the multitudes face to face with a happy smile. A few months ago they had stoned him, a few weeks ago they were still against him ; but now with silver tongue he had won back their hearts, and his people were with him again. Surely, few men have ever tasted such an hour. The procession reached the end of its journey. Then Mr. George called for silence and asked them to sing once more " Land of Our Fathers." In a moment there was utter stillness, and then they sang that great and solemn anthem. The darkness above us lent the scene a ghostly majesty ; the earnest, melancholy harmonies breathed an undying hope ; the sea of invincible faces gave a sense of vast, indefinable strength. The great hymn ended, and then in perfect quiet the great multitude dispersed. And so was a victory for courage and principle which in this election will hold a historic place second to no other.

CHAPTER II

I

Mr. Joseph Chamberlain—" The most striking figure in the House "—Debates on the Address —Kynochs, Limited—Mr. Lloyd George's speech.

IN the new Parliament of 1900, with its small, discordant Opposition, and its massive, often overbearing majority, nothing was more marked than the ascendancy of Mr. Joseph Chamberlain. The benches behind him regarded him with the same sort of affectionate awe which a school captain inspires in the fourth form, and it was only the most hardy veterans on the Speaker's left who were prepared to face him with any show of courage. It was not merely that his great dialectical ability made him a formidable opponent. That was at least as true of Mr. Balfour, of whom nobody stood in terror. But there was something of savagery in Mr. Chamberlain's methods wholly lacking in those of Mr. Balfour. The humour of the Colonial Secretary was never playful, and the victim of his onslaughts was seldom anxious to provoke a second attack.

It is a fact so obvious as to have escaped none of the commentators upon Mr. Lloyd George's rise to Parliamentary fame, that he owed much of it to the cool and pertinacious courage with which he not only stood up to Mr. Chamberlain, but challenged and provoked him to do his worst. His harassing pursuit of the Colonial Secretary was in a way a tribute to that statesman's pre-eminence. It will be remembered that, during his first session in the House of Commons, Mr. Lloyd George regarded an invitation to speak at Birmingham as " a glorious opportunity," and gave as his reason for attaching so much importance to the occasion " the representation of the town." [1] It was a healthy ambition which made him choose to stake his reputation upon contests with the most redoubtable champion in the lists.

[1] See Vol. I., p. 105.

Let me quote here an estimate of Mr. Chamberlain from a lecture on "The House of Commons" which Mr. Lloyd George delivered on more than one occasion at this period. "Who," he asked, "is the most striking figure in the House of Commons now?"

I am afraid it is some one with whom I am not a great favourite. Undoubtedly, for better or for worse, Mr. Chamberlain is the most powerful politician in the Empire to-day. He is an extraordinary man, who has made his way by sheer strength. His is a strong, forcible, but rather savage personality, and the secret of his success seems to be that he knows his own mind. Though his horizon is not very extensive, he sees very clearly what is within the range of his vision, and he goes straight for his purpose, ruthlessly and relentlessly, regardless of anything. Not an orator in the sense that Gladstone was, never displaying much imagination or flights of fancy, Mr. Chamberlain yet possesses the rare power of lucidity of utterance. In my opinion, his great weakness is that he is too impulsive and too impatient, and though the point is as yet in the region of controversy, I do not think the Colonial Secretary is a great statesman.

Something has already been said of Mr. Lloyd George's sincere belief in Mr. Chamberlain's desire for social reform. Later in this volume I shall have to tell the story of the rioting of the Colonial Secretary's loyal followers at Birmingham when Mr. Lloyd George endeavoured to address a meeting there. It is impressed upon the memory of Mr. Lloyd George's friends that at that very time, when excuse might have been found for some bitterness of feeling and of speech, Mr. Lloyd George expressed to them his unshaken belief in the excellence of Mr. Chamberlain's intentions towards the common people. He has always seen in him the Radical, if the Radical *manqué*. "It is a thousand pities," he said once, when his old opponent was in honourable retirement and he himself was Chancellor of the Exchequer, "that Chamberlain ever left the Radical Party. He could easily have made his terms with Gladstone over Home Rule. And he would have finished the House of Lords years ago."

I am unable to say how far Mr. Chamberlain reciprocated the very real admiration that his political enemy felt for him, although it is certain, as has been shown above,[1] that he recognised his ability and welcomed his co-operation in a social scheme. The Colonial Secretary might be forgiven, however, if he felt that Mr. Lloyd George dissembled his admiration, and it is impossible to read the speeches delivered by the member for the Carnarvon Boroughs during the war without recognising that it was not merely the desire to score in debate over the strongest available

[1] See p. 215.

opponent that distinguished them. Mr. Chamberlain had made himself responsible for what was in Mr. Lloyd George's eyes a wicked and ignoble cause. Indignation joined with ambition to produce the clever, bitter, and, above all, sincere speeches with which, in the country and in Parliament, the Colonial Secretary found himself assailed.

The House of Commons met to hear the Queen's Speech on December 6. On the 10th, Mr. Lloyd George moved an amendment to the Address which brought him into sharp conflict with Mr. Chamberlain. The amendment proposed to represent to Her Majesty " that Ministers of the Crown and members of either House of Parliament holding subordinate office ought to have no interest, direct or indirect, in any firm or company competing for contracts with the Crown, unless, the nature and extent of such interest being first declared, your Majesty shall have sanctioned the countenance thereof, and, when necessary, shall have directed such precautions to be taken as may effectually prevent any suspicion of influence or favouritism in the allocation of such contracts." Unusual interest in the question of Ministers and Government contracts had been aroused by the publication, before and during the General Election, of facts which showed that several members of the Colonial Secretary's family were shareholders in " Kynochs, Limited," a cordite-manufacturing company. In 1895, when the Liberal Government fell upon the cordite vote, Mr. Chamberlain had expressly claimed to speak as a member who had a connection—through his constituency—with the manufacture of cordite. He did not, he said, think the cordite was actually manufactured at Birmingham, but the firm of Kynoch & Co., whose headquarters were at Aston, a suburb of Birmingham, were cordite manufacturers, and, therefore, he had the legitimate interest in the matter which, as representing his constituents, he might be expected to have.

It may well be that, at the moment of making those observations, Mr. Chamberlain was oblivious of the fact that his brother was chairman of Kynochs, and that the total interest of members of the Chamberlain family in the concern, taking the shares at their par value, was £75,200. Further investigation showed that, in other companies which had in fact profited by the war, Mr. Chamberlain himself had an interest. Stated in that way, these facts could be made to look almost damning: they were, however, susceptible of a perfectly innocent explanation. One of the companies, for instance, was a " trust company," given a general direction by its shareholders to invest their money for them in other concerns, and had made an investment, of which Mr. Chamberlain had, and could have, no knowledge, in a concern which supplied boiler tubes to the Admiralty. He had sold out of Kynochs on entering public life. In a word, Mr. Chamberlain was in a position to prove, as few can have seriously doubted, that his personal integrity was as far beyond reproach as had always been believed. On the other hand, it could not seriously be doubted that there was proper matter for investigation in the facts. There was no doubt that Kynochs had been treated with exceptional partiality in the matter of War Office contracts. There was much to be said for the view that Government departments were not likely to be most vigilant when they were dealing with a firm in whose composition the members of a Cabinet Minister's family, some of whom lived under his roof-tree, figured largely. Mr. Austen Chamberlain, Civil Lord of the Admiralty, held six hundred shares in a firm which supplied a certain small quantity of ship's fittings to the Admiralty, and though, here again, a charge of corruption was ridiculous, there was, as it seemed to many, a question of principle involved. It was always the fashion to quote Mr. Joseph Chamberlain against himself, and some words of his upon the appointment of Sir Hercules Robinson (afterwards Lord Rosmead) as High Commissioner of South Africa were now quoted with effect :

I may admit that in no conceivable circumstances will Sir Hercules Robinson be improperly influenced by his previous connection with these speculations. But something more than that is expected of a person who has been appointed to represent the Queen in a Colonial Government. It is not only necessary that he should be pure, but, like Cæsar's wife, he must not be suspected.

Debates upon the Address, however unfruitful they may be, are often not lacking in interest. Visitors to the House of Commons on December 10, 1900, looked down upon a varied and very interesting entertainment. The debate on Mr. Lloyd George's amendment was immediately preceded by a peculiarly piquant discussion in which Mr. Balfour found himself called upon to defend the very substantial part which recognition of his own family's abilities had played in influencing Lord Salisbury's choice of a Cabinet. The satire of Mr. Gibson Bowles had enlivened a topic in itself entertaining, and it was in a very full House that Mr. Lloyd George rose. To any stranger who had derived his ideas of Mr. Lloyd George from the contemporary Press, and expected to see him, at the worst, a raging fanatic, and, at the best, an ebullient zealot, the speech he made must have come as a revelation. His manner was quiet and restrained, his criticism had the air of judicial detachment and impartiality which we are accustomed to look for in a barrister appearing as counsel for the prosecution. In the course of his speech an incident occurred which passed unobserved, save by very few. He had been speaking only a few minutes when a slip of paper was handed to him. This was a message from a clerk who had been sent to Somerset House to verify the facts as published in a London newspaper. It was characteristic of the caution which I have ascribed elsewhere to Mr. Lloyd George that he had not taken any facts or figures on trust. The slip of paper contained a correction of some item in the published statement. A copy of the newspaper in question was in Mr. Lloyd George's hand as he spoke, and Mr. Chamberlain's eye was no doubt upon it, although he wore that air of indifference and inattention which Ministers under fire are prone to assume. The speaker reached the point where a quotation of the inaccuracy seemed to be impending. Mr. Chamberlain became attentive : a moment later he was in his characteristic attitude, eager and ready to pounce. Mr. Lloyd George went on—not to quote the mistake, but to state the fact correctly. Mr. Chamberlain relapsed into his studiously inattentive attitude.

I quote the peroration of the speech :

I have stated the whole of the facts, and I am exceedingly obliged to the House for their kindness in listening to me so long. I put it again, that I brought the subject forward on the ground of the importance of ensuring that regulations of this character, as laid down by the right honourable gentleman himself, should be rigidly enforced. We have a proud pre-eminence as a country in this matter. One of the first things anybody hears after crossing the Atlantic is charges of corruption brought against public men in connection with public municipalities, and even the State. It is suggested that contracts are given purely from influence, and if any one draws a contrast between that country and this, his heart is filled with British pride at the purity of our statesmanship. I do not say that the Secretary for the Colonies or the Financial Secretary to the Treasury has done anything to lower the standard of proud pre-eminence which we enjoy as a country in this matter. What I do say is that they have given legitimate ground for uneasiness, and, above all, they have established precedents, which, if they are followed, would lead to something infinitely worse than anything I have spoken of to-day.

Mr. Chamberlain, as has been said, and as was to be expected, was able to show that there was nothing discreditable to himself in his connection with any company named. It is, however, I think a fair comment on a great part of his speech to say that it was an answer—an eloquent and adroit answer—not to Mr. Lloyd George, but to scandalmongers, real or imaginary, outside the House. He did not deal with and explain his plea for Kynochs in 1895. He took the line that the intention of his critics, among whom was Mr. Robson, who, at least, was not disqualified on the ground of being a "pro-Boer," was to attack his honour.

I have never complained of any attack made upon me in a fair field and in regard to my public action ; but this is not a fair fight, and I do think it hard that, after twenty-five years of Parliamentary service, in the full light of day, I should have to stand up here and explain to my colleagues on both sides of the House that I am not a thief and a scoundrel.

If Mr. Lloyd George's speech was comparable with that of a prosecuting counsel, Mr. Chamberlain's might be compared justly enough to the oration of a counsel briefed for the defence and masking the real point by a great display of forensic indignation. The plea was successful. The amendment was defeated by a majority of 142, a majority larger by forty than that which had rallied to support the Cecilian claim to a monopoly of all the talents.

II

A problem of civilised warfare—The concentration camps—Mr. Lloyd George's denunciation —Sir Henry Campbell-Bannerman on " methods of barbarism "—The Queen's Hall meeting—Differences among Liberal leaders—A portrait of Mr. Lloyd George.

Our generals in South Africa and the Government at home were confronted with new problems in the ethics of warfare. Of these none was more complex, and none in its solution aroused more bitter feeling, than that of the treatment to be accorded to the wives and children of Boers who were thrown upon the hands of our conquering but embarrassed forces. What was done, as all the world knows, was to house them in so-called concentration camps, a term which came to denote to the headlong Imperialist a kind of charitable shelter from the rigours of war and famine, and to the sterner critics of the Ministry a loathsome prison. On the one hand, it was said that, for good or ill, we had been forced into the policy of the concentration camps by the consequences of our original quixotic humanity. Lord Roberts had begun by making a sentimental blunder.[1] He had allowed Boers on parole in the Orange Free State to go back to their farms. The result was that every farmhouse became a fresh recruiting agency for the enemy, and after the men had gone back on commando the farmhouses occupied by the women became depots from which the Boer forces obtained supplies and information as to the movements of our troops. Thus the policy of farm-burning was justified. "We are not going to do anything," said Mr. Brodrick, "in order to please Exeter Hall, and some adherents of Exeter Hall in the House of Commons, that will put a difficulty in the way of Lord Kitchener in his work of bringing this campaign to an early conclusion." We had, however, continued to display a generosity that did us credit. We might have left Boer women and children to starve and die upon the blackened waste that our victorious troops had left behind them. Instead of that we had housed them with as much comfort as the circumstances allowed, and fed them with rations not inferior to those supplied to our own soldiers. It was necessary to admit that the infantile mortality in the camps had been deplorably high, but that was due in part to epidemics over which little control could be exercised, in part to the ignorance and insanitary habits of many of the Boer mothers.

On the other side it was denied that farm-burning had been adopted as a policy only in cases of treachery of the inhabitants. According to a Government Return between five and six hundred farms were burned between June 1900 and January 1901. "In a few instances," the Return stated, "they were burned without orders and by some persons unknown." In many cases the charge which was put forward to justify the burning was one of treachery in some form or other, but in the Orange River Colony 132 were destroyed in compliance with orders to lay waste the country because used as a base by the enemy, and fifty-four because the owner or occupier was on commando. "In no inconsiderable number of cases," said the Imperialist and Conservative "St. James's Gazette," "measures have been taken which cannot be justified by any canon of civilised warfare."[2] We could not even plead a military necessity, therefore, for the concentration camps, still less a sentimental generosity. Having incurred a grave and awful responsibility for the Boer women and children, we had herded them in camps, with so little forethought that no contributory negligence on the part of Boer mothers could avail us as an excuse. We had from ignorance or carelessness

[1] See Mr. Brodrick's speech in the House of Commons, June 17, 1901.
[2] May 16, 1901.

disregarded elementary precautions, and unbiassed critics, and even critics whose bias was against the Boers, united to condemn the arrangements of the camps.

Considerable feeling on both sides was aroused by the publication early in the summer of 1901 of a report by Miss Emily Hobhouse upon the condition of the concentration camps. Miss Hobhouse had gone to South Africa at the end of 1900, as the delegate of the Distress Fund for South African Women and Children, and had spent three months in investigation. Her report, while it did not impute any inhumanity to our soldiers, was a formidable indictment of the system, and it showed the existence of a problem of such difficulty and magnitude as to demand the strictest investigation.

The fault of the Government was that, strong in its invincible majority and sheltering in the folds of the Union Jack, it would never apologise or make admissions. Conscious of their virtue as of their strength, Ministers appealed from a prejudiced Europe to the verdict of posterity to recognise the sublime and unprecedented chivalry of their policy. The result was that they laid themselves open to charges of indifference which the sweeping reforms Mr. Chamberlain made later in the administration of the camps showed him not to deserve.

Mr. Lloyd George's attitude upon the subject may be gathered from a speech at Pwllheli on October 23, 1901 :

Some people are under the impression that these camps are another proof of what is called the policy of mistaken leniency. I have seen it said—in fact, it is one of the commonplaces of the war—that never in the history of the world has there been such quixotic tenderness displayed towards an enemy as to feed and care for his women and children whilst he was engaged in shooting down our men. Now what are the real facts ? They are carefully suppressed in the Unionist and Jingo Press. In order to render the country absolutely untenable by the Boer commandos, and to force them into surrender by sheer starvation, it was decided to go in for what was called denuding the country. What did that mean ? The villages were burnt to the ground ; all the farmhouses were blown up, so that there should be no shelter from one end of the country to the other for a single rover ; the cattle were swept away ; such of the grain as could not be carried away was burnt. Thousands of tons have been burnt. So determined were the military authorities that there should be nothing left for either man or beast that they destroyed all the agricultural implements, all the mills, and broke open the irrigation dams, so that the territory over which our armies had trodden was left a blackened, devastated wilderness. I am not criticising that policy for the moment. It may be said that it was a purely military operation, and the only comment I offer upon it is that the event has proved it to be, like every other measure of harshness, an acknowledged failure. But what was to be done with the women and children who dwelt in those villages and farmhouses ? Is it suggested that they should be left in this barren wilderness created by ourselves, without shelter or sustenance, to die of famine and cold ? And if the military authorities took the view that it was their bounden duty not to commit such a monstrosity, where was the excessive mercifulness of the proceeding which herded them in the depths of winter in thin, leaky tents, surrounded by barbed wire, where thousands of them have died from the privations they unnecessarily suffered ? If this conduct is to be defended on the ground of military tactics, let them do so, but at any rate do not let them add hypocrisy to the other crimes of this war. How did this mistaken leniency work for its victims ? Since the month of June we have been furnished with official figures showing the mortality in the camps. A good deal has been said about the splendid way these people were cared for. The answer to that is the number of deaths. Whosoever bears false testimony about the facts in Africa, at least death never lies. In June the death-rate among the children in the Orange River Colony camps was at the rate of 192 per thousand per annum, and in the Transvaal 233 per thousand per annum. In July the figures were 220 and 366 per thousand per annum respectively. In August they had risen to 250 and 468, and in September to 422 in Orange River Colony and to 457 in the Transvaal. These are truly appalling figures. It means that at that rate in two years' time there would not be a little child left in the whole of these two new territories of the King. The worst of it is that I cannot resist the conclusion that their lives could be saved had it not been that these camps had been deliberately chosen for military purposes. In the few camps near the coast there is hardly any mortality at all, and if the children had been removed from the Orange River Colony and the Transvaal to the seacoast, where they could have been easily fed and clothed and cared for, their lives might be saved ; but as long as they were kept up in the north there was a terrible inducement offered to the Boer commandos not to attack the lines of communication. Whatever may be the temporary gain, who is there who still believes in the control of Providence, who will not dread the punishment that must necessarily befall this treatment of the innocent and unprotected ? If I were to despair for the future of this country it would not be because of trade competition from either America or Germany, or the ineffectiveness of its army, or anything that might happen to its ships ; but rather because it used its great, hulking strength to torture the little child. Had it not been that this Ministry has shown distinct symptoms of softening of the brain, I would call the torpor and indifference they are showing in face of all this criminal. It is a maddening horror, and it will haunt the Empire to its dying hour. What wonder is it that Europe should mock and hiss at us ? Let any honest Britisher fearlessly search his heart and answer this question : Is there any ground for the reproach flung at us by the civilised world that, having failed to crush the men, we have now taken to killing babes ?

There were, of course, many to whom such comments seemed totally unjustifiable, whether the facts on which they were based were made out or not, and men who took that view were to be found as well in the Liberal as in the Conservative Party. This fact caused a considerable cleavage in the Liberal ranks. It is fortunately no part of the task undertaken in this book to relate in detail the controversies among the leaders of Liberalism which, while the war lasted, were the only theme of light relief at political meetings in the Tory camp. Lord Rosebery and Sir William Harcourt, who had both found the leadership uncongenial and untenable, had been separated by a wider gulf than ever. Sir Henry Campbell-Bannerman, in his attempts to carry out what Mr. Lloyd George called his *métier* of keeping the party together, laid himself open to the obvious criticism that he did not know his own mind. His ablest lieutenants gave him divided counsel. It was a day of mutual distrust. The existence of cabals was suspected on either side. In the words of Mr. Birrell, the history of the Liberal Party " was becoming painfully intestinal."

In the summer things came to a head, and Mr. Lloyd George was so prominent a figure in their development, that, although this is not a history of the Liberal Party, some account must be given of the course of events. It was upon the question of farm-burning and of the concentration camps that the crisis in the party definitely arose. On June 14 the National Reform Union, a body presided over by Mr. Philip Stanhope (afterwards Lord Weardale), entertained Sir William Harcourt and Sir Henry Campbell-Bannerman at dinner. The latter took occasion to deal with the means which we were employing in the war. My readers, remembering, as they must, the greatest achievement of Campbell-Bannerman's life, will be ready, as few Englishmen were in 1901, to see that his strong criticism of a policy which, however necessary from a military point of view it may have been, had as a probable consequence the embitterment of our relations with the Boers, was based upon a statesmanlike foresight. With the fullest sense of future responsibility, he laboured as leader of the Opposition to lay a sure foundation for the peaceful settlement which, as time showed, it was his destiny to inaugurate. In his speech to the National Reform Union he sternly censured the policy of the concentration camps and their deficient organisation, and he used a phrase which was fastened upon and repeated for years afterwards, in default of argument, by opponents who sought to overwhelm him with obloquy.

A phrase often used is that " war is war," but when one comes to ask about it, one is told that no war is going on—that it is not war. When is a war not a war ? When it is carried on by methods of barbarism in South Africa.

Mr. John Morley, who also spoke, was at pains to underline the speech of his leader. He could not for one moment doubt, he said, that they were not that night in any cross-current of Liberalism, not in any wayward or retrograde eddy, but they were in the main stream.

He found, he added, that many of his own friends in the House of Commons had forgotten that they ever supported this war.

Gentlemen, we have found it very difficult to persuade some of our friends that in politics there is a difference between right and wrong ; but there is a second great law of our moral being to which, I think, they are accessible, and that is that there is a relation between cause and effect.

The leader's " methods of barbarism " speech, as it came to be called, was followed on June 17 by a motion for the adjournment of the House by Mr. Lloyd George in order to call attention to the condition of the concentration camps. He made a fierce speech against the administration of the camps, and suggested with bitter sarcasm that what had happened there had entitled Lord Milner to his peerage. His speech was resented by many members on his own side of the House. Mr. Haldane,[1] who spoke for the Liberal Imperialists, said that he had yet to be convinced that there had been brought home to the Government or to the distinguished soldiers in command of the military operations any blameworthiness for a state of things which, if it was blameworthy, was blameworthy because of causes far deeper and reasons more far-reaching than any mere incidents that could happen in the course of a great military campaign. Sir Henry Campbell-Bannerman, however, supported Mr. Lloyd George's motion, and incidentally repeated and explained the passage in his own previous speech which had aroused so much comment.

Miss Hobhouse [he said] brings no accusation, and I assume none of us would do so—at least, speaking for myself, I never said a word that would imply cruelty or even indifference on the part of officers or men in the British Army. It is the whole system that I consider—to use a word which I have already applied to it—barbarous. There are no people in the world who feel that barbarity more than the unfortunate men whose duty it is to enforce that system.

[1] Viscount Haldane of Cloan.

Liberal Imperialists did not listen with any pleasure to the speech of their titular leader in the House of Commons. Two days later a demonstration was held at the Queen's Hall, London, which was for a long time held up to scorn by Tories as the extreme limit which pro-Boerism had reached. It was a ticket meeting, at which all precautions were successfully taken to exclude demonstrators of another colour, although an angry mob besieged the hall and threatened to do mischief. It was addressed by Mr. Sauer, who had come to Europe with Mr. Merriman in order to plead the cause of peace from the point of view of the Boers. Mr. Labouchere, the member for Northampton and Editor of "Truth," was in the chair. A resolution was proposed by Mr. Lloyd George which condemned the South African policy of the Government "as contrary to the highest interest and best traditions of the British people," protested against the continuance of "an unjust and dastardly war," and demanded "such an offer of peace to the Boers and the two Republics as a brave and freedom-loving people could honourably accept." Mr. Stead, the Editor of the "Review of Reviews," was on the platform, and he has left on record the impression he formed of Mr. Lloyd George, whom he then saw for the first time.

He excited immense enthusiasm, but the impression he left on me was that he was too slight in physique to be able to play a great rôle in an arena where stamina counts for so much. He had, however, evidently immense nervous energy, first-class pluck, and the knack of saying biting things in a most effective fashion.

However distasteful Mr. Lloyd George's sentiments were to the mass of the people, they were the outpouring of a sincere passion. "I thank Heaven," he cried, "for the spectacle of one little nation of peasants standing against the mightiest Empire in the world, preferring to die rather than prostrate itself with the other nations of the earth at the feet of the vulgar priesthood of Mammon."

Such sentiments, publicly expressed by a Liberal who had received the approval of Sir Henry Campbell-Bannerman, contributed to alienate still further the Imperialist wing of the party. Moreover, the chairman of the meeting and the mover of the resolution were both a little prejudiced by the action of the meeting, which refused to be content with the resolution and carried by acclamation an amendment declaring for the complete independence of the Boers, an ideal which, as has been seen, Mr. Lloyd George had definitely abandoned as unpractical.

II—4

The next evening Mr. Asquith, who held first place among the Imperialists, delivered himself of what was in substance a reply to the speeches of Sir Henry Campbell-Bannerman and Mr. Morley at the banquet of the National Reform Union ; and so began what was called by some wit a " war to the knife and fork " between the Liberal leaders. Mr. Morley's ironical sentences had rankled in Mr. Asquith's mind, as was perhaps not surprising, and he declared himself convinced that his country was engaged in no criminal adventure, but in a campaign not of her own seeking, out of which it was her purpose that there should arise, " upon the scene at present of so much desolation and ruin, the fabric of a free, federated, self-governing South African dominion."

On July 2, after an interval for reflection, Sir Henry Campbell-Bannerman returned to the charge at Southampton. He again condemned the management of the concentration camps, and pointed out with perfect truth and justice that the result of criticism had been that some of the objectionable features of Government policy with regard to them had already been removed, Two grounds of complaint had been, first, that women who had husbands on commando had been supplied with smaller rations than the others in the camps ; secondly, that persons had been detained in the camps who could have been supported adequately by their friends and relations outside. Both those charges had been admitted, and in each case a promise had been given in the House of Commons that the offence would not be repeated. As to the differences in the party, Sir Henry levelled a strong criticism at intriguers whose presence, rightly or wrongly, he suspected in the Imperialist ranks. He had occupied a difficult position and had refused to ally himself with any extreme section.

It is now seemingly impossible to preserve unity [he said], owing to the persistent schemes and efforts of a few men, who, under the influence of some personal jealousy or antipathy of their own, are constantly and actively engaged in magnifying and embittering such differences in political opinion as exist.

He would appeal to his fellow-members in the House, and if necessary, beyond them, to all true Liberals throughout the country, for their support in the effort to put down this disorder and to restore efficiency to the great historical party to which they belonged.

" C.-B. is doing well," Mr. Lloyd George wrote in a letter the next day. " His speech last night was excellent. He is showing his mettle and winning the respect of friend and foe."

There were, however, friends who were disposed to be more than candid, and there was a natural disposition among the foes of the party to take advantage of the confessed divisions in the opposite camp. On July 4, in the debate upon the second reading of the War Loan Bill, Sir Henry Campbell-Bannerman was told by Mr. Balfour that he had come off the fence and made " a frankly pro-Boer speech." The keynote of the speech which was thus described was a plea for such a conduct of the war as should not destroy all hopes of conciliation. If the Government were to go on shutting their eyes to everything except the main object of beating down the Boers, then they would leave behind them after the war was over a state of things with which it would be impossible either for the statesmanship or the power of this country to cope. Mr. Lloyd George took part in the debate and declared that the Government had caused the Dutch population of South Africa to hate the name of Britain. The Government, he said, in an impressive peroration, had taken the risks of war : was it not time that we had a statesman who was prepared to take the risks of peace ? In the course of his speech he denied that he was in favour of independence for the Boers, and Mr. Brodrick, who spoke after him, taunted him with the amended resolution carried at the Queen's Hall Meeting. " I have absolutely no responsibility for the amendment," he replied. Mr. Brodrick's retort was that he had no doubt voted for it. " The right honourable gentleman has no right to say that," Mr. Lloyd George answered, and Mr. Labouchere, who spoke subsequently, declared that his own responsibility for the amendment was limited to that of a chairman who is compelled to put to the meeting any amendment that has been formally proposed and seconded.

The breach between Liberal leaders had grown so wide that there was an attempt upon a grand scale to heal it. On July 9 a large gathering of Liberal members of Parliament, which included Mr. Lloyd George, met at the Reform Club and proceeded, as Lord Rosebery put it, to unite, or re-unite, " on the double basis of a hearty and undisputed allegiance to its leader and a complete liberty of action and dissent with regard to the one vital question before the country." [1] At this meeting Sir Henry carried out his promise to appeal to his fellow-members. In his speech he called upon the " solid, earnest, loyal men " he saw before him to lend him their aid in extinguishing cabals, and declared again that the party was divided, " not on account of real and essential divergences of opinion, but because of the

[1] See Lord Rosebery's open letter to members of the City Liberal Club, dated July 16, 1901.

operation of certain personal antagonisms which for the last half-a-dozen years had disturbed and paralysed the Liberal Party in Parliament." A resolution of confidence was proposed, and the result showed that the peace-makers had been at work. Sir William Harcourt, Mr. Asquith, and Sir Edward Grey all joined in supporting it. Mr. Asquith made a straightforward, downright speech. If there were cabals, he knew nothing of them. He had differed from his leader, but never had a body of men worked together with more cordial personal goodwill than the occupants of the front Opposition bench. It was useless, however, to fancy that you could get rid of differences by resorting to ambiguous formulæ. Sir Edward Grey also claimed " complete tolerance in regard to differences of opinion," and upon that foundation Liberal unity for the time being rested. Lord Rosebery, " ploughing his furrow alone," denounced the pious resolution as an avoidance of the question at issue, and trembled on the verge of applying to it the phrase which Beaconsfield applied to his own party—" an organised hypocrisy." [1]

It has been necessary to remind the reader of the course of the Liberal Party's history at the date with which we are dealing in order to make clear the position Mr. Lloyd George occupied within it. It was a position of complete independence. He had, as has been seen, made up his mind for himself after long cogitation, and certainly the authority of this or that eminent leader had no share in helping him to his decision. His own resolve had thrown him into the camp of Sir Henry Campbell-Bannerman, but he did not, as we shall see, shrink from even merciless criticism of that cautious leader when, as he thought, the occasion required it. The Tory Press of the day liked to picture him as Sir Henry's evil genius. According to the elegant analogy of one Ministerialist, he played the sinister part of Dr. Leyds to the Kruger of his pliable leader. No view of the relations between the two men could have been blinder or more foolish. But public men, as they are seen by the public eye, are often creatures as fabulous as the monsters or demi-gods of mythology. Some journalist or opponent labels a politician with a phrase, and it clings as closely as the mask to a Greek actor until the shifting scene calls for new disguise. He ceases to be a man and becomes a type.

Among Liberals Sir Henry Campbell-Bannerman was just beginning, in spite of feuds and dissensions, to come into his own, as Mr. Lloyd George pointed out in an interview which will be quoted presently. The Conservative Press, however, still portrayed him as a weak, shilly-shallying, nerveless leader, without

[1] Speech at the City Liberal Club, July 19, 1901.

courage and without backbone, and the great mass of its readers, at any rate south of the Tweed, being at this time ready enough to believe evil of any one to whom the label " Pro-Boer" had been attached, was content to accept the portrait. Similarly, Mr. Lloyd George was imaged as a wild and audacious leader of an openly disloyal faction. The least inspiring speaker on a Tory platform, the most insipid humorist upon the music-hall stage, could be sure of awakening enthusiasm in his audience by a gibe, however clumsy, at this typical " pro-Boer." According to one writer in the Conservative Press, this was a positive advantage to him.[1]

In reckoning the future of a public man the aptitude for attracting attention must outweigh most other qualities. It is the power of making yourself a storm-centre that tells—the power of making controversies rage round you personally, of making yourself the pivot about which conflicting factions revolve—this is the power that promises success in the world of affairs. It matters little whether you arouse a storm of approbation or a whirlwind of abuse, so long as your individuality stirs men's passions to the depths. It is of small consequence whether you are a public idol or the detested of the masses, so long as the very mention of your name thrills men's emotions—the transition from villain to hero is but a small one on the political stage, one that the changing limelight of public opinion effects automatically. The important thing is that the gaze of the audience should be riveted on you.

The article from which I quote was doubtless intended as a corrective to the crude picture drawn by opponents with less fairness and knowledge, and if it is not a sympathetic appreciation, it does show very clearly how Mr. Lloyd George appeared at the end of the 1901 session to a critic of considerable insight. There were, this critic wrote, many Radical stalwarts before the days of Mr. Lloyd George, men as advanced in their views, as violent in their opinions, as steadfast in their principles, as fierce in their utterances as he, men at the beginning of the session better known far to the man in the street than he. Then he arose, and in an instant all these prominent persons were referred to as Lloyd-Georgeites ; they became a mere mob of mediocrity, whose only claim to distinction was that they voiced the same opinions as the man who could catch the public ear.

Those opinions existed before Mr. Lloyd George had been tucked ; now they are notable and known chiefly because he holds them. The doctrines and doctrinaires alike shine only by reflected glory from the

[1] See an article signed " M." in the " Daily Mail," October 3, 1901.

man who has suddenly taken the centre of the stage and appropriated all the limelight. He is the actor—the rest are mere chorus ; they have dwindled into insignificance in the presence of the man who can make himself prominent.

The writer described Mr. Lloyd George as "a short, somewhat commonplace-looking individual," with nothing remarkable about him to reveal his special power.

He would by most be described as of insignificant appearance. With his fresh-coloured complexion, his slightly unruly dark brown hair, combed up from the forehead, his small dark moustache, his sharp features, and his quick eyes, he suggests nothing more important than a very ordinary member of the middle classes ; he might, with his straight, unremarkable frock-coat and dark, uncreased trousers be doing well in a small way of business, or else be taken for a valuable assistant in a large concern. Certainly there is nothing about his exterior that would have led one to prophesy that he would so soon make his mark in the councils of the nation. His manner, too—the jaunty self-assurance, thoroughly in keeping with his appearance—is not one that in itself would assure him success in all circles.

Yet even in private intercourse one's first impression of the man immediately gives way to a feeling that there is a something about him out of the common. He speaks with a decision and a certainty that carry conviction. You feel as you talk to him that he has something to say worth listening to—that he is not, after all, of the common ruck. He makes no pretence at fine polish, but there is that about him which, despite his appearance and his manner, impresses you with a sense of authority and almost of dignity. He has a self-assertiveness, a self-assurance that make him stand out in any company. He could never be overlooked. You always know he is there.

It is not mere bumptiousness, no mere vulgar impudence that effects this. It is something far more solid, more imposing—a grand, unhesitating belief in his own ability. Where mere bumptiousness would irritate you into scornful pity, this man compels your attention. He makes you feel there is solid ground for his confidence in himself. He is always so positive, so definite, not with the dogmatism of common impudence, but with the unreasoning certainty that is impatient of opposition. You feel as he speaks that he looks down with contempt on all who hold views different from those he expresses, and the fact impresses you.

From a character sketch which, it will be agreed, well deserved to be rescued from the limbo of the files, I must quote one more passage. It is in part a comparison between Mr. Lloyd George and his great antagonist, in part a prophecy which time has

shown to be none too optimistic, although few would have given
it credence when it was written :

There is, indeed, a very remarkable similarity between the Lloyd George
of to-day and the " Joe " Chamberlain of twenty years ago. The man of
now, like the man of then, has an indomitable, unquestioning self-confidence, an irresistible pushfulness. Sprung from no exalted parentage, he
has forged his way to prosperity by the same dogged tenacity, the same
relentless business ability as made Nettlefolds one of the best-known
names in the commercial world.

Like his prototype of two decades ago, Mr. Lloyd George began his
parliamentary career careless of personal appearance, and with side-
whiskers. With the advent of fame—or notoriety—the side-whiskers
vanished, the hair was cut and groomed, and a band-box smartness replaced
the careless *négligé*.

Look at him in debate, leaning forward, eager, keen, alert, hand to
ear, ready to spring on his prey and rend him to pieces—the reflection of
what his great adversary once was. His very manner of rising is reminis-
cent—the sudden leap to his feet, the momentary pause to shake out his
coat-tails and stretch his shirt-cuffs ; it was done just so almost in that
very place years ago.

The moment he opens his mouth to speak the similarity is so striking
as to make the listener start involuntarily. Listen ! The same clear,
low-pitched, cruel voice ; the same keen, incisive phrases ; the same
mordant bitterness ; the same caustic sneer ; the same sardonic humour ;
the same personal enmity. It is the very re-incarnation of the present
Colonial Secretary in his younger days—a spectre of his dead self arisen to
haunt him. A little more excited, you say, a trifle more violent in gesture,
more impassioned in delivery ; yes, more than Mr. Chamberlain now is,
but recall the turbulent outbursts of his earlier days, the fire and
impetuosity of his vigorous youth, before he had learned the secret that
the cold, bitter vitriol bites deeper than the glittering knife.

The very substance of his speech is as a far-away echo of a well-remem-
bered eulogy of our present foes—Mr. Chamberlain's splendid advocacy of
the Majuba compromise. Will time, that has had so mellowing an influence on that great Imperialist, work a similar change in the virulent Little
Englander ? Will he a score of years hence be the tower of strength of
the Imperial or the Parochial party ? None can now say, but that he will
by then be one of the foremost men in the nation's Parliament is beyond
question. His faults are the faults of inexperience, of strength untried
and untrained ; but strength, force of character, individuality are there
without a doubt. . . . To-day the little Welsh lawyer is a man to be
reckoned with in the councils of the nation ; to-morrow he will be a con-
trolling voice on one side or the other. . . . His views may not now be
acceptable to the people of this country, but here time is on his side. He
is of the type that moulds public opinion to his own.

III

In October and November Mr. Lloyd George addressed a series of peace meetings in Wales.[1] By this time there was little of the war fever left in that country, and he met with a great reception. It is interesting to observe how his speeches to his own countrymen are filled always with picturesque touches racy of the soil. As an instance, let me quote a fragment from a speech delivered in Welsh at Llangeitho :

In the village in which I was reared, at the foot of Snowdon, there was a mill which was worked by a small stream, and in order to keep the water up to the level of the wheel the miller had to build an embankment. I remember that the village children used to make a hole in the embankment and so prevent the water from reaching the mill wheel. Then the miller would wonder what had happened : he would oil his machinery and see that it was in perfect working order, but the sacks of corn would keep on accumulating until at last he found out the real cause. Then he would fill up the breach and the water would flow on towards the wheel, and the sacks of corn would be ground into flour.

The British Parliament is still in existence, the machinery is in perfect working order, but the motive power is wanting. People go to the mill at Westminster and say, " Make us a sackful of land laws." Others want a sackful of temperance legislation, and others a sackful of disestablishment; but nothing is turned out from the mill. What is the matter ? There is a wicked child of the name of Joseph Chamberlain who has made a hole in the weir, and the river of national enthusiasm and energy and strength is running to South Africa.

At Llanelly he dealt, in a very typical passage, with the charge that he was a pro-Boer and that his speeches were encouraging the Boers in the field. He was given his cue by the interruption of a " voice," which seemed to be inevitable at political meetings in those days, " What about Majuba ? "

Yes, what about it ? I will give you an answer. You have sown Africa with Majubas. Disaster after disaster has befallen the men who went there to show how much better they could do the thing than Mr. Gladstone. . . . There is a certain class of man who thinks he has disposed of any argument by simply calling one a pro-Boer. That is the silly delusion of silly men. You settle nothing in a controversy by calling your

[1] Llanelly (Oct. 7), Llangeitho (Oct. 18), Pwllheli (Oct. 23), Merthyr Tydfil (Nov. 15), Carnarvon (Nov. 22).

opponent nicknames, except it be your own weakness and intellectual sterility. It is not worthy of the dignity of a great controversy. It reminds you rather of a certain type of bird that is always using the same words time after time, without any sense of relevance and without even comprehending what they really mean. You know that bird. And I say that to be calling your opponents pro-Boers is not the device of a statesman, it is the trick of a political cockatoo. . . . I should like to ask: When John Bright opposed the Crimean War, was he a pro-Russian? Did he not rather oppose it in the best interests of his own country? But I should like to remind you of this—the Crimean War was far more popular with every class in the country than this Boer War. There were fewer men opposed to it: everybody said it was the right thing. Is there any one who does not now admit that it was a colossal blunder? Mr. Chamberlain denounced the Afghan War in 1879 and 1880—was he then called a pro-Afghan? More than that, Mr. Chamberlain signed a document charging Sir Frederick Roberts and his army with barbarism [1]—was he a traitor? Mr. Chamberlain also opposed the Zulu War. Was Mr. Chamberlain a nigger because he did so? Why then should they say that men who, entirely in the interests of their country, believe that this war was a mistake, a folly, a blunder—that these men are pro-Boers. These men are pro-Britons.

We may be all right, we may be all wrong. Time will tell. Do not forget that time has shown that most of the wars this country has been engaged in were blunders from the point of view of the people. At any rate, do give us the credit for being sincere in our motives, and as honest in our desire to promote the interests of Great Britain in this matter as you are.

Well, now, there is another cockatoo phrase very frequently used, and it is this. In criticising this war, they say, you are encouraging the Boers. Well, now, let us deal with that. It is really the stock argument. In the first place it is not true; in the second place it is not a genuine charge. Let me put this to you, and my Unionist auditors on the other side. Do they intend this canon of criticism for the military situation? I should like to know what their propositions are. Do they say you may criticise the military position, but you are a traitor if you criticise the political side of it? Why, what is the difference, from the point of view of encouraging the Boers? Now I will show you for a moment that this is a matter for calm discussion and argument. I do not want to appeal to any passion. My sole desire is to convince your reason, and if I do not succeed in that my visit here will be a failure. If you have read the Unionist papers during the last few days—there is a long list to-day of extracts from these papers in the " Daily Mail," all of them shaking their heads most pitifully, and saying how disquieting the outlook is—I ask every fair-minded man amongst my opponents, which is the more likely to give heart to the Boers: a speech from a member of the minority—and a very small minority, I admit—in Parliament, urging the Government to admit

---

[1] The reference is to a Memorial to Lord Salisbury, dated February 1880, and signed by Mr. Chamberlain.

the Boers into the Empire on the terms which have been given to the French in Canada, and which have already produced excellent results there; or a speech from a Unionist M.P. or an article in a Unionist paper, saying, for example, that our troops are weary and worn out, our generals are no good, that we cannot enlist enough men, that the whole position is very serious. Which of the two, I ask you, will give most encouragement to the Boers to go on ?

Immediately following this was an interesting allusion to Mr. Winston Churchill :

Last week there was a very interesting speech delivered by a brilliant young Tory member, Mr. Winston Churchill. There is no greater admirer of his talents, I assure you, than the individual who is now addressing you, and many a chat have we had about the situation. We do not always agree, but at the same time we do not black each other's eyes. We know too well that that is not the way to settle disputes, and we do not take each other by the scruff of the neck and fling each other down stairs. Well, what does he say ? If you read his speech he says that the situation is serious and disquieting, and the position is as momentous to-day as it was two years before the first shot was fired. That is not my statement. That is the statement of a strong supporter of the war, known to the Boers, do not forget. Now, Mr. Chamberlain said that every speech delivered in this country is read in Africa by the Boers. All I can say is : It is not very creditable to our Generals, who are supposed to be hustling them about, that they should have sufficient leisure to read speeches. Supposing it is true, and I have no doubt it is quite as true as most things Mr. Chamberlain says, what does it mean ? The Boers will read Mr. Winston Churchill's speech. They will say, " We know him : that is the young fellow we caught in the armoured train ; a bright, intelligent young lad he is." And they will say, " Here they are, for two years they have been exerting the whole strength of the Empire to crush us " ; and these Unionist members say that the position is just as bad as it was at the beginning of it. [A voice: " That encourages the Boers."] I ask that intelligent gentleman whether a statement like that of Mr. Winston Churchill is not much more likely to encourage the Boers than any poor speech that I can deliver.

The future colleagues had had their first encounter in the House on February 18, during a South African debate raised upon the Address. " I am going to stay in the House," Sir William Harcourt was heard to say to Mr. Lloyd George on that occasion, " to see the cock-fight between you and young Churchill." Mr. Lloyd George's speech that day had been an attack upon some aspects of the military conduct of the war. He had expressed the horror he felt at a policy which, as he believed, was using the sufferings of Boer women and children as a means of coercing Boer soldiers.

"The moderation of the amendment," Mr. Churchill said in his reply, "was the moderation of the honourable member's political friends and leaders, and the bitterness of the speech was all his own."

That there was bitterness in Mr. Lloyd George's speeches it would be idle to deny. Upon his theory of recent South African history bitterness of feeling was not merely excusable in, but to be demanded from, any man of sentiment and spirit. As the war went on, and entered upon its later phase, his bitterness became intensified. I will give the reason of this in words of burning eloquence of his own :

I am not going to discuss the origin of the war. As an old man said in the Sunday school once, " The question is not how sin came into the world, but how are you going to get it out of the world." Do you know that there have been two wars in Africa since October 11, 1899 ? The first was the war to repel invasion. I am not going to discuss now what brought that about or who was to blame. The second object was to establish equal rights. The third object, or at least the third avowed object, was to redress the grievance of British subjects in the Transvaal. That was the first war. Lord Salisbury said about a month after it commenced : " We seek no territories, we seek no goldfields." What has become of that war ? It came to an end with the capture of Bloemfontein, when the Boer forces were overthrown, beaten, and demoralised. That ended the first war. A sensible Government would then have brought it to an end. All wars—do not forget this—are so horrible in their incidents, so uncertain in their events, that sensible statesmen always, so long as they can achieve the object for which they entered upon war, will bring it to an end at the first convenient opportunity. The worst of it is, we have no statesmen at the head of our affairs. What did the Government do ? Instead of bringing the war to an end when the Boers were really beaten they changed the whole purpose of the war. Instead of making it a war to remedy grievances they suddenly said, No shred of independence—not a *shred*, mind you. The French in Canada within our Empire have internal independence, the inhabitants of Australia under the British flag have absolute internal independence. They can pass their own laws, they can tax our goods, and we dare not meddle with the management of their local affairs. The Boers might have had independence within the Empire. Lord Salisbury said, Not a shred. Then commenced the second war, a more inglorious, more protracted, more desperate, more disastrous, more costly war, and a war of which no man can foretell the end. Do not forget these two wars. I am here to-night to denounce the second.

In his view peace should and could have been made honourably and advantageously at three separate crises of the war. The first was after the capture of Bloemfontein.

The next was after the capture of Pretoria ; and here I will quote an authority that the strongest man will not challenge—that of Lord Milner. The passage is of such enormous importance that I will read it all to you. Lord Milner is talking about the recrudescence of the war, and says : " What is more serious, to my mind, than the mere material distraction of the last six months, is the moral effect of the recrudescence of the war. I am thinking especially of the Orange River Colony and of that portion of the Transvaal which fell so easily into our hands after the relief of Mafeking—that is to say, the country lying between Johannesburg and Pretoria and the borderland of Bechuanaland. Throughout this large area the feeling in the middle of last year was undoubtedly pacific. The inhabitants were sick of the war. They were greatly astonished, after all that had been dinned into them, by the fair and generous treatment they received on our occupation, and it would have taken very little to make them acquiesce readily in the new *régime*. At that time the feeling in the colony was better than I have ever known it. The rebellious element had blown off steam in an abortive insurrection, and was glad to settle down again." Why was not that " very little " suggested that would have brought in the Boers on our own terms ? The answer is unfortunately an obvious one. It is because we had a mere electioneer and not a statesman at the head of affairs, a man who had his eye not on Africa but on British polling-booths.

The third occasion on which peace could have been established on our own terms was in February 1901, when Lord Kitchener and General Botha met at Middelburg to discuss a settlement :

Now for the third occasion upon which peace could have been established on our own terms. It was when Lord Kitchener entered into negotiations with General Botha. Lord Kitchener states that he made it perfectly clear to General Botha that a recognition of Boer independence was out of the question. He declined even to discuss it with him, and he then proceeded to lay down generally an outline of his proposals for the establishment of peace. What was the first ? I will give it in Lord Kitchener's own words : " I said that, subject to correction from home, I understood that when hostilities ceased the military guard would be replaced by Crown Colony administration, consisting of nominated executive with elected assembly to advise administration, to be followed after a period by representative government." Mark now the very next words used by Lord Kitchener. They are most momentous. He says about General Botha— " He would have liked representative government at once, but seemed satisfied with above." Think for a moment what that means. In the month of February last the Commander-in-Chief of the Boer forces seemed satisfied to accept the annexation of the Republics as an established fact— a British governor, with an executive nominated by that governor—provided the people of the country were allowed to elect a council to advise that governor. How is it that when both Generals seemed to have arrived at an understanding satisfactory to them, and certainly satisfactory to this country, peace was not concluded ? Just follow the sequence of events.

Lord Milner was consulted upon these proposals. He approved in the main of Lord Kitchener's action. Both Lord Kitchener and Lord Milner referred the matter to Mr. Chamberlain for his final sanction, and then the mischief came in. Mr. Chamberlain, 6,000 miles away from the scene of danger and of blood, denounces Lord Kitchener's proposal with regard to the government of the Transvaal as " preposterous," and declines to approve of it. The negotiations broke off, the war was resumed, millions more treasure have been squandered, thousands more of brave British lives lost, many equally brave African peasants killed, and thousands of innocent little children sacrificed. Who is to blame ? It is not Lord Kitchener. The man who knew what war meant strove to make peace. It is not Lord Milner. He knows something now of the horrors of war, and he also did not withhold his sanction from Lord Kitchener's efforts. All these deaths lie at the door of one man, and it is with him the public of this country have to reckon. I know it is said that afterwards General Botha claimed independence. Having regard to what happened in the Middelburg negotiations, how can any one be surprised ? General Botha evidently trusted Lord Kitchener as a manly, straightforward British soldier, but Mr. Chamberlain's conduct in repudiating so contemptuously the Kitchener terms proved to the Boers that he had something behind which was not revealed to them, and they made up their minds once and for all that as long as he had the direction of affairs, at any rate, it was idle to trust their future to such a ruler. What pains and perplexes me more than anything is the fact that Liberals should uphold such action. I can understand their attitude with regard to the origin of the war. Although in my humble opinion they are wrong, it is all a question of fact ; but surely they must condemn the conduct of a man whose only motive seems to be to render every endeavour to effect a peaceful arrangement abortive. It is all very well for millionaires like Mr. Perks to instigate the Government to prosecute this war to the bitter end. What personal difference would it make to him, or to men like Lord Salisbury, Mr. Balfour, Lord Rosebery, the Duke of Devonshire, Mr. Chamberlain, and Mr. Cecil Rhodes, if this war went on for another ten or twenty years ? They would still be in receipt of an income of thousands a year. And so they indulge their own personal pride, which they mistake for national patriotism, at the expense of the less fortunate members of the community. Those who have read what followed the Napoleonic wars know well what war means for the household of the man who earns his bread by the sweat of his brow. Poverty, privation, suffering are his lot. Has it never occurred to you to inquire why every member of the House of Commons who represents labour, or who has ever lived the life of the people, is bitterly and angrily opposed to this war ? By supporting it they would have gained much popularity, even amongst their own class ; by opposing it they have many of them risked their own careers. It is because they know what this huge expenditure means, what this absorption of national energy upon schemes of aggrandisement means to their class—that is what has dictated the course they have, amid slander and scurrility, pursued, and that is why I am prompted to come here to-night to beg you, for your own sakes, for the sake of the people everywhere in this land and in Africa, to help us to put an end to this conflict on the only terms which can produce permanent peace in Africa and reflect lasting credit upon the name of Britain.

A passage in the same speech dealt in a spirit of bitter irony with the Archbishop of York's suggestion that a national day of humiliation should be observed :

The Archbishop of York, in writing this message to his clergymen, suggested a day of humiliation. He tells them that he has discovered the source and fountain-head of the Boer inspiration to fight on. What do you think it is—pro-Boer speeches, or pro-Boer articles, or foreign encouragement? No; he says that the fount—the one great thing that inspires them to struggle on—is the Bible. That is not my opinion ; it is the opinion of the Archbishop, and Heaven forbid that I should challenge such an authority. Let Mr. Chamberlain reflect on this. I think it is a case really calling for another proclamation. This book which encourages the Boers ought to be proscribed, every copy throughout South Africa should be surrendered under the most dire pains and penalties for any man that should be found in possession of so seditious a print. I am not sure but that every patriotic chapel ought to close its doors against a book which encourages Boers to resist in this fashion [A well-known Churchman in the audience cried "Rot!"] Rot! Fancy a Churchman calling what an Archbishop says rot! Ladies and gentlemen, I must tell you that I am afraid that gentleman is a pro-Boer. Now, before I get away from the Archbishop—I love to linger on that topic—I must say a word about this day of humiliation. What does he propose? He says we are not getting on as we should like in thrashing the Boers, so we had better have a day of humiliation. Not long ago I read a speech from a boastful Cabinet Minister, in which he said that we would finish this war in spite of anything on the earth beneath or in the Heaven above. Ah, they are beginning to discover that they cannot force God to unconditional surrender, but we are to have a day of humiliation—we are to try the other tack—humiliation on terms. We are to approach the Throne and say : We, the greatest Empire in Thy world, upon which Thy sun can never set, we humble ourselves for a whole day before Thee, but upon the distinct expectancy that Thou on Thy part shalt help us to finish that troublesome creature Naboth, so that we may enjoy his vineyard in his place. Gentlemen, it needed a Bishop—an Archbishop—to dare suggest such blasphemy to the nation. Let us have no more of that. I am not going to tell you that we need no day of humiliation. What Empire is there, or nation, or individual, that stands in no need of it? But I tell you this—it will avail us nothing until as a people we are prepared to say, " Thy will be done in Africa, as everywhere else on the earth."

In the midst of his Welsh tour he found time to visit Edinburgh on October 31, in order to address a large meeting organised by the Young Scots Society. The chairman was Mr. Thomas

Shaw, Q.C., afterwards Lord Advocate in Sir Henry Campbell-Bannerman's ministry, and, at a later date, Lord Shaw of Dunfermline. Mr. Shaw welcomed the guest as "a brilliant and courageous colleague," who, "in a time when to question the policy of the hour was to be confounded by every force and device of obloquy, numbers, fashion, and passion," had "come forward manfully to dare and defy them all."

The Colonial Secretary himself undertook a Scottish tour in October. Mr. Chamberlain was never prone to confess failure, but at Edinburgh he had "pleaded guilty" to the charge that the Government had failed to foresee the length or the difficulties of the war.

I admit frankly that we were not wise enough to pierce into the future further than the rest of the world. What others did not see we failed to see, but it was not for want of trying. We consulted everybody who by any possibility could be considered an authority upon this subject. We saw and spoke to Boers and Afrikanders, British subjects and loyalists, whether Dutch or English, civilians or soldiers; and I say that, as far as I know, there was not one single man who was entitled to the slightest confidence, or even pretended to be an authority upon the subject, who anticipated the prolonged resistance which we have incurred.

This confession, to which, as Mr. Shaw put it, eight thousand persons, gathered together for an evening's amusement, listened with amazement and stupefaction, came oddly from the man who in 1897 had declared that a war against the Boers in South Africa would be a long and costly war. It assorted even less with a speech Mr. Chamberlain delivered only four days later at Cupar [1] when he referred to his presage of 1897 and made this comment upon it :

I should have thought that one inference to be drawn from these observations would have been that I should be the last man to enter upon the war if I did not think it absolutely necessary for the honour and interests of the country. I, who had foreseen—as indeed every one who had studied the question must have foreseen—that a war of this kind would be a serious war, a long war, and a costly war—is it likely that I, or any other statesman in my place, would have lightly forced the country into such a conflict ?

Quite as interesting, Mr. Lloyd George said, as the misrepresentations in Mr. Chamberlain's speech—"fourteen first-class misrepresentations and a whole fleet of second-class cruisers "—was the revelation of what was passing in his mind.

[1] October 29, 1901.

He told us that he was " surprised at the prolonged character of the war." What was really wanted, he said, was a true prophet. Well, Mr. Chamberlain had true prophets—and he stoned them, while he called the men who misled him loyalists and patriots. Mr. Chamberlain is defiant, insolent, and arrogant, but it would better become the man whose mistakes have cost thousands of lives to walk humbly before the Lord for the rest of his days. . . . Mr. Chamberlain appears to have extraordinary notions as to how the war is to be settled. After two years' experience, after finding out the men who misled him and were not reliable advisers, he is exactly where he was. He has not the slightest grasp of the main fact, and that is the Boer character. The war will never be finished until we have a statesman who has the courage first of all to find out the truth, in the next place to believe the truth, then to tell the truth, and lastly, to act upon the truth. None of these qualifications is in Mr. Chamberlain's statesmanship.

It has been seen that Mr. Lloyd George strongly urged the view that peace could have been made in February or March 1901. If that view be regarded as correct, a terrible responsibility is placed upon the Cabinet by its failure to guide the negotiations of Middelburg to a successful issue. It was at any rate a view which received countenance from Lord Rosebery some months later. At Liverpool, on February 15, 1902, Lord Rosebery reminded his audience that in March 1901 General Botha was in a mood to negotiate. He was " by no means sure," he said, that " a wise statesman " would not have concluded peace with General Botha at that date.

If that be so, what does it mean ? We are now in the middle of February this year [1902]. Even if peace were concluded next month, of which there is not the slightest probability or possibility, that fact would have cost us £60,000,000 ; it would have cost us numerous valuable lives, and it would have indefinitely postponed what we all have to look to as statesmen—the permanent settlement of South Africa.

To that extent, then, the position taken up by Mr. Lloyd George at the end of 1901 was adopted by so detached a statesman as Lord Rosebery in the early part of 1902. But Mr. Lloyd George went much further. He believed that while peace could have been made without great difficulty in March 1901, wise statesmanship would have endeavoured to end the war in June 1900, when the tide of success had turned decisively in favour of the British arms. He made this clear in a speech delivered at Leigh, in Lancashire, on November 7, before an audience of two thousand persons. At that date, he said, the Boers were more hopelessly beaten than they had ever been since—they were a mere rabble. They would have accepted any terms short of losing their national independence. When national independence became the issue of the contest, the burghers " became transformed, transfigured." It was no longer a question of defending Kruger, of defending any party, any policy—it was a question of defending the independence of their native land. No man worth calling a man would have given up his rifle after that.

On December 4 a special meeting of the General Committee of the National Liberal Federation was held at Derby. Notice was given of two official resolutions. The first of these urged upon the Government that immediate steps should be taken to remedy the deplorable condition of the concentration camps. It aroused little opposition, and was eventually carried with unanimity. The second called upon all Liberals to unite in demanding from the Government a public announcement of the terms upon which they were prepared to conclude peace. Its form showed clearly enough that it was the result of a compromise, and it found no favour with the members of the party who were opposed to the war. These wished to see, for one thing, a definite acknowledgment of Sir Henry Campbell-Bannerman's leadership. Further, they were dissatisfied with the suggestion that a Government which knew how to make neither war nor peace should be appealed to submissively for its considered ultimatum. There were several amendments placed upon the paper. Mr. Lloyd George had been chosen as the spokesman of the malcontents, if it be permissible so to term men who turned out to represent a large majority of the party. He interviewed the executive in friendly conference. It had already been persuaded to incorporate with its motion an amendment regretting the suspension of constitutional government and the extension of martial law in Cape Colony, and another declaring confidence in Sir Henry Campbell-Bannerman as leader of the party in the House of Commons. Mr. Lloyd George bent his efforts to the task of persuading the executive to accept, in place of the demand for a public statement of terms, a declaration that the time had arrived when " negotiations should be entered upon with a view to the conclusion of an honourable and durable peace, and that for that purpose it was essential that a Special Commissioner should be dispatched to South Africa." This was another of the occasions on which he talked over unwilling listeners. It was a time, it must be remembered, when differences within the party were acute, and the relations between old comrades strained to and often beyond the breaking-point. " Party feeling," a wit has

said, "is the feeling we have against men of our own party."
There was a great deal of "party feeling" of this kind at the
time of the war, and it was no small achievement to win over
the executive to a proposal the expediency of which some of the
members profoundly distrusted. The result showed that they
had been well advised to listen to Mr. Lloyd George. No other
resolution would have secured such unanimity, and when a
delegate from Sheffield insisted on proposing an amendment as
to terms of peace, framed on the lines of the original resolution,
he found only an insignificant body of supporters.

Mr. Lloyd George's reception from the delegates when he rose
to speak showed that the boldness of the course he had taken
had made him not only prominent but admired in Liberal ranks.
Perhaps it also showed that the supporters in the Liberal Party
of what he had called during his Welsh tour "the second war"
were far fewer in number than those who had acclaimed or
acquiesced in the first. As he rose, a greeting in Welsh was heard
from the back of the hall. "Ah!" he said, "they are trying to
crush out a nationality six thousand miles away, but here is one
close at hand speaking a tongue that has not been crushed yet."
His speech was an endorsement of a plea for unity which Mr.
Birrell had just made. He took a strong view on the war himself, he said, and probably most of the resolutions on the paper
would fail to incorporate his views. For instance, he would add
a few adjectives where the name of Mr. Chamberlain came in.
He appealed to the precedent of Canada and Lord Durham.
"The men to build the Temple of Peace are not the men who
have taken part in the war." "The Boers will never accept an
olive-branch from hands stained with the blood of their children."
What was wanted was that somebody should go out to South
Africa with a fair, impartial, unprejudiced mind to investigate
the whole circumstances, and to tell them what ought to be
done. Lord Durham had not gone out to Canada with certain
peace proposals in his pocket. The first thing to be done was
to declare that they were in favour of negotiations; the second,
to follow the suggestion of Sir Henry Campbell-Bannerman, who
had got "a good sound Scottish head on his shoulders," and
send out a man in what Mr. Birrell had called the "spirit of
conciliation." He suggested, with regard to the other branch of
the resolution, that in the expression of confidence in Sir Henry
Campbell-Bannerman the words "in the House of Commons"
should be omitted, so that it should be made clear that his leadership of the party was recognised. The chairman did not allow
that suggestion to be adopted, but its reception from the dele-

gates made it abundantly clear that it was welcomed. The resolution advocated by Mr. Lloyd George was adopted unanimously. " My verdict is that C.-B. is irremovable. The hostile cave is in ruins," Mr. Massingham wrote exultantly in the " Daily News " the next morning.

Mr. Lloyd George, however, was anxious, for his own part, that Lord Rosebery should not be driven definitely into the camp of reaction. He hoped, on the contrary, that the former leader would use his great gifts in order to make easy the way of peace. Lord Rosebery was to speak at Chesterfield in the middle of December. Speaking at Carnarvon on November 22, before an audience which was not perhaps inclined to receive the noble name with great respect, Mr. Lloyd George made a very genuine appeal to him. He knew no one, he said, better qualified than Lord Rosebery to deal with the question of the war. His position and influence, and the fact that during the progress of the war he had been outside party strife, gave him opportunities possessed by no other statesman.

Meanwhile it had been planned that Mr. Lloyd George, as the guest of the Birmingham Liberal Association, should make a speech in the Town Hall there on December 18, two days after the Chesterfield utterance. It was, as will be seen, his purpose to deal in his Birmingham speech with the advice Lord Rosebery had offered to the nation. The fate of the Birmingham meeting must be told in a separate chapter. At Chesterfield the Liberal Party was bidden by its retired leader to " wipe its slate clean and consider very carefully what it was going to write on it in future." To the plea that " no alternative Government " was possible, Lord Rosebery replied that " the nation that could not produce an alternative to the present Government was more fit to control allotments than an Empire." Upon the war he had more practical and less oracular advice to give. He condemned the doctrine of unconditional surrender and the proclamation issued in August by which Lord Kitchener had declared the war at an end and made it known that all commanders who did not surrender before September 15 would be " permanently banished from South Africa." Searching inquiries were necessary into the administration of martial law and of the concentration camps, and other matters, but, on the other hand, Lord Rosebery acquitted the Government of any " barbarity " and declared that martial law was a " necessity of the situation." He pleaded for " a regular peace and a regular settlement." Overtures of peace from any responsible quarter should be welcome, especially if from the exiled Boer Government in Europe. Some of the greatest settlements in the world's history had begun with an apparently casual meeting of two travellers in a neutral inn, and some such fortuitous meeting under the auspices of His Majesty's Government and the exiled Boer Government might well lead to very good results.

"In this country," said Lord Rosebery at the end of his speech, "I understand you like a man who speaks his mind. Well, I have spoken mine." Two days later Mr. Lloyd George went to Birmingham, there to speak his.

CHAPTER III

IN the annals of Birmingham's political history two instances
of successfully organised rioting stand out conspicuously.
The first of these belongs to the unregenerate days of
Birmingham's Radicalism, and its victims were Conservative
statesmen. In 1884, a great party demonstration at Aston,
organised by the Conservatives, ended in a riot from which some
of their leaders had difficulty in escaping without injury. Sir
Stafford Northcote and Lord Randolph Churchill, the two principal speakers, were only saved from capture and violent assault
by good fortune and the prompt action of their supporters. Lord
Randolph, as his son tells us, was carried away in the arms of
a burly admirer from Wolverhampton; Sir Stafford Northcote
was dragged at full speed out of the reach of his assailants, and,
even so, narrowly avoided capture. Mr. (afterwards Mr. Justice)
Darling made his escape from the window of a room in which he
had taken refuge. The responsibility for those Aston riots was
laid by Lord Randolph Churchill at the door of Mr. Chamberlain
and his caucus. " The contest in Birmingham," he said, " is not
a contest, such as is carried on in other constituencies in England,
between party and party. It is a contest between popular self-
government and a corrupt oligarchy ; between electoral freedom
and Russian despotism ; between open dealing and Venetian
espionage ; between individual security and public order and all
the resources and ingenuity of terror and intimidation." In
Parliament Lord Randolph moved a vote of censure upon Mr.
Chamberlain for speeches which encouraged interference with
freedom of discussion and incited to riot and disorder. " The
noble lord says I might have stopped it," said the right honour-

able gentleman. "My answer is that I could not have stopped it if I would, and I would not have stopped it if I could. Why on earth should I have stopped it ? " Mr. Chamberlain escaped censure by a majority of thirty-six. "No evidence was ever produced to sustain any charge against Mr. Chamberlain of having himself fomented the disorders," says Mr. Winston Churchill, "but," he adds in a delightful sentence, "an impression was created that the whole affair showed that he had been only partially successful in exerting those influences of moral restraint which are so much to be commended in political leaders during times of popular excitement."

When the second striking example of Birmingham's capacity for concerted violence is considered, it is as well to keep in mind the parallel case of 1884. The analogy, it is true, is far from perfect. The excuse put forward for the riots of 1884 was that Conservatives were endeavouring, by importing holiday-makers into Birmingham, to make it appear that a great mass meeting of her own citizens had supported a policy which her elected representatives denounced. The rioting of 1901 was occasioned by a meeting of the Liberal Association, and nobody could possibly have supposed that any but the members of that body were pledged to such resolutions as were passed. So far as the workings of the mind of a mob can be conjectured, or any reasoning detected in the columns of the newspapers which aroused the mob, the argument seems to have been that Birmingham would be disgraced if a man who had opposed the war and attacked Mr. Chamberlain were allowed to address a meeting of his friends in Mr. Chamberlain's city and to leave it unharmed.

It had long been customary for the Liberal Association of Birmingham to hold one or more meetings annually in the Town Hall, and to invite prominent spokesmen of the party from outside the constituency to address them on these occasions. In the summer of 1901 the executive of the Association resolved to invite Mr. Lloyd George to be the chief speaker at a meeting in December. The voice of Liberal Imperialism was far from silent in the counsels of the party in Birmingham, but the officers of the Association were agreed that a speech from Mr. Lloyd George would tend to promote unity in the ranks of their members. It was settled, as the time for the meeting drew near, that Alderman William Cook, a well-known member of the Imperialist section of the party, should take the chair for Mr. Lloyd George.

When the day of the meeting had come and gone, and the tragic events which it now becomes necessary to chronicle had happened, an impudent attempt was made by the instigators of disorder to blame the Lord Mayor of Birmingham for allowing the Liberal Association the use of the Town Hall. The Birmingham Liberal Association represented at that time broadly one-third of the population of the city. Its chief officers were men well known in every department of public life. If the Lord Mayor, who, as it happened, was a Conservative, had refused the Town Hall to such a body, it would have been impossible for him to justify his action on any intelligible ground.

It was announced in December that the meeting would be held on the 18th of that month, and there were soon signs that a section of the population of Birmingham would regard the holding of it as a treasonable offence. The laws of England, through what seemed to these full-blooded patriots a regrettable lacuna, provided no punishment for critics of the policy of the Colonial Secretary even when that policy included war, and it began to be hinted that a Birmingham mob might supply the deficiency of the criminal code. Two Liberal-Unionist newspapers, the " Birmingham Daily Mail " and the " Birmingham Daily Post," besides publishing articles strongly denouncing the audacity of the local Liberals, threw open their columns to letters, mostly anonymous, in which more or less covert threats of violence were made. The Conservative papers, while they did not yield to their Unionist colleagues in their denunciation of Mr. Lloyd George and his views, were on the side of law and order, and published nothing which could be construed as an incitement to riot or uproar. It may be that they had not forgotten the riots of 1884 : at any rate they were properly reluctant to accept responsibility for methods which have not in the end brought credit either to Radical or Unionist Birmingham. For some days before the meeting, therefore, the two Unionist papers contained much more exciting reading than did their contemporaries.

The first hint that trouble was brewing seems to have come from a letter in the " Mail " for December 12, over the initials R. V.

Although a Unionist [said the writer], I hope no one will object to the pro-Boer meeting in the Town Hall, as I have no doubt Mr. Lloyd George and his friends will meet with a reception from the Birmingham people that they do not expect. For my part I should think they must be under a very wrong impression to think of holding a meeting anywhere in Birmingham, after the reception they received in London.[1] I suppose no one will be admitted without a ticket, so that they can fill the hall as far as possible, for those are the tactics they always pursue. If so, I trust some one will " organise " a meeting outside the hall in opposition.

[1] The reference is to the disorder outside the Queen's Hall meeting.

On Saturday the 14th the " Mail " announced that " it was feared " that there would be a disturbance in connection with the meeting which " the pro-Boer Member of Parliament, Mr. Lloyd George," was to address. " It will be a ticket meeting," said the " Mail," " and this fact has aroused a lively sense of indignation." If the suggestion was that a meeting thrown open to the public would have been less of a challenge to disorder, the logic of the argument is difficult to follow. If it were true that only a handful of people in Birmingham opposed Mr. Chamberlain's policy, there could not be much harm done to Mr. Chamberlain's prestige by allowing them to congregate in a corner of the Town Hall. On the other hand, an attempt to hold a large public meeting in Birmingham to oppose the war might have called for opposition, though it could not have excused violence.

A non-party politician [the article went on] declared to a " Mail " reporter to-day that the town was not going tacitly to acquiesce in such an arrangement, nor was it going to be permitted that the meeting should, as was a notorious pro-Boer gathering, be taken outside Birmingham as representative of the opinion of the city.

On the 16th leading articles on the subject of the meeting appeared in both the " Mail " and the " Post." The " Mail " had in two days completely changed the ground of its attack. Its objection was no longer based on the fact that admission was to be by ticket, but on the fact that the meeting was to be " public "—which, as the " Mail " had already complained, nobody could or did pretend that it was. The activities of the Unionist Press in Birmingham during those days can best be judged from extracts. A leading article published in the " Mail " two days before the meeting declared that the indignation that had been aroused was growing rapidly. There were signs that a counter-demonstration was to take place outside the hall, and it was possible that there would be some imitation of the scenes witnessed at the " infamous " Queen's Hall meeting. Many of those still formally connected with the Liberal Association, it said, resented the invitation given to " this most virulent anti-Briton " as strongly as the most vigorous Unionist :

Possibly those responsible will not be disturbed by the withdrawal of Liberal Imperialists from their ranks, as it would leave them a small but happy body who could meet and denounce in the choicest Billingsgate Mr. Chamberlain, Lord Milner, and the soldiers at the front. It will not require a very spacious room for the meeting; in fact, Alderman Martineau's drawing-room would suffice; but the vigour of the language and the strength of the adjectives would no doubt be sufficient to make the Town Hall ring with fiery declamation. But this alleged public meeting in the Town Hall is another matter. Mr. Lloyd George has studiously acquired the reputation of the most violent pro-Boer in the country. He is not a man of many parts, but among nonentities even mediocrity may become prominent. This Welshman has used language respecting the Ministers of his country and the soldiers of the King which, if uttered respecting any Continental Ministry, would have caused him to be arraigned for treason, and sentenced to a very considerable term of imprisonment. A hundred years ago in England he would have stood a very excellent chance of losing his head, a feat which, metaphorically, he performs every time he addresses a public meeting. His particular antipathy has always been towards the Colonial Secretary, and he has described the member for West Birmingham by every insulting epithet from Judas downwards.

He has declared in effect that the policy of putting the children in the concentration camps is an imitation of the plan pursued by Herod of old to crush out the race he feared. And this man who would make out our soldiers and our Ministers to be absolutely inhuman butchers is the individual the Birmingham Liberal Association are delighting to honour.

Mr. Chamberlain can afford to disregard the personal malice toward himself which instigated the petty clique concerned to issue their invitation to Mr. Lloyd George, but the mere fact of bringing this " politician " to Birmingham, the city which has given so nobly and so freely of her sons to fight her battles, which has made so many sacrifices in order to maintain through the medium of our wonderful fund the homes and families of the men at the front—to invite such a man as Mr. Lloyd George to speak in the Town Hall is an insult to the city, and to every loyal inhabitant. No doubt care will be taken to sedulously select the audience, no one will be admitted without a ticket ; we may be sure those pieces of paste-board will only be issued to the chosen worshippers of their brother Boers.

Whether the Liberal Association managers desire to imitate their friends of the Queen's Hall and engage prize-fighters and similar gentlemen to protect the entrances, we cannot say ; but we are doubtful if the professional pugilists of Birmingham would consent to accept engagements in such a cause. A correspondent ironically suggests that Mr. Lloyd George shall venture out into Chamberlain Square, and address a public meeting there, when he would meet with a reception which would leave him in very little doubt as to the opinion of the people of Birmingham respecting himself and the views he expresses.

Sir Henry Campbell-Bannerman may be listened to with contemptuous tolerance ; no one takes Mr. Labouchere seriously : but we fail to see how patriotic Englishmen can sit quietly under the tirade of foul calumny and vulgar abuse which generally follows when the Welsh member airs his views on the war.

The members of the Birmingham Liberal Association have forfeited the respect of the best of their political friends ; they have utterly cut themselves adrift from the overwhelming majority of the electors of Birmingham, and they have bound themselves hand and foot to that discredited and discreditable faction which is invariably in favour of the enemies of this country. It is not for us to object to their committing political suicide, but in the name of the city we protest against Mr. Lloyd George being brought to the Town Hall to write the epitaph.

All through the week of the meeting the correspondence columns of the " Mail " and " Post " were full of the letters of eager and, for the most part, anonymous patriots. " Brum " wrote that he hoped that Mr. Lloyd George might be induced by Alderman Cook to address an overflow meeting " say in Chamberlain Square." " I am sure the reception he would get would be worthy of the man and the cause he advocates." " Hydra " blamed the Liberal Association for not knowing " that the name of Lloyd George stinks in the nostrils of those who have the welfare of their country at heart, be their political opinions what they may," and charged him with having " ever made the foulest aspersions upon the conduct of our brave soldiers at the front." " Truly Birmingham should give a great reception to Mr. Lloyd George."

One letter (signed " Empire " and published in the " Post ") contained this gem upon the ethics of free speech : " It is right to allow all parties the use of the Town Hall, and especially so when they happen to be numerically weak; but for any Association to bring forward on the platform of the Town Hall a man of so notorious a type, a self-confessed enemy of the country in which he happens to live—for such a man has no country—is so scandalous a thing that no one could have blamed the Lord Mayor for refusing to concede to such a proposal." " Pax " wrote to say that a riot was inevitable if the meeting were held ; " Cymro," who professed to be a Liberal and a Welshman, to declare his disgust that one of his fellow-countrymen should " gain notoriety " by exhibiting his personal malice and antipathy towards Mr. Chamberlain.

On the day before the meeting the " Mail " published an article headed " Rioting Feared," which gave colour to the complaint of Liberals that the " Mail's " emotions were akin rather to pleased anticipation than to dread. " There is every reason to believe," it began, " that Birmingham is menaced by the prospect of serious rioting to-morrow night."

Feeling in the city runs very high on the subject, and it is being discussed in most of the clubs and places of public resort. Many men who have lost brothers, or sons, or intimate friends in the war are expressing great indignation that such a meeting should be allowed to be held in the Town Hall; the returned soldiers and Welshmen are displaying an anxiety, which is not mere curiosity, to see the man who lauds the country's enemies and accuses our troops of barbarism.

The daily objurgations of the Press had a powerful effect upon a large section of the population. It was not difficult to persuade men who in every phase of Mr. Chamberlain's career had been his loyal votaries that the honour of their city and their idol was at stake. The scandal of a " pro-Boer " meeting in the Town Hall which had so often resounded to the plaudits of Imperialists acclaiming Mr. Chamberlain was canvassed in every club and every workshop. It was determined by secret organisers that the hall should be filled not by adherents of the Liberal Party but by the stalwarts of the opposite camp. At the beginning of the week of the meeting it came to the knowledge of the Liberals that forged tickets were in circulation. On the 17th (Tuesday) the Secretary of the Liberal Association published an advertisement which announced that all tickets issued would be recalled, and substitutes issued. This is how the " Mail " dealt with the incident :

Influential business men without keen political convictions are seriously questioning the wisdom of tolerating the meeting, which will be duly reported to the burghers in the field, and will necessarily have a stimulating effect. *How keen is this feeling* was shown yesterday by the circulation of hundreds of forged tickets, evidently printed with the deliberate intention of enabling interrupters to secure entrance, and to break up the meeting.

A rumour was put about, and repeated in the Press, that some " well-wisher of the Boers " had imported into Birmingham a gang of " Irish roughs " to assist in ejecting interrupters. The Liberal Association denied any knowledge of such an importation, and indeed it was not suggested, at any rate in print, that they were responsible for it. Events sufficiently disproved the charge, which was always vague in its terms. No published account of the rioting suggests that any such "roughs," " Irish " or otherwise, were present to support Mr. Lloyd George, or that the behaviour of the stewards in the hall was anything but good-humoured. But the rumour was seized upon with eagerness by the newspapers and made the foundation for what can fairly be construed as incitement to riot.

It seems incredible [said the " Mail "] that the Birmingham people should be challenged by a display of force of that kind, but unfortunatley there is reason for believing the statement to be accurate. It is to be hoped that the person who hired the Irishmen for to-morrow's meeting will reconsider his decision ; otherwise a riot of very serious dimensions may be provoked.

It is a little curious that the organisers of disorder should on this occasion have accused their victims of employing roughs, for the accusation had an historical parallel. A reference has already been made to the Aston riots. When Mr. Chamberlain was taxed in the House of Commons with responsibility for them, his answer was that his constituents had acted " almost entirely in self-defence." They had been subjected to " almost intolerable provocation." In support of this charge Mr. Chamberlain produced a number of affidavits, signed by three men, including one " Larry Mack," which charged a Mr. Jarvis with hiring roughs on the Tories' account. At a subsequent criminal assize " Larry Mack " was found guilty and sentenced to six weeks' imprisonment for criminal libel upon the strength of the affidavit which Mr. Chamberlain had been induced to accept and to offer to the House of Commons as truthful testimony, and his counsel admitted that there was no truth whatever in the allegation which the affidavit contained.

The Liberal executive were of course aware by this time that the meeting would be held in circumstances of difficulty and danger. Unless they had been very blind they could not have failed to realise this fact, which had become patent. While the newspapers confined themselves to prophecies of a tumult which they made some show of deprecating, some of their readers were at work to ensure the fulfilment of the worst forebodings. It was not necessary to be in the councils of the plotters to know that mischief was brewing. Notices were to be seen posted on the walls of factories and workshops summoning meetings to decide upon a plan of campaign. Crowds eager for battle assembled in the roads, and for some days work was partially neglected.

On one point the " Mail " was able to reassure readers whose patriotism was tempered by considerations of economy. It attributed to the Lord Mayor the statement that " an assurance had been given that if any damage were done the Liberal Association would be liable to make it good."

Meanwhile, Mr. Lloyd George was warned by the Liberals at Birmingham of the danger that threatened him. His reply was that he hoped the Association would go through with the meeting at all costs. A few days before the meeting a representative of one of the Unionist papers called at the house of Mr. William Evans, a prominent Welsh citizen of Birmingham, who was well known to have been long on terms of friendship with Mr. Lloyd George. The object of the visit was to persuade Mr. Evans to use his influence to procure the cancelling of the engagement. Mr. Evans communicated this warning to his friend, and was answered by a decided refusal to abandon the meeting. "The view I take," Mr. Lloyd George said afterwards, "is that no man has the right to make a kind of ring fence round a part of the country, and say, 'These are my preserves.' I went to Birmingham deliberately to protest against the insolence of such a claim."

The Chief Constable of Birmingham, Mr. Rafter, was urged to dissuade Mr. Lloyd George from carrying out his programme, and wrote in courteous terms to acquaint him of the danger he would incur. The reply was that he had accepted an invitation of long standing, and intended to fulfil it.

The Liberal Association seems to have done what it could to remove any pretext for disorder. In a communication to the Press it emphasised the fact that the meeting did not purport to be a public meeting, and it also announced that it would not be an "anti-war" meeting. On December 17 the "Birmingham Post" had the following paragraph :

Prominent members of the Liberal Party are anxious that it should be made widely known that the meeting at the Town Hall to-morrow night, at which Mr. D. Lloyd George, M.P. for the Carnarvon Boroughs, is to be the principal speaker, is in no sense a pro-Boer meeting, or even a public meeting. The gathering has been arranged under the auspices of the Birmingham Liberal Association, just as other meetings are organised, and only members of the Association are expected to be present. Admission will be by ticket, and the opinions expressed, whether on the war or on the many other subjects which are of interest to the Liberal Party, will be merely the opinions of the meeting, and it is not claimed that the gathering will be representative of the city, or that it will voice the feeling of the whole city, for it is not an open public meeting.

It was added that the conveners of the meeting were waiting to read the terms of the speech which Lord Rosebery was to deliver that night at Chesterfield before definitely framing the resolutions to be put to the meeting.

The next day the "Post" was able to announce that the resolution would "consist of three clauses."

The first will be a vote of thanks to Mr. Lloyd George for his visit and speech ; the second will express the unabated confidence of the meeting in the Liberal leaders in Parliament, Earl Spencer and Sir Henry Campbell-Bannerman ; while the third will welcome the speech of Lord Rosebery at Chesterfield.

On the previous day the "Mail" had called for the publication of the resolutions to be proposed, and had doubted the assertion made by the promoters of the meeting that "it was not an open one, but a gathering of the Liberal Association." As has been already pointed out, the "Mail" was curiously inconsistent. The fact that Mr. Lloyd George was to address a "ticket" meeting from which aggressive Imperialists would be excluded had at first been made a ground of protest. When Liberals pleaded that in fact it was and professed to be a "ticket" meeting, the "Mail" was sceptical and more indignant than ever.

It is now semi-officially announced that the meeting is not an open one, but a gathering of the Liberal Association. The curious feature of the matter is that the meeting has been advertised as if tickets were procurable by any one.

The only sentence in the original advertisement of the meeting which could be said to lend any colour to this assertion was the modest announcement that "a limited number of reserved tickets" would be issued "for the side galleries and front of great gallery at 2s. 6d. each." But the advertisement, which had appeared a week before the meeting, and before the rage of the Unionist Press and their correspondents had been excited, was prominently headed "Birmingham Liberal Association," and did not purport to call a public meeting of all citizens, or in the vernacular of local Birmingham politics, a "town meeting." [1]

The "Mail," unwilling to be convinced that the meeting could be of an innocuous character, next argued that, as tickets had been sent to some people who had not asked for them and were opposed to the holding of the meeting, it would be "the most curious Liberal Association meeting ever held in Birmingham." The same paper, misunderstanding an announcement that Mr. William Evans, who had undertaken the distribution of tickets to members of the Welsh colony, would give out new tickets in place of the old at his offices in the evening, caused him considerable embarrassment and annoyance by suggesting that anybody

---

[1] It is as well to publish the advertisement as it appeared in the "Birmingham Daily Mail" on December 12 :—

BIRMINGHAM LIBERAL ASSOCIATION.

TOWN HALL MEETING, WEDNESDAY NEXT, DECEMBER 18.

CHIEF SPEAKER—MR. D. LLOYD GEORGE, M.P.

Chair to be taken at 8 o'clock by Alderman Cook, J.P.

A limited number of reserved tickets will be issued for the side galleries and front of great gallery at 2s. 6d. each, and may be had from the offices, Coleridge Chambers, Corporation Street.

who applied could obtain tickets from him. The result was a disconcerting rush of applicants to whom tickets were of course refused.

It had been arranged that Mr. Lloyd George should be the guest of Mr. and Mrs. William Evans at their house in Hagley Road. On the morning of the 17th the sub-editor of the " Mail " called upon Mr. Evans to inquire if the report that he was to be Mr. Lloyd George's host were true. Mr. Evans replied that it was, but begged the journalist to regard the fact as private. Otherwise, he urged, unnecessary trouble and risk would be caused not only to Mr. Lloyd George, but Mr. and Mrs. Evans and their household. As it was, police had been told off to protect the house, and it was not desirable to publish information which might make it necessary to add to their numbers. The sub-editor would make no promise : he claimed the " right of a free Press to publish all matters of public interest." At Mr. Evans's request the Chief Constable attempted, but in vain, to obtain a promise that the address should not be published, and in the end representations were made to the paper by the Lord Mayor. On the day of the meeting the " Mail " published this paragraph :

In the ordinary course of things we should have published to-day the address of Mr. Lloyd George's host, and other details which are customary when a speaker whose visit arouses great interest is coming to the city. Influential representations, however, have been made to us that to give the address might be to cause a hostile demonstration, if not something worse, at the house. The fears thus expressed are probably groundless. Men who regard to-night's meeting with something akin to horror would scarcely display any resentment to the promoters in their private capacities ; still less would they attack a house in which women and children were living. Still, out of regard for the gentleman from whom the request has come, and in order that a few unruly spirits may have no chance of injuring a patriotic protest, we have suppressed the information.

On the day of the meeting work seemed to have come to a standstill. Sandwichmen were parading the town bearing placards which called upon the citizens to assemble at the Town Hall " to defend the King, the Government, and Mr. Chamberlain," and to denounce " Brum Boers." It was known that Mr. Lloyd George would arrive during the afternoon, and an edition of the " Mail " announced, in a prominent space specially reserved for late news, that he would reach New Street Station at twelve minutes past three. While a huge and hostile crowd surrounded the Liberal Club and the offices of the Liberal Association, another mob filled the platform at which the train was expected.

When the train steamed in a rush was made for the carriages. Men peered into them, even looking under the seats, and the astonished passengers found themselves surrounded by a jostling crowd and were, some of them, roughly handled. The crowd realised at last that the object of their search was not in the train. A rumour spread that he had got out at Castle Bromwich. The guard was questioned on the subject. " If he did," he replied, " he must have had a bad time, for the train did not stop."

The fact was that Mr. Lloyd George had arrived by an earlier train, a few minutes before three. It had been arranged that the President and officers of the Liberal Association should meet him, but the crowd which besieged the Club, where most of them were at lunch, was menacing, and the officials felt that even if they tried to force a way through, their presence at the station would have the undesirable result of identifying their guest. The result was that Mr. Lloyd George was met only by Mrs. William Evans and her niece, a little Irish girl of about four years of age. He passed out of the station with his hostess and the child, unrecognised by the handful of people who had already gathered in the hope of giving him a Birmingham welcome.

The " Mail " in a later edition published its account of what it called " A Disappointment at New Street Station," stating with what seemed to be a note of regret that Mr. Lloyd George had " missed a reception." The "Mail" showed signs of anxiety that the Welsh speaker should not so easily escape the attentions of the crowd in the evening. It can hardly have been solicitude for his welfare or a belief in his popularity which led the gentlemen conducting the paper to publish a likeness of him in a special edition and upon the posters that advertised it.

At Hagley Road the state of affairs was explained to the guest whose coming had so disturbed the normal equilibrium of life in the city. He learned then that Alderman Cook would be unable, much to his own regret, to carry out his promise to take the chair. The Alderman was a man of advanced years and in indifferent health. He had received numbers of threatening letters, and had been warned from various sources that if he attempted to leave his residence on the day of the meeting he would be shot. To give matters an even more serious air, a menacing mob of persons had gathered round his house. With great reluctance he submitted to his doctor's advice not to undertake the duty of presiding.

A telephone message was sent to Mr. A. C. Osler, another well-known Liberal Imperialist and a personal friend of the member

THE RIOT AT BIRMINGHAM TOWN HALL.

(*From a drawing by Allan Stewart.*)

for West Birmingham. He readily agreed to take the chair, and at once called to see Mr. Lloyd George and discuss the resolutions with him. While this conference was proceeding the Chief Constable telephoned to the house. He spoke to Mr. Lloyd George, and gave him a final warning that the risk he ran would be considerable unless the meeting were abandoned. Mr. Lloyd George repeated what seemed to him the only possible reply. Then, after dining with his hosts and a few members of the Liberal Association, he drove in a closed carriage with Mr. and Mrs. Evans to the Town Hall.

Meanwhile a crowd had begun to assemble to receive him. It was said afterwards that no such multitude as gathered that night had ever assembled within living memory except on the day when King Edward VII.'s accession was proclaimed. Then the crowd had been orderly and unanimous. On this night the mob that collected as the time for the meeting approached was for the most part angry, resentful, and ripe for disorder. It was a crowd that contained many highly respectable citizens, some of them merely sightseers, many of them full of what they conceived to be a righteous indignation. These honest men, armed with nothing more dangerous than penny Union Jacks, were reinforced by a strong detachment of students from the University, bent upon having an evening of riotous relaxation from their studies. The most dangerous, though not the largest element in the mob, was composed of men whose manner of life had habituated them to encounters with the police, and taught them what weapons would do most deadly work in a street brawl. Before the evening was out not less than 30,000 people must have gathered round the Town Hall. The Chief Constable had taken the precaution of drafting about 350 policemen into the vicinity.

Mr. Lloyd George reached the hall at about half-past six, some time before the crowd had swollen to its largest dimensions. Already, however, there was a large throng in the streets, and many, including the police officials, doubted whether the speaker would reach the building in safety. Somehow his carriage ran the gauntlet unsuspected, and he entered by a door in Victoria Square unmolested and unperceived except by some of his supporters and by the police officers who were lining the street. His supporters cheered, and the police constables themselves, though probably few enough of them had much sympathy with the views of the man it was their duty to protect, were moved by a sudden enthusiasm at his daring to wave their helmets and join in the cheers that welcomed his safe arrival.

II—6

About a quarter of an hour afterwards the "early doors" were opened for those with special tickets of admission, and the hall began to fill, at first chiefly with supporters, many of them ladies, whom the prospect of disturbance had not discouraged. With the opening of the ordinary doors the scene became uproarious. Entrances were stormed, and people with spurious tickets or no tickets at all were at no disadvantage under conditions which made careful scrutiny of credentials impossible. The result was that the majority of those in the hall desired and intended to wreck the meeting. A compact body of medical students on the floor of the hall led the forces of disorder within. At first a vociferous rendering of the strains of "The Soldiers of the Queen" and "Rule Britannia" satisfied their warlike vigour, but the din had become so deafening, even before the first speaker had arrived upon the platform, that a young man had mounted upon a form to appeal to his friends to "reserve themselves" lest the arrival of the enemy should find their lungs exhausted. His appeal had only a temporary effect, and a variety of noises—"cat-calls, dog-barks, screams, shouts, yells, cheers, and groans"—soon broke out afresh. Finally the heartfelt emotions of the citizens found expression in a parody of one of Moody and Sankey's hymns, which they intoned lustily:

"We'll throw Lloyd George in the fountain,
And he won't come to Brum any more."

While the audience in the hall was thus warming to its work, Mr. Lloyd George was within earshot of its vocal efforts. He was among his friends in an ante-room, and those who were there saw no sign of perturbation in his manner. "Whatever his feelings may have been at that moment," says a lady who was of the party, "he was outwardly calm, kindly, courteous, and interested in every detail, and he conversed smilingly with each person presented to him."

There was still some time to elapse before the meeting was to begin, and this interval he filled up by going, accompanied by his hostess, Mrs. William Evans, into the body of the hall itself. It was probably the unexpectedness of this step which saved him from recognition by the enemy, and to this day possibly many who were among the hostile crowd in the hall do not know that before the meeting the object of their detestation walked quietly amongst them. When a little later he appeared with his friends on the platform, the uproar broke out with such force as quite to eclipse the previous tumult. In some parts of the building the cacophony was organised with as much system as an orchestra. It was observed that as one section of the audience relaxed, from sheer exhaustion, its performances with drums, whistles, horns, tin cans, and the infinite resources of the human voice, a fresh relay would take up the task. Mr. Osler, the chairman, was able to shout a speech into the ears of the reporters. "One would think," he said, "from all the hubbub, that the Liberal Association had invited some great criminal to be present—a man, for instance, who made or planned a raid into a friendly country, instead of one whose pride it is that he pleaded for peace when the war spirit ran high."

When Mr. Lloyd George rose to speak the cheers of the Liberals in the hall only served to swell the continuous tumult. It was quite clear that not a word of his speech would be heard except by the reporters and those next to him upon the platform. He rose, slowly took off his overcoat, and, leaning his arm on the desk before him, and smiling at the tumultuous scene, stood waiting for silence. He managed to make a few sentences heard by the reporters, who clambered on their benches to be nearer to him. "This is rather a lively meeting for a peace meeting," was the first of them.

We are told [he said] that speeches delivered in this country reach the ears of the Boers. If that be so, the Boers will know when Birmingham Unionists promise them free institutions how to interpret the promise. I have been called an enemy of my country. Why? Because, in common with thousands of others, I have not allowed my judgment to be swept away by the unthinking clamour of the multitude. The real enemies of the country are men who decline to discuss a matter of so much moment to the future of their native land with the calmness and fairness which such an intricate problem demands.

He was glad, he added, that a resolution was to be submitted which included in it a word of welcome to Lord Rosebery on his return to active political life.

His last audible sentences were in criticism of the amazing scene before him :

The Union Jack is the pride and property of our common country, and no man who really loves it could do anything but dissent from its being converted into Mr. Chamberlain's pocket-handkerchief. It is enough for me to emphasise the fact that the Press of Birmingham, which used to be the champion of free speech, has for days been stirring up its friends to deny liberty of debate to us solely on the ground that we are an insignificant minority in this town. And in this respect I may also add—because it has a significance of its own—that the Liberal Unionist Press has behaved more disgracefully than the Conservative papers of the town.

This was the last sentence which the reporters were able to record. The noise had become so insistent and so deafening that a person addressing his next neighbour could only be heard with difficulty. A tempest of noise and a waving forest of Union Jacks filled the scene. Cheers for Mr. Chamberlain and " the boys at the front " were distinguishable among more incoherent cries. Mr. Lloyd George saw that the reporters' task and his own were alike hopeless. However, typewritten copies of the speech he had intended to deliver were handed to the Press. He suggested to them that they should go on writing as if they were taking the words down as he spoke them.

Suddenly, and, as it seemed, at a signal, the crowd in the body of the hall made a rush for the platform, and were confronted by a force of policemen who had been stationed beneath it. There was a very ugly struggle, and according to those who witnessed it from the platform many of the attacking force were armed with such weapons as sticks, hammers, and knives, while some of them used a particularly deadly weapon of offence, a brick tied up in barbed wire, which seems to have been in common use outside the hall also. There seems to have been some considerable bloodshed.

I quote from an account kindly given me by one of the courageous ladies who were on the platform :

" During all this Mr. Lloyd George was calm, and it was only with great difficulty that he was at last induced to leave the platform, and then only when he was almost carried off by a number of detectives in plain clothes. The crowd then attacked those on the platform with stones, ' barbed ' bricks, bottles, cans, and the like. The Chief Constable asked every one to leave the platform, saying that the crowd was too desperate and that lives would be lost if we remained. However, some only of the party consented to go : others, knowing Mr. Lloyd George's wish not to allow the opponents to hold a meeting, explained their reasons for remaining. The Chief Constable replied that he would endeavour to clear the hall. By this time the crowd outside had joined in the attack, and the beautiful glass dome of the Town Hall over the platform and organ began to fall in upon us. Huge stones and other missiles were being thrown from outside. ' Barbed ' bricks were also being thrown through the side windows at those on the platform."

One by one the constables who remained guarding the hall were injured by the missiles which hurtled through the windows. In the words of the lady I have quoted, " the organisation of lawlessness was complete." Outside concerted attacks were being made upon the doors of the building, while mob-orators of local fame inflamed the passions of the crowd. Inside organised detachments carried out carefully laid plans.

It is impossible to attempt any connected account of what went on outside the Town Hall. The crowd, which was superficially good-humoured early in the evening, worked itself later into a frenzy. Every window and every pane was shattered. Had not the framework of the windows been of solid iron, the mob would have effected an entrance into the building, with results which it is not necessary to contemplate. The besieging force, with a unanimity which seemed to show the plan of campaign to have been thoughtfully devised, concentrated its efforts upon one particular door of the building, which almost yielded. Some say that revolver shots were fired.

That Mr. Lloyd George would leave the building uninjured seemed hopeless to his friends. They felt that he would be fortunate if he got away alive. I quote again from the account of the same eye-witness—an account which comparison with reports published in the Press at the time shows to be in no way exaggerated :

"Finding his men would soon all be incapacitated, the Chief Constable, as a last resource, suggested to Mr. Lloyd George that he should leave the hall in a line of police constables, and added that, by arrangement with the officers outside, he could get a passage through the crowd for the men, provided that Mr. Lloyd George would consent to wear a policeman's coat. This Mr. Lloyd George emphatically refused to do. It was only under great pressure that he gave way, when the Chief Constable pointed out that it was a last and only chance, and that by doing it he might save his friends from injury. The doors could not much longer be held, and there might be a great inrush of the mob, with terrible results. The fact that his friends might be injured if he persisted in his refusal was the only argument that prevailed with Mr. Lloyd George. That the crowd outside sought his life seemed not to weigh with him.

"When the Chief Constable had made his arrangements the doors flew open, and the little procession marched out in order. The doors quickly closed behind them, but not before those inside heard what they thought was identification—a shout from one quarter, ' Quick, it's the little man ' ; from another, ' He's the fifth from the end.' We all felt he had gone to certain death. There was not a word spoken, but some of us offered up a silent prayer, as we felt that it was only by a miracle that he could be spared.

"The Chief Constable then quietly gave orders that the wounded were to be attended to, and asked us to descend to the basement of the Town Hall so that all strength might be available in the hope of holding out. We could still hear shrieks and howling and the smashing of doors and windows. The Chief went outside twice, and standing on a chair informed the crowd that Mr. Lloyd George was not inside the Town Hall. It was when the Chief saw he could not hold out any longer that he gave orders that we were to leave the building one at a time, each in the centre of a number of policemen, some in borrowed clothes lent by the wife of the curator."

Nobody can quite explain how Mr. Lloyd George escaped violence that night. It is certain that in spite of his disguise he was identified by at least one man in the crowd, who was, however, fortunately ignored. At any rate he got back safely to Hagley Road, where a detachment of police guarded Mr. Evans's house until Mr. Lloyd George left it the next morning. The rioting outside the Town Hall continued till after ten o'clock. A city councillor and a member of the School Board were among the mob-orators who throughout the evening had harangued the crowd. "Men of Birmingham," cried one of them, "I am proud of you to-night. Not a word has been heard in the Town Hall. The pro-Boers have got in there and cannot get out, and now I want you, a hundred thousand Birmingham citizens" (this was an exaggeration not unpardonable in the circumstances), "to pass a resolution expressing your confidence in His Majesty's Government and your pride in the Colonial Secretary." The acclamation which greeted this proposal fully justified the speaker in dispatching, as he did, a telegram to Mr. Chamberlain, to which, it is said, a gracious reply was sent.[1]

Shortly after ten o'clock a heavy snow-storm considerably thinned the crowd, but its most dangerous element remained, and seemed to be bent upon storming the now empty hall. By this time there were few windows left to break. Some of the mob possessed themselves of a scaffold pole and used it as a battering ram upon one of the doors. Just before this a police constable had been felled and stunned by a stone, and in the struggle with the gang who were making this assault upon the door, another officer was badly injured. Matters were so serious that the Chief Constable ordered a baton charge upon the mob.

---

[1] The telegram was in the following terms: "Lloyd George, the traitor, was not allowed to say a word. Two (sic) hundred thousand citizens and others passed resolutions of confidence in the Government, and of admiration for your unique and fearless efforts for King, country, and people."

The order was promptly obeyed, and the mob was effectively dispersed. Most unhappily a young man, Curtis by name, met his death during the charge. It was said by some that he fell accidentally and struck his head against the kerb, but according to the verdict of the coroner's jury he was struck down by an unidentified policeman. Twenty-seven persons who had been injured at one time or another during the rioting were taken to the hospital, and many more were treated in their own homes.

The citizens of Birmingham had such satisfaction as the wrecking of their own Town Hall (at the expense, it is true, of the organisers of the meeting) could afford them. One parallel to these riots has already been noticed. Observers of the scene with a knowledge of the history of the city could not fail to be impressed by another. Near the Town Hall, and opposite the little door by which Mr. Lloyd George escaped from it, stands the statue, erected in 1873, of Priestley, the great scientist, who was a Nonconformist minister of religion in Birmingham at the end of the eighteenth century. In 1791 the rage of his fellow-citizens descended upon him because of his known sympathy with the French revolutionaries. Always practical in the expression of their emotions, they burned down his chapel, sacked and destroyed his house and laboratory, and made away with the records of his scientific and philosophical inquiries which it had been the work of years to collect. After eighty years repentance came tardily. His statue was erected to commemorate the greatness of the man whom loyalists had proclaimed a traitor. So the whirligig of time brought in its revenge. The apostles of liberty are fortunate indeed if it is not left to posterity to honour what their contemporaries denounce.

Upon his safe return to Hagley Road, Mr. Lloyd George's only anxiety was for his wife and his uncle, Mr. Richard Lloyd. They had not, he knew, been in fear of any disturbance. He had kept from Mrs. Lloyd George all knowledge of the threats and warnings which had reached him. It was impossible to tell what reports the morning newspapers might contain, and he was eager to reassure them at once. He promptly telephoned to the offices of the London " Daily News," and Mr. Harold Spender was able to send a message to Mrs. Lloyd George, who was in London, and a telegram to Mr. Richard Lloyd at Criccieth, to acquaint them of his safety. The reporter of the " Daily Post " interviewed him soon after his return. The interview was short and pithy. " How did you manage to escape unnoticed ? " asked the reporter. " The portrait published in the ' Birmingham Daily Mail ' did not serve its purpose," was Mr. Lloyd George's reply.

All night the house was watched by the police. Early the next morning Mrs. William Evans's little Irish niece, Ellaline, ran into Mr. Lloyd George's room eager to warn and protect him. Inspired by a precocious genius for strategy and reminiscences of the Christmas pantomime, she exclaimed, "You've been naughty, and they've come for you! Shall we make the poker very hot, or will you get into the big bearskin rug in the dining-room and go out as a bear?"

Mr. Lloyd George was cautioned by the police that there was extreme danger of further rioting, but he decided none the less to leave by the 10 a.m. express. He drove to the station, and on the way he was recognised by divers magnates of the city who were being driven to their business houses. These worthies instructed their coachmen to keep abreast of Mr. Lloyd George's carriage and ostentatiously hooted and hissed at him. In spite of the attentions of these gentlemen he was able, by taking an unaccustomed route, to avoid those of patriots of coarser grain, which might have been equally malignant and more dangerous. On his arrival at New Street Station, where arrangements had been made that he should reach the platform by a subway, he discovered that Mr. Chamberlain was leaving by the same train by which he intended to travel. The police pointed out the danger of further rioting if he courted observation by entering the same train with the hero of the disorderly element, and prevailed upon Mr. Lloyd George to wait for a later train. The mob continued to search the city for him until the evening papers made it known that he was in London. "They failed to inflict even a scratch upon me," he wrote home, "although they had sworn to do for me." In the same letter he expressed his grief at the death of young Curtis and the injuries to the police.

According to current reports in the newspapers, Mr. Chamberlain, who had been staying at his residence near Birmingham during the rioting, expressed an opinion upon it in the course of conversation with a friend before he left by the train for London. He did not blame the people for stopping the meeting, he was reported to have said, but he regarded the attack on the Town Hall and the riotous proceedings generally as disgraceful, and very much to be deplored.[1]

A few days later, however, the "Birmingham Daily Post" claimed to be authorised by Mr. Chamberlain to say that he had made no public statement whatever on the subject of Wednesday night's meeting, and that he had not been interviewed by anybody connected with the Press. "It may be hoped," added the

[1] See the "Birmingham Daily Argus," December 19, 1901.

" Post," " that this definite contradiction may dispose, once for all, of the reports circulated by some of the pro-Boer newspapers as to a supposed, but entirely fictitious interview." Apparently what had horrified the " Post " was the dreadful suggestion that Mr. Chamberlain could possibly have " deplored " the riots.

Another comment was attributed to Mr. Chamberlain by Mr. W. T. Stead. Mr. Lloyd George's old friend Mr. W. S. Caine, " in his genial, ruffianly fashion," accosted Mr. Chamberlain in the lobby of the House of Commons a day or two after the breaking up of the meeting. " What's the matter with Birmingham ? " he asked. " Every one expected you would kill Lloyd George. Why did you let him escape ? " To which Mr. Chamberlain replied, " What is everybody's business is nobody's business." [1]

It would, however, be unfair to place any responsibility upon the member for West Birmingham except for one of those " acts of omission " which lawyers, if not moralists, are inclined to treat tenderly. No doubt he might, by a word, have checked the incitements in the Unionist Press and prevented the riots. He did not do so. Not for the first time in his career, as we have seen, he failed to exert " those influences of moral restraint which are so much to be commended in political leaders during times of popular excitement."

On the other hand, the Conservative, as distinct from the Liberal Unionist Press of Birmingham, strongly censured the disorder it had done its best to prevent. The " Gazette," after saying that it " yielded to no one in its detestation of the line which Mr. Lloyd George had taken since the war began," declared that the riot " was a discredit to the city and no service to the State." " We fear that those who organised the demonstrations of pseudo-patriotism were not very particular as to the tools they employed for their purpose."

The " Daily Argus," expressing no greater love for Mr. Lloyd George's opinions, was not less emphatic in its denunciation of the too successful efforts of the Unionist Press. I quote its leading article, which shows the view taken by those supporters of the policy of the war who had not permitted prejudice to blind them :

We sincerely trust that the representatives of the infamous type of journalism which instigated last night's riot in Birmingham are pleased with their work. They have gathered to the full the fruits of violence, which for a week past they have been industriously engaged in sowing. They can boast now that a man has been killed to prove the success of

[1] " Review of Reviews," October 1904.

their agitation, that thirty or forty people have sustained personal injuries, that the Town Hall has been wrecked, and that an orgy of blackguardism has been witnessed in Birmingham such as few cities would have been capable of producing. Measured by the standard of their own aims, they are to be congratulated on an unmitigated success, and we trust they will not be too coy to give themselves the pleasure of attending such funerals as may be amongst the miscellaneous sequels to their achievement.

The process of instigation to which the proceedings of last night were due was not difficult to follow. The right of one political party to deny by force a hearing to its opponents was assumed as a matter of course. The flames of blind passion were carefully fanned day by day, until the eve of the meeting, by allusions to well-known methods of disorder. The use of force was not indeed recommended in so many words, but the idea was kept before the minds of the lower orders until the suggestion had been safely lodged and its successful development was assured. Every facility was offered to those disposed to assault the promoters of the meeting. Mr. Lloyd George's portrait was published on the day of his arrival. The train by which he was expected to reach the city was conspicuously advertised in a space reserved for specially important announcements. The question of a disorderly demonstration at the house at which the speaker was staying was discussed at length, the address being withheld in consequence of a significant intimation from the Chief Constable. The disorderly element were informed in a casual way that any damage which might be done to the Town Hall would have to be paid for by the promoters of the meeting, and the hint, as last night abundantly testifies, was not thrown away. The cowardice which now proceeds to blame the Lord Mayor for giving impartial facilities to both political parties, and to complain that the Chief Constable ordered his men to charge a ruffianly crowd after several members of the force had been injured, is what one might expect from those who gather missiles for their less cunning dupes to discharge.

We need enter no further into the controversy as it affected Birmingham and its reputation. Grumblings continued in the Unionist papers against the Lord Mayor, the Chief Constable, the Liberal Association. The " Mail " and the " Post " were unrepentant. I cannot refrain from quoting two passages from the latter paper which may serve to show the kind of proposition which a writer *in extremis* may be driven to support:

The executive of a political organisation is supposed to be in close touch with popular sentiment. It is supposed to know to a nicety how far it is safe to go in opposition to that popular sentiment. In choosing its speakers at any public demonstration it is expected to ascertain exactly the support those speakers may count on receiving from within the party, and how much hostility they will provoke from outside.

In fact, they should choose their speakers as some modern

newspaper proprietors choose a policy for a paper ! This is the second passage :

Nothing could have been more unwise than for the pro-Boers of Birmingham to invite such a man to make a public speech here, and the citizens rose to the occasion. It was all very well to suggest that Mr. Lloyd George would only address Liberals : *his presence in the city was distasteful*, and many Liberals saw the folly of arranging for such a meeting.

I have ventured to italicise a pregnant sentence. Mr. Lloyd George's crime was that he entered the Holy City of Imperialism : for that iniquity many of its citizens had adjudged violent injury or even death to be a fitting penalty.

Outside Birmingham diverse morals were extracted from the Birmingham riots. According to the "Times" they "illustrated the fact, which even some continental journals had begun to find out, that the working-classes in this country were Imperialist to the core," a comment upon Imperialism which would, one thinks, have been treated with contumely had it come from a "pro-Boer." Most people of all parties will prefer to accept the lesson drawn from the incident by Mr. Asquith in a speech which he delivered at Bilston on the next day :

It will be a very bad day if it ever dawns—and sometimes one is tempted to think that it is nearer than we ever expected—when the free expression of opinion in this country is not going to be tolerated, and is going to be put down by force, by terrorism. Where is there any man amongst us— I do not care what views he holds—who has not read with shame and indignation the accounts of what appears to have been the organised and concerted rowdyism by which, in a town not very far from here, a man who is supposed to hold unpopular opinions was deprived on Wednesday night of the opportunity of expressing them ? I do not suppose, if those intended speeches had ever been allowed to be made, that I should have found myself in entire agreement with what was said. But what has that got to do with the matter ? There is no possession which an Englishman values more highly than the inestimable and inalienable right of free speech. If you don't like my views, and have not got the good sense to listen to them in good temper and in silence, then stay away. If you wish to choose the more excellent part, go and hear the views of the person from whom you differ, and very likely you will go back strengthened and confirmed in your own. One thing that is not allowable, because it strikes at the very foundations of democratic freedom and democratic government, is that a man whose views do not happen to be those of the majority should not be allowed a fair hearing.

It was a gross outrage upon the elementary rights of citizenship.

The " Birmingham Mail " had prophesied exultantly that at least Mr. Lloyd George would not be likely to set foot in the city again. That prophecy was destined to be falsified. Five years later, when a reaction had set in, which seemed very distant in 1901, the man whose voice the howls of Birmingham had silenced, whose life the stalwarts of Birmingham had sought, came again to the city and its Town Hall as the guest of the Young British Liberals' Federation.[1] On that occasion, which, at the risk of seeming to anticipate, it may be well to mention now, the " Mail " was pleased graciously to compliment him on a " singularly felicitous " anecdote with which he commenced his speech. He told his hearers that when he was taking his ticket at the London terminus the booking clerk asked him innocently, " Would you like to insure, sir ? " " What special risks do you think I run ? " the hardened traveller replied. He seemed to feel, he went on, that he had been in that place before. It looked familiar, and he had a faint recollection of a crowded but not exactly enthusiastic audience—perhaps he might say, an audience of conflicting enthusiasts. He also seemed to remember that there was an overflow meeting in the square of men who were anxious to get inside but somehow failed to do so.

Something has been said already of the fact that, in spite of the bitterness of their many duels, Mr. Lloyd George has always regarded Mr. Chamberlain with something akin to admiration. In 1906 he made references to him, untinged with bitterness, which show that the man whom Birmingham had willed to sacrifice in proof of her devotion to the greatest of her sons cherished no rancour and bore no malice. A few words from the speech of 1906 may serve as a charitable epilogue to the incident :

I have never thought that Birmingham was permanently lost to democracy. As a matter of fact, the very quality which has, in my judgment, led Birmingham astray, is a democratic quality—its devotion to its chief; not that sycophancy and snobbery which surrounds some who gain position and power without merit, but loyalty, the loyalty of the people to the man whom they have chosen from among themselves to lead them.

[1] October 22, 1906.

I append to this chapter the note of the speech he had intended to deliver which Mr. Lloyd George handed to the reporters :

He said that he quite approved of that portion of the resolution which bore upon Lord Rosebery's speech. There was much in it which every friend of peace must contemplate with great satisfaction. There was one thing at least which must gratify every Liberal in connection with it, and that was its reception by the majority of the Tory journals in this country. There was not that chorus of praise which generally followed speeches delivered by certain Liberals of the Imperialist persuasion, praise which he very much regretted was often deserved, from the Government's point of view. It was true that one or two of the Ministerial papers approved, but he found that to-day on full reflection they hesitated. From the extreme north to the south of this island they jeered and carped. That in itself predisposed all Liberals to regard that speech with some partiality. One felt instinctively that there would be a deal of good in an utterance which was attacked by the " Standard," the " Scotsman," and the " Birmingham Daily Post," and which the " Times " liked less and less the longer they reflected upon its contents. Liberal foundation was unobtainable without unity, unity could not be achieved except on the basis of peace, peace was impossible except on the basis of freedom. The application of Liberal principles could alone save South Africa to the Empire ; that was why he emphasised his anxiety for unity so long as there were any hope of this being effected on Liberal lines. Lord Rosebery's speech held that unity of action could be obtained without sacrifice of principle on either side. Unity of action did not imply uniformity of opinions. If it did co-operation in any walk of life would be impossible. Before he entered into any discussion upon the suggestion made by Lord Rosebery, he wished to point out one object at least which had been promoted by his speech. Up to the present the mind of the people had been directed solely to consider the most effective methods of prosecuting the war. Lord Rosebery had set the nation thinking about the best means of concluding peace. He had done more ; he had made it clear that a durable peace was only possible on the lines of a liberal treatment of our foes. Once the incorporation of the two States within the Empire were conceded, Lord Rosebery advised the concession of liberal if not lavish terms. Once the British people started from that point, they were too direct and too practical a race to allow the trivialities that trouble pedantic minds to deter them from reaching the goal. If they wished to realise how much we have progressed towards unity as a party through Lord Rosebery's influence, let him point out one important fact. Immediately it had been delivered, Mr. Asquith and Sir Edward Grey got up and accepted its doctrines in their entirety. How much that meant for the Liberal Party, and especially for those who had striven towards common action on the lines of a conciliatory policy, would be instanced by dwelling for a moment on one or two of Lord Rosebery's proposals. Let them take his attitude towards the confiscatory proclamation of September 15. As they were well aware, that was

Mr. Chamberlain's. Sir William Harcourt at the time of its issue mercilessly condemned it, and expressed the opinion that it would embitter controversy, make the Boers desperate, and thus prolong the war. On the other hand Mr. Asquith defended it. What had Lord Rosebery to say about it ? He used his own words : " That proclamation has done unmixed harm in prolonging the war, and in driving the Boers to desperation," and he unhesitatingly counselled its annulment. When Sir William Harcourt and Lord Rosebery agreed on any proposition, they might depend upon it that there was much to say for it, and it must not be forgotten that whilst Sir William Harcourt and Sir Henry Campbell-Bannerman denounced the proclamation, Mr. Asquith got up in his place in the House and defended it. He was glad now to see that he supported Lord Rosebery's demand for its cancelment. The next point was a much more important one. Lord Rosebery referred to the Kitchener-Botha negotiations. It would appear that Lord Kitchener proposed as part of the terms of settlement a general amnesty, but Lord Milner and Mr. Chamberlain disapproved. That was in itself enough to prevent the conclusion of peace. No brave and honourable man would ever consent to accept a peace which involved abandonment of his comrades in arms to punishment as criminals. Now let them mark what happened. The terms proposed by Lord Kitchener were altered everywhere by Lord Milner and Mr. Chamberlain. Sir Henry Campbell-Bannerman supported Lord Kitchener ; Mr. Asquith's friends in the House backed up Mr. Chamberlain's action in throwing over Lord Kitchener and said that Mr. Chamberlain had gone to the extreme limit of generosity. But what did Lord Rosebery say at Chesterfield ? He condemned Lord Milner's policy, and said he would unhesitatingly have voted for Kitchener's proposal for a large and liberal amnesty. Lord Rosebery rightly attached great importance to this; he thought the question of the amnesty was the greatest obstacle to peace. Was it not significant that on the question that Lord Rosebery considered the most difficult he and Sir William Harcourt, Mr. John Morley, and Sir Henry Campbell-Bannerman should be on the same side ? He was exceedingly glad to find that Mr. Asquith and Sir Edward Grey were now also on the same side. There was another point in these negotiations where Lord Rosebery backed up Lord Kitchener as against Mr. Chamberlain and also as against his own Imperialist friends. Lord Kitchener had proposed to General Botha that the Boers should have a voice in advising the Provisional Administration which he proposed to set up. He also suggested that the Administration should be followed, after a period, by representative government. What said Mr. Chamberlain ? He would have no Boer representation, and as for representative government, he would only concede it at three removes. Lord Rosebery's friends in the House of Commons approved of Mr. Chamberlain's action in this respect. Lord Rosebery himself on Monday not only backed up Lord Kitchener's views but went considerably further along the same road. Surely it was not without some pleasure that they noted the fact that the leaders of the Liberal Imperialist Party in the House of Commons were now prepared to recede from the reactionary position they took in March last and introduce suggestions which were very similar to, if not identical with, those already made by Sir Henry Campbell-Bannerman on this point. Let him give another illustration. Lord Kitchener recommended that the Government should furnish the Boers with money to rebuild and restore their farms. In this he was supported by Lord Milner. Mr. Chamberlain, however, declined to accept the suggestion, and offered instead a contingent and conditional proposal for lending some part of the money required. Lord Rosebery, agreeing in this respect with Sir Henry Campbell-Bannerman, now strongly advocated the dealing out of money with a lavish hand for the purpose of re-settling the farms. On this point he goes beyond Lord Kitchener. Unfortunately the Liberal Imperialist leaders in the House of Commons thought fit to support Mr. Chamberlain's action against Lord Kitchener. Now they accepted the much more thorough and Liberal proposals of Lord Rosebery. They could now see how far they had been led along the road of unity, and they considered that on three such cardinal questions as this Lord Rosebery had induced his Liberal Imperialist friends to come into line with the leader of the Liberal Party. It was said that Lord Rosebery had thrown over the Derby Resolution, but that was hardly so when they came to consider what he actually proposed. The Derby Resolution said the time had arrived for opening negotiations. In that Lord Rosebery fully concurred. All he did was to contribute a suggestion as to the best means of bringing the parties together. It was true they advocated the sending out of a Commissioner to South Africa, while in Lord Rosebery's opinion there was a better chance of securing peace by negotiating with the exiled Boer Government in Holland. That could only be done by means of special envoy. Lord Rosebery would have a special Commissioner in Europe—the Derby Resolution suggested South Africa, so that even on that point there was substantial agreement. There was one other service which Lord Rosebery had done in the interests of the fair and effective discussion of this great question. He had treated with scorn the doctrine of the infallibility of Lord Milner. He was not sure that this new dogma of papal infallibility was not the most serious obstacle in the path of the unity of Liberal action for the moment. Any suggestion that was made, whether by Sir Henry Campbell-Bannerman or any one else, if Lord Milner did not approve, or if in any way it involved the slightest slur upon him, was not even considered on its merits. Those were some of the reasons why he took a hopeful view of the results of Lord Rosebery's utterance. He need hardly say that there was a great deal in the speech with which he could not possibly agree, and he had no doubt at all that no one would be more shocked than Lord Rosebery if he found that those who had opposed the war through and through, and still considered it both unjust and unnecessary, were in agreement with everything he had said.

CHAPTER IV

I

THE season of peace and goodwill which followed immediately upon the Birmingham adventure had scarcely ended when Mr. Lloyd George had to prepare himself for another meeting which promised at one time to be not less exciting. He had been under a promise to speak at a meeting at Bristol at the end of November. But for a few days his health had failed him under the strain of strenuous propagandist work, and the engagement had been postponed to January 6 in the New Year. The result was that he had scarcely escaped from Birmingham when he found himself called upon to face whatever risks were incident to a meeting at Bristol. There was much in the prospect that was disquieting. It could not be said of the Bristol meeting that it was a commonplace assembly of local Liberals. On the contrary, it was definitely a " Peace " meeting, called to advocate the cessation of the war by a combination of bodies, which included the Bristol Conciliation Committee. It was, however, to be a ticket meeting, and the people of Bristol had at first shown no disposition to be perturbed by the prospect of it.

In November the Vestry Hall of St. Philip's had been hired by the organisers without any kind of difficulty being raised. After Birmingham had shown the lengths to which some of the advocates of the curtailment of freedom of speech were prepared to go, the Overseers' committee, in whom control of the hall was vested, took alarm. At first they decided to refuse to let it for the purpose proposed at all : finally, after prolonged negotiations, they were induced to alter their decision upon terms which absolved the Corporation from any possible financial liability. It was agreed that the promoters of the meeting should be held liable for any damage done to the building, and further, that they should make no claim against the Corporation under the provisions of the Riots Act. The fact that such an agreement was considered necessary showed that the situation was not regarded by local opinion as free from gravity, and many of Mr. Lloyd George's friends, concerned for his safety, begged him to cancel, or, at any rate, to postpone the engagement. He would not listen to their appeals, and was as firm in his resolution to carry out his promise as he had been when danger threatened at Bangor and at Birmingham. Unionists professed to believe that Birmingham had taught the Peace party such a lesson that there would be no fear of further Peace meetings. That in itself was enough to persuade Mr. Lloyd George that, at all hazards, the Bristol meeting must not be abandoned. His friends, finding their remonstrances to be in vain, contented themselves with doing what lay in their power to mitigate the dangers; and Mr. William Evans, who had been his host at Birmingham, went to Bristol to give such advice to the conveners of the meeting as his experience of the Chamberlain Square encounter suggested.

In Bristol itself little had occurred to suggest that the peace would be broken. On the day of the meeting, however, a London newspaper, the " Daily Express," published an account of an interview with Mr. Lloyd George in which he was reported to have uttered a truculent and provocative challenge to the Unionists of Bristol. He was stated to have said that, whereas at Birmingham they had been unprepared for attack, they were now ready. " If the Bristol people want a fight, they can have it. We are ready for them." The head-lines under which this interview was published served to emphasise the invitation to physical combat which it seemed to offer. " Trailing his Coat," " Lloyd George's challenge to Bristol Loyalists," were the headings, and in a leading article the " Daily Express " laid further stress upon the suggestion they contained. The writer accused him of openly and aggressively daring Bristol to repeat the reception given him by Birmingham : " no Donnybrook Irishman had ever more pointedly invited the public to tread on the tail of his coat."

The report of this interview was widely circulated in Bristol, and the " Daily Express " poster for the day, with the words " Mr. Lloyd George challenges the Unionists of Bristol," was exhibited prominently all over the city. In this way a certain amount of indignation was aroused, which again awoke fears of a disturbance.

Throughout the day handbills were distributed in the streets calling upon the citizens of Bristol to assemble in their thousands to protest ("in an orderly manner") against "this tricky attempt to hold a pro-Boer meeting in the heart of the city, to prejudice the country's cause and strengthen the hands of Britain's bitter foes."

However, the precautions which had been taken to keep the peace would have been ample, even if really serious danger had threatened. As it was, the crowd which gathered seems to have been, with few exceptions, good-humoured and attracted rather by curiosity than any sinister purpose. Still, it is an extra-ordinary fact, from which no doubt very diverse morals will be extracted, that to safeguard the right of one member of Parliament to make an unpopular speech it was thought necessary to adopt measures which could not have been considered inadequate if a royal progress had been on foot. We read that barriers were thrown across two of the roads leading to the Vestry Hall, with a strong body of police to guard each barrier. During the day the windows of the Vestry Hall were barricaded. Over one hundred police constables were on duty in the neighbourhood of the hall at six o'clock, two hours before the meeting was to begin; and about 150 more, together with a section of mounted men, were being held in readiness at the nearest police station. Before the meeting ended most of the reserve men, with the exception of the mounted men, had been called out. After half-past seven the doors were closed: none but ticket-holders had been admitted, but it was discovered later that some of the tickets were forged.

On the steps outside the hall a fire-hose, guarded by firemen, dominated the approach and served to strike terror into the hearts of any who may have contemplated a rush upon the building. Nothing so exciting took place. The worst that happened was that some hundreds of people managed to get into the space beyond the barriers. Some of them were ticket-holders who had arrived too late to gain admission; others were intruders, and perhaps the majority of these were hostile to the meeting. At any rate, they were beginning to get a little noisy, when a body of police bore down upon them from two directions and swept them in a surprisingly short time behind the barriers. Outside the barriers there was a press of many thousands, but their attitude does not seem to have been unmixedly hostile. One rush was made upon the barriers, without effect; and there was a good deal of hooting. On the other hand, it was claimed afterwards by the organisers of the meeting that a great many in the crowd were friends, bitterly disappointed at not being able to get in, and it was said that one man who tried to move a resolution in favour of the Government and the war, found that he had mistaken the temper of those near him and had to fly from their wrath. On the whole, the crowd seems to have been more curious than enthusiastic in any sense.

The meeting inside was, on the whole, a friendly one, and those who had got in with forged tickets made no attempt to disturb the proceedings or to interrupt them, except by occasionally interjecting questions. The Vestry Hall, which held two thousand people, was quite crowded. Mr. Lloyd George, whose arrival in Bristol early in the afternoon had passed unnoticed, reached the building on foot. He was accompanied by a few stalwart supporters, mostly Irish Nationalists, of whom it was said afterwards that they were a little disappointed that no one offered to molest the man they guarded. At the hall a telegram awaited him from one of those eccentric people who find pleasure in dispatching such anonymous missives of abuse. "That Bristol will go one better than we did," it said, "and crack your skull, is the sincere wish of all Birmingham."

It has been said already that, as the war proceeded, the bitterness of Mr. Lloyd George's tone became more marked. Perhaps, considering events at Birmingham, it is not surprising that when he found himself facing an audience of warm admirers and friends at Bristol, he showed no disposition to be half-hearted in his denunciations. One may think, too, that the same instinct of pugnacity which made him the more eager to hold his meetings when violence was threatened urged him to make it very clear that he was in no chastened mood.

He began by commenting upon the conditions under which the meeting was held. It had been found necessary to barricade the hall, and to trust, not to argument alone, but very largely to the well-developed muscles of their own friends in the town. After centuries of struggles for free speech, argument was to be thrust aside, and men were to trust to brute force rather than to the intellect with which, in varying degrees, God had endowed most of them. He condemned as an incitement to riot the article published in the morning by the "Express." He based his argument upon the war on his belief that Lord Kitchener, left to himself, would have been able to make peace with General Botha—a belief which, as has been seen, Lord Rosebery was inclined to share. "Why," he asked, "was peace not made?" There were cries from the audience of "Chamberlain" and "Judas." He took up the parable and emphasised it : "Judas," he said, "only finished himself—this man has finished thousands!" Then, after claiming that the terms suggested by Lord Rosebery at Chesterfield were the very terms which the poor pro-Boers had been urging upon their countrymen for months, he prophesied that a time would come when the rage of the people would be turned against those who had led them into the war instead of against those who tried to stop it. He went on to attack in strong terms the policy of farm-burning and the concentration camps. When the Boer farmer found charred and blackened ruins in the place where his homestead had been, and learned of the death of his children, was it likely that he would ever come back to be a loyal British subject? "Do you believe in the Boers?" a voice from the audience asked him. No nation, he answered, had a monopoly of scoundrels. No braver race would they find, and courage covered a multitude of sins. In a peroration which pictured Britain, her prestige shaken after a vast expenditure of blood and treasure, threatened with disasters which might leave her as prostrate as other great empires of the past, one striking sentence stands out: "I have a few superstitions left," he said, "and one of them is that the government of this earth is not in the hands of great imperial syndicates."

The meeting was over before ten o'clock, the streets cleared quietly and rapidly, and Mr. Lloyd George, escorted by his Irish bodyguard, walked home in safety. On the way a local journalist managed to interview him, and questioned him as to the statement attributed to him by the "Daily Express." There had been an interview, he said, but it had been "written up" so as to misrepresent him entirely. He had said: "If the Bristol Jingoes really want to break up the meeting, we are ready for them," adding that he did not think the Bristol people wanted a row, as he believed they had better sense. The latter remark, he said, was not printed. The former was misrepresented. Whatever hopes may have been founded upon the provocation of the "Daily Express" interview were luckily disappointed, partly because of the good sense of the people of Bristol, partly, no doubt, from an application by the Peace party of a maxim which they do not commonly quote with approval: if you want peace, prepare for war.

One veteran reformer, the late George Jacob Holyoake (for whom the collocation of Birmingham and Bristol must have had a strange significance, since it was in the course of his walk from the former to the latter city, in 1842, that he delivered the lecture which led to his trial and imprisonment), wrote to the "Manchester Guardian" to express his admiration of the courage of the Member for Carnarvon:[1]

[1] "Manchester Guardian," January 14, 1902.

It is one of the most unusual victories of the age. Nothing accomplished in South Africa has been more brilliant than this achievement. No victory over the Boers has been attended with more danger than Mr. Lloyd George encountered, and no general has been in more peril than he. His safety depended on the timely and judicious construction of stout, Todleben fortifications. But for these he would not be living now. That he overcame the allied forces of our Home Boers—the Imperialist battalions of intolerance and brutality—was a military feat of no mean order, and the Victoria Cross, or other insignia of honour, for skill, intrepidity, and distinguished success in the field, ought to be awarded to him, with official recommendation for promotion.

To the average man, sentiments such as Holyoake's seemed extravagantly paradoxical, and there was no general disposition to attribute any credit to Mr. Lloyd George for his courage. He was regarded, however, with what is the best to be expected from excited opponents, wonder at his audacity. In some quarters the result of the Birmingham meeting was made an excuse for refusing to allow him to speak at all. In the borough of Islington, for instance, the Town Council rejected the request embodied in a memorial by six hundred ratepayers, that a meeting should be permitted in the public baths at which it had been arranged that Mr. Lloyd George should be among the speakers. By a substantial majority the Council carried an amendment to the effect that in view of the violence at Birmingham, the Council was compelled, in the interests of law and order, to forbid the use of the hall by the Liberal Associations, unless those bodies gave an undertaking that Mr. Lloyd George should not be one of the speakers. That undertaking was refused, but just ten months afterwards, Mr. Lloyd George was able to make merry, from the very platform that was denied him in January, at the expense of the councillors who had regarded him " as a dangerous individual likely, if he were permitted to enter the borough, to arrive at the head of a Boer commando " with intent to capture their valuable property.

II

Lord Rosebery and Sir Henry Campbell-Bannerman—Mr. Lloyd George's views of the latter —A meeting at the St. James's Hall—The Cawley amendment: an unsuccessful manœuvre—Mr. Lloyd George's sarcasm—" Pawning the heirlooms of Liberalism "—Lord Rosebery at Liverpool—Mr. Lloyd George on " the clean slate "—The N.L.F. at Leicester—The Liberal League.

The Chesterfield speech had raised high the hopes of those Liberals who believed that the return of Lord Rosebery to active leadership was essential to the prosperity of their party. Such a belief was very general. Sir Henry Campbell-Bannerman's great qualities were firmness and honesty of purpose, and these virtues, by their very nature, cannot make their appeal to the public conscience until the statesman who possesses them has been long in the public eye. Sir Henry Campbell-Bannerman, though known to those with any close knowledge of affairs as a very valued Minister and trusted colleague, had never been before his election to the leadership of the House of Commons one of those characters in politics upon whom the limelight shines. His qualities, like those for which the Vicar of Wakefield chose his wife, were such as would wear well. To his durable qualities he added few of the superficial charms which easily evoke popular enthusiasm. Were it not for his personal *bonhomie* and tact, one might say that he had the advantage of no such natural endowment. When he was brought into the glare of prominence, it was to be represented by that section of the Press which for the time being had the upper hand, as a sort of pinchbeck traitor, the weak tool of a gang of disloyalists of whom Mr. Lloyd George was the chief. As time went on and the elected leader got increased opportunities of meeting his followers and making his voice heard by them, he began to find the way to their hearts. Indignation at the language used of him by Mr. Chamberlain and smaller men in the Unionist Party served to increase his popularity. But few Liberals, and fewer Tories, realised how that popularity was growing in the ranks of Liberalism. Lord Rosebery had all the qualifications of a popular favourite, and even those members of the party to whom his leadership would have been unacceptable, seldom showed or felt any confident belief that the man who was shepherding his errant followers through the desert places would be the leader chosen to enjoy the rewards of entry into the promised land.

An instance of the ridicule which the Tory Press was accustomed to throw upon any suggestion that Sir Henry Campbell-Bannerman was to be considered seriously is provided by the amusing comments of an interviewer who gave a version in the " Pall Mall Gazette " of a conversation with Mr. Lloyd George.[1] When Mr. Lloyd George told him that Sir Henry " had enormously strengthened his hold upon the public during the last two years, and especially the past six months," the journalist " glanced at the window with a mute appeal for breath," thought that " this was recklessness with a vengeance," and " ceased to wonder why Birmingham was roused." Mr. Lloyd George went

[1] January 3, 1902.

on to say that Sir Henry carried with him the Centre in the Liberal Party, men not associated with either the extreme imperialists on the one side, or the strong anti-war party on the other. " You may look as surprised as you like," he told his interviewer, " but I have done a lot of platform work, and I have been surprised at the success Sir Henry has achieved during this late campaign of his up and down the country. Since Gladstone we have had no names on our side, like Chamberlain, Balfour, and Salisbury —I am thinking of Chamberlain in particular—which can thrill an audience into a cheer whenever they are invoked. But Sir Henry, I think, is beginning to strike the Liberal imagination ; and though he has never been a fighting man, he has courage of a dogged sort, and when I say he has obtained a triumphant series of meetings I am not using exaggerated language."

These words represented what was the fact, but it was a fact to which, at that date, many people were blind.

In spite of Mr. Lloyd George's admiration for Sir Henry Campbell-Bannerman, it was not long before he found himself seriously in conflict with him. Before we come to that occasion it is necessary to say a word about intervening events. One of the first fruits of the Chesterfield speech was a meeting held on January 13 at St. James's Hall to inaugurate a body newly come into existence under the style of the London Liberal Federation. At this meeting the principal speaker was Sir Henry Campbell-Bannerman. The hall was crowded. The various schools of Liberalism were represented on the platform, Mr. Perks, the Nonconformist Liberal Imperialist, and Mr. E. T. Cook, whose services had been transferred, in consequence of his views upon the war, from the " Daily News " to the " Daily Chronicle," sitting cheek-by-jowl with advanced opponents of the war. Mr. Lloyd George was unable to be present, a fact which there is reason to believe that some of the promoters of the meeting had learned without any deep regret. But those who regarded him as a stormy petrel of politics, and hoped that his absence might conduce to a calmer atmosphere, were doomed to disappointment. Cheers were raised for his name before the meeting started. When the chairman read a short letter of apology from him, hats and handkerchiefs were waved amid a storm of cheering and cries of " Shame on Birmingham !" When the time came to read a letter from Lord Rosebery, in which the hope was expressed that the Federation would aim at securing the unity of " common-sense Liberalism and would proceed on broad national and progressive lines," there was a very different demonstration. There were shouts of "Traitor!" "Return his letter,"

"Don't read any more," and so forth. Leaflets had been distributed among the audience by persons other than the promoters of the meeting, warning them of "a conspiracy" to supplant Sir Henry Campbell-Bannerman on the part of Lord Rosebery, Mr Asquith, and Sir Henry Fowler, and they would seem to have fallen upon fruitful ground. Sir Henry Campbell-Bannerman had prepared a speech in which he held out an olive-branch to Lord Rosebery, but he delivered it under conditions which boded ill for the prospects of unity. His mention of Lord Rosebery's name was received with prolonged hooting, groans, and hisses. But he persevered, and refusing to be led by the meeting, ultimately succeeded in leading them, and in enlarging upon the main thesis of his speech, which was that, after all, he and Lord Rosebery were not very far apart. He professed to find an indication in the Chesterfield speech of Lord Rosebery's willingness to renew co-operation with his old friends, and there is no doubt that he would have welcomed Lord Rosebery none the less sincerely although his return to politics would probably have meant Sir Henry's supersession as leader. This was Mr. Lloyd George's opinion : "It is a mistake," he said, "to imagine that there is any personal feeling against Lord Rosebery ; there is absolutely none. If he really becomes leader, and takes the country along with him, we shall all be delighted, and Sir Henry Campbell-Bannerman will be as pleased as any one, simply because of his loyalty to the Liberal cause."[1]

The beginning of the Session found the official organisers of the Opposition engaged upon the interesting though futile task of drafting an amendment for which all sections of the Opposition would be able to vote. Liberals differed profoundly in opinion ; the puzzle was to reconcile them in words. The amendment which finally emerged from the hands of the skilled artificers of unity proposed to represent to the King " that this House, while prepared to support all proper measures for the effective prosecution of the war in South Africa, is of opinion that the course pursued by your Majesty's Ministers and their attitude with regard to a settlement have not conduced to the early termination of the war and the establishment of a durable peace." Mr. Cawley, a Lancashire member of little more than local celebrity, who had not hitherto been accustomed to take any part in the debates of the House, was selected to move the amendment, perhaps because his name was not likely to arouse the suspicions of any section. This duty he performed on January 20. On that day Mr. Chamberlain made a long contribution to the debate,

[1] " Pall Mall Gazette," January 3, 1902.

in which he adopted a more conciliatory tone than usual in dealing with the prospects of peace.   He expressed partial agreement
with Lord Rosebery's Chesterfield speech, and while insisting
upon " unconditional surrender," promised that no harsh terms
should be exacted from the beaten foe.   The amendment he
denounced as dishonest and a sham.   The wording of the resolution
adopted at the Queen's Hall meeting by " the citizens of London " [1] (" Some of them came from Wales, I think," the Colonial
Secretary commented) showed that the Liberal Party possessed
draftsmen who could, if they liked, express themselves without
ambiguity.   He argued that those who had supported that resolution could not, if they cared to preserve any rag of consistency,
support the Cawley amendment.   It soon appeared that the
withers of the " pro-Boers " would be unwrung by this hypo-
thetical criticism.   They had no intention of exposing themselves
to a charge of inconsistency, and felt, or at any rate yielded to,
no apprehension of the consequences of a logical adherence to
their principles.   Mr. Dillon, the Irish Nationalist, moved an
amendment to the amendment of Mr. Cawley, which struck out
the reference to " the effective prosecution of the war," and
flatly condemned the conduct of the war as contrary to " the
recognised usages of civilised war " and as " barbarous."   Nine
members of the Liberal Party went into the same lobby with
Mr. Dillon and the rest of the Nationalists.   One of these was
Mr. Lloyd George : the others were Mr. Channing, Mr. Cremer,
Mr. J. D. Hope. Mr. Thomas Shaw, Mr. Lough, Mr. Pirie, Mr.
Labouchere, and Mr. J. H. Wilson.   It will be perceived that Mr.
Lloyd George was the only Welsh member who went so far in
this extremely unpopular course.

The result of Mr. Cawley's well-meant attempt to bridge a
chasm with a formula may serve as a warning to all politicians
who are tempted to seek by similar devices to present the semblance of a united front.   On the second day of the debate,
which had stood adjourned after Mr. Dillon's amendment had
been defeated by an overwhelming majority (the voting was
285 to 66), it was noticed that Sir Henry Campbell-Bannerman,
Sir William Harcourt, and Mr. Morley had not the company on
the Front Opposition Bench of the leaders of the Liberal Imperialists, Mr. Asquith and Sir Edward Grey.   A rumour that Mr.
Churchill, who had moved the adjournment the night before,
intended to make an attack upon the Government, had filled
the House.   Rumour was falsified, for the criticism in his speech
was friendly.   It was not until after nine o'clock that Mr. Lloyd

[1] See p. 257, above.

George spoke. Meanwhile, Sir William Harcourt had uttered an impressive condemnation of the Colonial Secretary's aggressive policy and of the statesmanship which gloried in the enmity of other nations, and boasted of our " splendid isolation "; and Mr. Gibson Bowles, from his accustomed place behind the Treasury Bench, had poured vitriolic criticism upon the devoted head before him. The debate had lapsed into dulness during the dinner hour, and the House began to fill rapidly when Mr. Lloyd George rose. Most of the Liberal Imperialists were purposely staying outside the Chamber, but before Mr. Lloyd George had been speaking long a little knot of them had gathered behind the Speaker's chair. From that vantage-ground Sir Edward Grey, Mr. Haldane, Mr. Emmott, and Mr. Strachey listened to Mr. Lloyd George's speech and, with darkening countenances, heard him, in the face of the enemy, pouring scorn upon the attempt to rally the discordant forces of the Opposition to a colourless flag. The right course, he urged, would have been to frame an amendment embodying a declaration of the principles enunciated by Lord Rosebery at Chesterfield. As it was, one set of gentlemen were asked to support what they regarded as a criminal enterprise as an induce-ment for another set of gentlemen to vote for a proposition they did not believe to be true. One set of gentlemen were told that if they would vote what they considered black to be white, an-other set of gentlemen would vote what they considered white to be black. They would never get unity on those terms, and he sincerely regretted it, because he believed that unity was necessary for peace, and that, at least on the single question of the terms of settlement, unity was obtainable.

His disappointment at an error which he believed to go deeper than mere tactics led him to level at Sir Henry Campbell-Banner-man a jest which had a tinge of bitterness. The Liberal leader had been captured, he said, by the Imperialists and, it was to be feared, had been treated by his captors in the way the Boers treated their prisoners—stripped of all his principles, and left on the veldt to find his way back the best way he could. In the circumstances of the day that piece of satire had a sting which, after the lapse of time, it is not perhaps easy fully to realise. Feeling was running so high that the ties of personal friendship which in this country often bind men sundered by political enmity had been strained in many instances, and broken in some. Sir Henry Campbell-Bannerman, it was felt, had deserved the respect, even if he could not command the allegiance, of every member of his party. He had been made the object of gross political, and sometimes personal, abuse. Of all the sneering criticisms aimed at him the most fashionable was the charge that at a great crisis of the nation's history he played the part of a mere trimmer. Liberals resented, as they had a right to do, these attacks from the enemy upon a man whom they knew to be distinguished beyond most politicians by a guileless devotion to principle. And so, when Mr. Lloyd George held up his leader's tactics to the ridicule of the delighted supporters of the Government, his speech undoubtedly angered many of his political friends. Nobody took it in better part than Sir Henry Campbell-Bannerman himself, who was too old a campaigner to be affronted by a jocular criticism, even if its wit was barbed. He contented himself, when he spoke, with the dignified retort that Mr. Lloyd George "might have expressed his difference from his friends quite as effectively with more respect to them." Sir Henry had, at any rate, the satisfaction of knowing that two of the Liberals who had supported Mr. Dillon's amendment, namely, Mr. Pirie and Mr. Channing, voted, contrary to the intention they had formed, in favour of Mr. Cawley's amendment, rather than identify themselves with an attack upon their leader.

On the other hand, Mr. Balfour was given an opportunity, to which no one was better qualified to do justice, of making merry at the expense of the flouted leader. In a sentence, prompted perhaps by his reminiscences of Mr. Gibson Bowles and other candid friends of his own, he declared himself to be perfectly aware that, at all events under modern conditions of Parliamentary procedure, it was allowable for one's friends to use much stronger adjectives about one than one's opponents, and he disclaimed the power to match the epithets which had been hurled at Sir Henry Campbell-Bannerman's head by Mr. Lloyd George :—

The hon. member, in a speech of extraordinary conciseness and pungency, gave his view of not merely the expediency and propriety, but the common honesty of the amendment to which we are now asked to address ourselves ; and unless I do the hon. gentleman's rhetoric a great injustice, I think that the epithet "shuffling" was almost the mildest with which his ample vocabulary supplied him to hurl at the proposal which, after all, was moved by the Leader of his party in the House of Commons, and which therefore, according to my view, at all events, of Parliamentary propriety, might have been objected to, but need hardly have been abused by him with the violence which he adopted. But, at all events, it has absolved me of the task which I should otherwise have had to undertake, and I am sure that anybody who heard the hon. gentleman's speech will acquit me of flattery when I say that I am perfectly certain that no amount of premeditation would have enabled me to accumulate so much bitterness in so short a speech as the hon. gentleman has contrived to do in the observations he has made.

Mr. Lloyd George's speech affords us proof that, at this stage of his career, he was still as much a free-lance as when he entered the House of Commons, and that he was still not afraid to face unpopularity even on his own side of the House. He had long ago decided that " courage and a thick skin " were essential to success in politics. The speech indicated a difference between his policy and that of his leader, which, if not wide or fundamental, was something more than fanciful. Sir Henry Campbell-Bannerman believed that though the war could have been avoided and should have been concluded at the earliest possible moment, it should be waged, while it lasted, with every legitimate resource available, and consequently that it was the duty of the Opposition to support the Government in their military operations by voting supplies. Mr. Lloyd George felt it to be inconsistent with his strong view that the war was a wicked war to vote money for its continuance, and impossible to square with his conscience a vote in favour of its prosecution. Not everybody will consider the difference great enough to justify such outspoken revolt. If the revolt is to be justified, it is on the ground that open divisions are, in the long run, less fatal to unity and leadership than a breach imperfectly concealed. The incident, although it caused transient resentment on the Liberal benches, and some small addition to the contemptuous exultation which was at that date the prevalent emotion on the other side, had, and was meant to have, no kind of permanent effect except the healthy one of checking a disposition to gloze over differences.

The peroration of the speech, with its fine protest against " pawning the heirlooms of Liberalism "—one of those *lumina ingenii* which flash even upon the written pages of his oratory— will show his view of the attitude that would have become a leader committed to a belief in the injustice of the war at its inception. The country, he admitted, was " stubbornly bent on pursuing the war," but it was sick of the war none the less, and would attribute the failures of the campaign rather to some defect in Ministers than to lack of strength in the Empire :

As in the Crimean war, and in every other war, the penalty of failure must be paid by Ministers. That does not mean the abandonment of the war, but it might mean that the " alternative Government " would have its chance, and I ask members who are going to vote for the amendment, if their party came into power would they vote for the prosecution of an unrighteous war—for that is the policy of the amendment—a war which they regard as a disaster to the Empire ? Would they go on with such a war ? If not, then what is the meaning of this amendment ? If they are prepared to go on with it, what do their denunciations of the war in the past mean ? No, there is only one party in the country who can prosecute the war effectively—I do not say only one Ministry, but only one party—and that is the party that believes in it. You cannot prosecute a war with a halting conscience. You must put your whole heart, your whole strength, and your whole might into it ; and I am proud to believe that the right hon. gentlemen on the Front Opposition Bench could not do that. Their position is a clear one—or at least it ought to be. It is to say : " The war is your business. We can have nothing whatever to do with it." I appeal earnestly to right hon. gentlemen now not, by voting for this amendment, to accept any share of the responsibility for the war. It is a mistake, even if it brings temporary popularity to the party, to pawn, as it were, the heirlooms of that party in order to buy off unpopularity. At any rate, so long as they face it they will have the respect of the country. On the other hand, if they do adopt that course they will simply substitute for an unpopularity which is undeserved, as long as it comes from adhesion to a definite principle, a contempt which is thoroughly well merited.

When the division was taken, Mr. Lloyd George abstained from voting. The members of the Opposition who joined him in that course included, besides his Welsh colleague Mr. Bryn Roberts, Mr. John Burns, Mr. Thomas Shaw, and Mr. Labouchere. The Irish Nationalists walked out in a body; and, so true it is that extremes meet, Sir Edward Grey led out a small band of Liberal Imperialists. The Ministerial majority was 210.

Thus ignominiously ended an inglorious field-day. It was followed by no estrangement between Mr. Lloyd George and his leader. In view of the course of the internal history of Liberalism, such an estrangement would have been impossible, even if the differences between them had been sufficiently grave to warrant it. For in the early months of 1902, Lord Rosebery went gradually further in his policy of jettisoning principles long associated with Liberalism, and Sir Henry Campbell-Bannerman became more and more resolute in their vindication. At Liverpool (in February) the former Liberal Prime Minister expounded afresh his doctrine of " the clean slate," and spoke of those who dissented from it as men " identified with some of those somewhat musty programmes which had crushed the Liberal Party in the past," by which they thought " it would be a glory to the Liberal Party to be crushed for all time to come." In particular he definitely abandoned any larger measure of Home Rule for Ireland than was covered by the term " devolution."

In the Chesterfield speech Mr. Lloyd George had seen a real and valuable contribution to the cause of peace in South Africa. The adjuration to cleanse the party slate was not, in the terms in which it was expressed in 1901, sufficiently clear or unambiguous to point to a definite abandonment of any principle. It could be interpreted as a mere exhortation to the expediency, and indeed the necessity, of presenting to the electorate a reasonably small and clear-cut programme. It might be agreed even by the most courageous politicians that there was no sense in going to the country with a collection of assorted pledges which the short life of a single Parliament could never enable the party to redeem. There could be no objection in principle to a policy of Liberalism by instalments or in small doses. But at Liverpool Lord Rosebery appeared to contemplate, not so much cleaning the slate as breaking it. At the best he proposed to inscribe upon it, not a few of the more urgent principles of the Liberal programme, but a series of platitudes upon which men of all parties might be content to unite, swept into a kind of lax cohesion by disgust at the inefficiency of the Cabinet.

In such a policy a Radical could have no part or lot, and Lord Rosebery's declaration of it marked the final destruction in Mr. Lloyd George's mind of any lingering hope that the former Prime Minister could ever again lead a united Liberal Party. On the day after the first Liverpool speech Mr. Lloyd George had an opportunity of expressing his views upon it at a meeting of the Metropolitan Radical Federation.[1] Lord Rosebery, he said, having cleaned his slate, wished to write nothing at all upon it. Like Moses, he smashed the tables, because, having come down from the mount, he found that the people had taken to the worship of strange idols. He seemed to think that because Liberals had been beaten they should give up everything. They in Wales had been beaten seven times on Disestablishment, but they were firmer than ever. Lord Rosebery, beaten on Home Rule, said, "For Heaven's sake, don't go on." If he were one of Lord Rosebery's followers, he would not know on which side of the House to take his seat, for there was nothing proposed in the Liverpool speech which could not be accepted on the Unionist side. What a curious Liberalism it was! No taxation of ground-rents, no Welsh Disestablishment, no Home Rule for Ireland—nothing but remounts (a reference to Lord Rosebery's criticism of the War Office) and recantations. The nation would never accept Liberalism from a man who handed it to them with a pair of tongs.

Lord Rosebery's reason for abandoning Home Rule was that

[1] Chelsea, February 15.

some Irish members had made indiscreet speeches. He might have remembered the galling provocation to which they had been exposed. At any rate, there were no better Liberal or Radical fighters than the Irish members.

A few days later the annual meeting of the General Committee of the National Liberal Federation took place at Leicester.[1] On this occasion a distinctly more Imperialist tone was prevalent than in the previous year at Derby. There was still, however, a general desire for unity, although the undercurrent of sectional feeling was strong, so strong indeed that information had reached the executive that an offer had been made to pay the expenses of delegates if they would vote for the election of certain selected candidates to its body. An official resolution was couched in terms carefully modelled upon Lord Rosebery's Chesterfield speech. It condemned the policy of unconditional surrender, affirmed the conviction that the future contentment and security of South Africa were bound up in obtaining a regular peace on broad and generous lines as the result of a regular settlement, and welcomed the impetus given to this policy by Lord Rosebery. Finally, by way of reconciling the divergent leaders, it called upon Liberal members loyally to support Sir Henry Campbell-Bannerman in advocating it and pressing it forward in the House of Commons. Amendments were moved by representatives of the " League of Liberals against aggression and militarism " on the one side, and the " Liberal Imperialist League " on the other, which aimed, the one at reaffirming in terms the Derby resolutions, the other at emphasising the welcome to Lord Rosebery. They were, however, both withdrawn. In the evening, Sir Henry Campbell-Bannerman made a speech to the delegates, which, if it did not promise very well for the desired co-operation, showed no lack of resolution. He declared himself to be no believer in the doctrine of the clean slate. He was not prepared to erase from the tablets of his creed any principle, or measure, or proposal, or ideal, or aspiration of Liberalism. He reasserted his allegiance to the Gladstonian policy for the settlement of the Irish question. " Firm and unfaltering," Mr. Lloyd George wrote of the speech from Leicester that evening to his brother. It had sufficed to restore the faith that a recent episode had perhaps shaken.

Sir Henry had pressed Lord Rosebery to declare whether he spoke " from the interior of our political tabernacle or from some vantage-ground outside." The answer was immediate. " I remain outside his tabernacle, but not, I think, in solitude," Lord Rosebery wrote in a letter published two days afterwards in the

[1] February 19, 1902.

"Times." At this moment of definite separation the Liberal
League was formed, with Lord Rosebery as its President, Mr.
Asquith, Sir Edward Grey, and Sir Henry Fowler as its vice-
presidents.

III

A scene in the House, March 20, 1902—Mr. Chamberlain and Mr. Dillon — Mr. Dillon's
suspension—Mr. Lloyd George's speech—Peace—The Boer Generals in London.

Thus the war had, as it seemed, rent in twain the party of
progress. The Irish were unchastened and resentful. When
Mr. Asquith, declaring that his principles had suffered no change,
gave his adherence none the less to the policy of Home Rule by
stages, Mr. Redmond scornfully warned him that he and his
associates would soon lose their place in the Liberal Party, and
might look to see a Cabinet formed of men " like Lloyd George "
when next Liberals obtained office. In the House of Commons
the Irish openly declared their belief in the righteousness of the
Boer cause and their desire to see the victory of the Boer arms.
The rage which they excited upon the Tory benches was balm
to their souls. But Tory Imperialists were not satisfied to rage
furiously against the Nationalists. Mr. Chamberlain led a campaign of increasing acrimony against Sir Henry Campbell-Bannerman and his followers, whom he insisted upon describing at each
available opportunity as pro-Boers. On a night in March, the
dangerous elements which had gradually gathered force in the
House of Commons burst into a savage storm. The resentment
of the Leader of the Opposition at insults long and tolerantly borne,
the Colonial Secretary's fierce mocking of his vanquished political
foemen, the Irishmen's passionate repudiation of any part or
lot in the glory of our victories or the bitterness of our defeats—
all these conspired to swell such a tempest of angry recrimination
as had not yet been witnessed even since new and profound
animosities had been stirred by the breath of war. Of the
speakers on that night of unpleasant memory two at least, however deep their feelings, bore themselves with an unruffled
demeanour, and inflicted burning wounds upon their opponents'
sensibilities with a cold and unerring precision. Of these one was
Mr. Chamberlain, the other was Mr. Lloyd George.

In the speech with which Sir Henry Campbell-Bannerman
began the debate he charged the Government, in words which,
heated as they were, had been carefully chosen and prepared, with
meeting inquiry and criticism by personal attack, and even

RT. HON. D. LLOYD GEORGE AND HIS UNCLE RICHARD LLOYD

(Photograph taken at 11, Downing Street.)

personal insults. When Sir Henry complained that any one who ventured to impugn the wisdom of the Ministry laid himself open to be called—as he himself had been by the Leader of the House—a pro-Boer, a few Ministerialists ventured to cheer. " The little cheer with which that statement has been met," the leader of the Opposition continued, " shows that the school of Parliamentary manners opened by the Government contains a number of very apt pupils." Allegations that his speeches reinforced the Boers he described as " malignant slanders." To these tactics of vituperation and vulgar abuse, by which he and his friends refused to be intimidated, the Government, he said, added " the tactics of the curtain, of the shrugged shoulder." They had failed to inform themselves, and to inform the House, of the course of events in South Africa. He was old enough to remember a phrase much in vogue, and used by a memorable witness in a great trial, *Non mi ricordo*. This was not the Government of " I do not remember," but the Government of " I do not know."

The Opposition welcomed their leader's unexpectedly aggressive invasion of the enemy's territory with defiant cheers. He proceeded to a strong criticism of Lord Milner's policy in the administration of martial law, laying stress upon the need of so conducting the war as to preserve for the day when peace should be made the elements of good government and prosperity. When he sat down Mr. Chamberlain, only too ready for an encounter in which a strong attack gave him some excuse for dropping the polite pretence of civility, threw across the table the retort that " malignant slanders " might best be looked for from a gentleman who had " never lost any opportunity of slandering his countrymen." If he objected to the phrase " pro-Boer," how would he describe " a man who thought that the Boers were right and his country was wrong, and who supported the Boers in every incident of the campaign, who found no fault with them in anything they had done, who had never once lifted his voice against any of the crimes that had been brought to their charge, while he had never ceased to take every possible opportunity in order to bring insinuations against his own countrymen "? He, at any rate, would continue to call the Leader of the Opposition a pro-Boer. It was soon evident that the phrase " malignant slanders " with which his antagonist had innocently provided him was to be the refrain of the Colonial Secretary's speech. Its recurrence brought first Sir Henry, and then the Speaker, to their feet, and

[1] March 20, 1902. The occasion was the third reading of the Consolidated Fund (No. 1) Bill.

the expression was ruled unparliamentary. By this time the
temper of the House had risen to a degree which made an out-
burst of disorder possible at any moment, a fact not surprising
when it is considered that a Cabinet Minister was using to the
full his powers of cold and merciless invective, with a zest which
appalled some among the less precipitate of his supporters, to indict
a former Cabinet Minister and the leader of a great party upon a
wanton and grotesque charge of treacherous calumny. The out-
burst came when Mr. Chamberlain, to prove that the Boers were
carrying on a struggle recognised on all hands to be hopeless,
pointed with pride to the fact that between 3,000 and 4,000
burghers, men who had formerly borne arms against us, were
now fighting for us and against the Boers. One of these men
he named—General Vilonel. At the mention of that name Mr.
Dillon, from the Irish benches, threw in the words : " Vilonel is
a traitor." " The honourable member," the Colonial Secretary
said frigidly, " is a good judge of traitors." The Speaker, appealed to by Mr. Dillon, declined to rule that the Colonial Secretary was under the necessity of making any withdrawal. " I
desire to say, Mr. Speaker," Mr. Dillon then said, taking the law
into his own hands, " that the right hon. gentleman is a damned
liar." Immediately Mr. Dillon's suspension from the service of
the House was moved. Six Liberals joined with the Nationalists to make up a small minority of forty-eight who voted
against it. Of these Mr. Lloyd George was one.[1]

Soon after Mr. Chamberlain had concluded his speech, which
he continued quite imperturbably after this interruption, Mr.
Lloyd George had his opportunity. Mr. Llewellyn, a member
who had come back from service in South Africa, where he had
administered a district under martial law, was the speaker who
immediately preceded him. Mr. Llewellyn's speech was short
and humdrum. It was based upon the familiar recipe for Tory
speakers at the time : its main theme was that the speeches of
" pro-Boers " had encouraged the Boers to a prolonged resistance. It contained, however, one original argument, based on
the speaker's own experiences. The complaint was made, Mr.
Llewellyn said, that persons had been deported without being
told the charge against them. But it was unnecessary to tell
them, because they knew already. Mr. Llewellyn, a butterfly of
debate, was promptly broken on the wheel. He had uttered, Mr.
Lloyd George declared, the most complete possible condemnation of martial law. The principle of English law was that every

[1] The others were Mr. Channing, Mr. Cremer, Mr. Labouchere, Mr. H. J. Wilson,
and Mr. Corrie Grant.

man was assumed to be innocent until he was proved to be guilty. Martial law said that a suspected person must be assumed to be not only guilty, but so guilty that he was to be sentenced before he had heard the charge.

Having disposed of Mr. Llewellyn, Mr. Lloyd George turned his attention to Mr. Chamberlain, who, with his accustomed reluctance ever to admit failure, had declared that he was " prepared to defend all the estimates of the past " touching the casualties among the Boers :

Well, he would defend anything. He is prepared to defend the fact that we have annihilated the Boers three times over, and still he has proved to-night that there are 9,000 still left. Encourage the Boers! There are no Boers to encourage, and it makes no difference what speeches you deliver. They are simply a phantom army.

Just as Mr. Chamberlain's taunt had fallen like a spark to gunpowder upon the Irish benches, so Mr. Lloyd George's was more than Tory flesh and blood could endure. He was dealing, as we have seen him deal before, with the foolish talk of " avenging Majuba," when an interruption came. He expressed his surprise that our generals should have rejoiced at a victory over the Boers because it was achieved on the anniversary of Majuba. That was a trifling affair of outposts. Since the present war broke out, British arms had suffered eighteen defeats of far greater magnitude than Majuba.

" And the pro-Boers rejoice at it," muttered Sir William Cayzer, a sturdy Tory.

Immediately there was a volley of cries of " Withdraw " from the Radical benches. " That is a perfectly insolent remark," said Mr. Lloyd George calmly. The Speaker interfered, and Sir William Cayzer explained first that he did not mean it to be personal, then that it was not aimed at anybody in the House. " It is a horrible thing," Mr. Lloyd George went on, " that a man should accuse any one of exulting over the death and mutilation of his countrymen."

This rebuke gave an opportunity for another interruption. A few days before, the Irish Nationalists, deprived for the time being of the leadership of Mr. John Redmond, who was not in the House, had in a fit of wantonness greeted with cheers the news of Lord Methuen's defeat and capture at Tweebosch. The memory of those cheers, which was to rankle long in the minds of Englishmen, was still fresh and poignant. And so when Mr.

Lloyd George spoke of the horror of exulting over our countrymen's mutilation, it is not surprising that another member, Mr. Plummer, was prompt to rise and cry that only the other night the Irishmen had done that very thing. This brought Mr. Redmond to his feet, with an appeal to the Speaker, who was not inclined to be sympathetic, since, as he pointed out, it was "notorious" that the Nationalists had cheered a British defeat. The excitement simmered, and the resentment with which the rest of the speech was heard by the Tories was displayed only in one or two interjections. The concluding passages summarise its arguments, and will perhaps explain Tory indignation :

Let me just sum up what I consider the main features of the present military situation. The summer campaign has ended worse than last year's summer campaign. It has left the Boers strong in ammunition and in the fighting qualities of their men. That is admitted by Lord Milner. They have done things that, from the military point of view, they would not have dared to do three years ago, and they have a prospect of an unlimited number of recruits from the Cape. All these things are bound to be taken into consideration when we come to consider the question of settlement and the terms we are to give. We may wear the Boers down, but there is one thing which the campaign in Cape Colony has proved, and that is that a very small body of the enemy can employ a very large body of our troops. . . . What is the use of giving a four, five, or nine months' estimate ? The right hon. gentleman knows very well that these are only tentative estimates. He has got to take into account the words of Sir Gordon Sprigg: "The war will not be ended till the last man is killed or captured, and the last cartridge fired." When we consider what has been done we ought to take all these matters into consideration. What are we fighting for ? We are told, for equal rights for all white men in the Transvaal. Lord Salisbury, who stated that he had some information in November which showed that the whole thing was coming to an end, said we were fighting for security. How is he going to get the security without a Government with whom to make the settlement ? It needs 270,000 men to keep under 20,000, or 9,000 according to the Colonial Secretary. When the 40,000 prisoners come back, how many shall we want to keep them under ? You cannot keep arms out of the country now. The "Times" correspondent mentioned the capture of a Cape cart carrying ammuntion to Delarey which had clearly been imported into the country, and if we cannot keep arms out of the land how are we going to control it ? How many rifles have been surrendered ? Less than half of the number of men accounted for. Where, then, is your security ? The moment we are in difficulties, the moment we are embarrassed with a foreign nation, and there is a serious war, these men will take their opportunity. Can we then send out 250,000 men to reconquer the country ? There will be an end of that security then. It is a new form of terminable security. Is there no greater security in dealing with a settled and responsible Government than in dealing with 40,000 irresponsible individuals ? You will want hundreds of officials to govern this country, and I doubt whether the Empire can produce 500 discreet officials. You are bound to get a few ill-informed, tactless, and hostile—I am not sure we have not got them now in high positions—with a faculty for treading on every corn the Dutchmen have, and then there is a scrimmage, a quarrel, if not bloodshed, and the whole thing is precipitated. That is the security. It depends on the wisdom of every officer you send out for years to come. But if you had a responsible Government you would then have a responsible administration who would know ; and those who blundered would be held responsible for the horrors of war. The war will have taught wisdom to both sides. We shall have no more ultimatums on the Boer side, and I do not believe we shall have any more Highbury picnic speeches on our side.

We are told that the terms we favour are absolute surrender to the Boers ; that is nonsense. Taking the very outside, we have gone to war to establish equal rights. Does anybody doubt that we could get them at the present moment ? Is it an absolute surrender to get what you went to war for ? It is evident we could have control of the foreign relations. The Boers are willing to give us the control of foreign relations, an equal franchise, and an indemnity. The terms imposed on France by Germany were considered humiliating : what if the Germans had proposed these terms ? What are the terms we offer to the Boers ? A British Government, a British Executive, and the British language to be the official language, the Boer language to be tolerated. Suppose we got to a war with Germany; that there was an invasion of this country ; that the country was annexed.

[An hon. member : Who declared the war ?]

What a stupidly irrelevant question ! Let me put the case. A German Government is appointed—German judges—the German language becomes official.

[An hon. member : Is the German Emperor sovereign of this country ?]

Really, Mr. Speaker, I sometimes think he is, from the way the Government behaves. Where is the suzerainty of the Orange Free State ? That State was as independent as Great Britain is at the present moment. The only difference is that we are a great Power and they are a small one. Does that make any difference at all in the inherent justice of the war ? Have you the right to be unjust to a man because he is poor and weak and insignificant ? Every honest man would say you should treat him with more generosity. There is an unpleasant flavour of Panama about this. The shareholders have been gulled by false statements from time to time as to the wealth that will await them, and as to the cost of the enterprise. We were told the whole thing would be finished, the whole job through, and the directors were re-elected on that statement. Who is guilty of the falsehood I know not, but one thing I do know, and that is, that the men who profit by it sit on the Government Bench.

Mr. Brodrick, when he rose to reply at eleven o'clock, said truly enough that no other audience in the country would have heard such a speech with the consideration the House had shown. " I fully admit that," Mr. Lloyd George acknowledged. Encouraged by his supporters' cheers, the Secretary of State for War went on to a fierce attack upon the member for Carnarvon. He seemed to be disappointed, he said, that there were not more disasters to gloat over. " That," Mr. Lloyd George answered, " is untrue." The debate ended in another storm of cheers and counter-cheers. It was the last in which Mr. Lloyd George took part during the war. Two months later peace was declared, and his subsequent speeches upon South African affairs were made in a calmer atmosphere.

One small incident may be worth relating here, as it illustrates the admiration and enthusiasm which the gallant resistance of the Boer generals had inspired in Mr. Lloyd George. In August 1902, Botha, Delarey, and De Wet came to London to interview Mr. Chamberlain at the Colonial Office. One of Mr. Lloyd George's friends looked in at the National Liberal Club one evening, and found him in the smoking-room. " I have just seen the Boer generals," the friend said. " Where ? " said Mr. Lloyd George. " At Horrex's Hotel." In a moment Mr. Lloyd George had snatched up his hat, and was off, half running, towards Norfolk Street, anxious to get a glimpse, as one of the crowd, of the heroic strangers who were now his fellow-citizens.

IV

Mr Lloyd George's anti-war crusade discussed—Its motive—Its methods—Its result.

In the foregoing pages of this volume the attempt has been made to give the reader the material upon which he may form his own judgment upon Mr. Lloyd George's activities during the war. It is possibly desirable here, without departing from the intention of this biography, which is to narrate rather than to weigh or criticise, to endeavour to focus the impressions derived from the bare relation of his policy and speeches. The subject seems to divide itself naturally into a consideration first of the principles or impulses upon which the policy was grounded; secondly, of the manner and method of his campaign; thirdly, of the relations into which it brought him with other politicians; lastly, of its effects, temporary or permanent, upon his career.

First of all, then, what were the principles that guided him ? There may be critics who will be disposed to say that " impulses " would be a better word than " principles," and there is no doubt that when, upon his return from Canada, he sat down to some hard thinking upon the general problem of the Transvaal and the more intimate question of the votes he was to give, it was hardly upon any abstract principles of justice that he made up his mind. To say this is no disparagement. If he could have surveyed the problem in the calm atmosphere of pure reason, it may be that he would have been left undecided in the bewildering maze of pros and cons. In the essential affairs of life, at every crisis of their fate, most men who live on a plane below the arid and sterile heights of bleak and barren philosophy are moved rather by the impulse of their hearts than the abstract principles of pure reason. The Celtic temperament, at any rate, does not regulate its sympathies by a schedule of categorical imperatives. Given an attack upon the Empire by a great Power, given a cause which could have been truthfully described as that of the weak and the oppressed, it may well be that the glory of war rather than its sordid horrors, the grandeur of Empire rather than its glittering delusions, would have been the theme of his speeches. He started, as we all do, with a bias, a " will to believe," but it was not an anti-patriotic bias; it was the bias of nationalism. There had been bred in his bones the belief in small nations ; when he saw one attacked his instinct was to fly at the aggressor. It was not that he loved Empire less, but that he loved Nationality more. During the war he himself contrasted the attitude of Wales towards the Empire with that of Ireland.[1] The attitude of Ireland, he said, was hostile, and perhaps not unjustifiably so, while that of Wales was friendly. Was not the British Empire founded by Elizabeth Tudor, a Welshwoman ? Wales objected to attempts to make the Empire the monopoly of the English, and, speaking for himself, he was enough of an Imperialist to want a share in the concern. But Imperialism in the Disraelian sense was not to be confused with Patriotism. Patriotism meant love of one's own land : Imperialism meant lust for the lands of others. We might add, enlarging upon his definition, that his own love for his native land amounted to a passion which made every other sentiment subservient to it. He put himself and his compatriots in the place of the Boers. He pictured Wales invaded by hostile legions—" The British Army against Carmarthenshire ! " From such a picture he could not but turn filled with a zeal that nothing could quench for the deliverance of the little nation. In the light of the zeal kindled by those generous impulses, all other considerations paled.

To anybody who is insensible to the claims of nationality, no

[1] In a lecture delivered to the London " Cymru Fydd " Association, January 1901.

better advice can be given than the recommendation to read the passage in De Wet's book upon the war—as noble a passage as any in literature—in which he describes the signing of the terms of peace.

To every man there, as to myself, the surrender was no more and no less than the sacrifice of our independence. I have often been present at the deathbed and at the burial of those who have been nearest to my heart —father, mother, brother, and friend—but the grief which I felt on those occasions was not to be compared with what I now underwent at the burial of my nation. There was nothing left for us now but to hope that the Power which conquered us, the Power to which we were compelled to submit, though it cut us to the heart to do so, and which, by the surrender of our arms we had accepted as our ruler, would draw us nearer and ever nearer by the strong cords of love.

Readers to whom the sentiment of that passage appeals will understand the motive of the Welsh Nationalist's fight for another nationality: those who find in it only the spurious metal of sentimentality never will.

The manner in which he presented to his fellow-countrymen the cause he championed was characteristically vigorous. He did not mince matters or scruple to go the logical length of his confirmed convictions by attacking fiercely and even savagely the Minister upon whom in his belief the responsibility was properly fixed. Let it be remembered that the Minister he was opposing was a man, with convictions no doubt as sincere as his own, who never hesitated brutally to beat down opposition, and that the Minister had the advantage of having force and the weight of numbers on his side. Hard words break no bones when they are uttered by the leader of a small minority; they may sometimes have that practical effect when the man who uses them commands a large and excited following. The charge of glorying in British defeats and of deliberately encouraging the resistance of the Boers, was a terrible charge, but it was made freely, sometimes by implication, often in express terms. It is not surprising that it was vigorously repelled.

It is interesting to observe that Mr. Chamberlain and Mr. Lloyd George, fundamentally as they differed upon the issue of the war, were perfectly agreed as to the duty of men who honestly believed the war to be wrong. In other words, if Mr. Chamberlain had been in Mr. Lloyd George's place, if, like him, he had been satisfied of the original injustice of the war, his course of conduct, it is safe to say, would have differed little from that of his critic. The regular leaders of the Opposition, when they consented to vote supplies, got no thanks from the Colonial Secretary. They were only told that if they thought the war unjust, they were dishonest to vote for its continuance. Out-and-out condemnation of his policy was a thing Mr. Chamberlain could understand and sympathise with : compromise was not.

It has been pointed out already that as the war went on, and as opportunities of peace were lost or thrown away, the strength and bitterness of Mr. Lloyd George's attacks increased. In his view, while the " first war " was unjust, the " second " was an infamy ; and he deemed this to be so, not of its objects only, but of the means by which they were pursued. But it is untrue to say that he ever encouraged those among foreign commentators who imputed inhumanity to our soldiers.

" I want you to understand," he said to an interviewer at the beginning of 1902, " that we, whom you call pro-Boers, here have nothing to do with the blackguardly liars who have spread false reports on the Continent about our troops. For myself, I have had no communication whatever with any foreign advocate of the Boer cause. I challenge all the world to find in any of my speeches a single word accusing our troops of brutality. I have neither part nor lot with Continental pro-Boers, either Press or public. They have lied shamelessly." When Parliament voted a grant to Lord Kitchener in recognition of his services during the war, he supported it by his vote and regretted the decision of the Irish Party, with whom two Liberals joined, to vote against it. In his most fervid attacks upon the administration of the concentration camps, he did not put the blame upon the soldier.

One further word must be said of his speeches upon the question of the concentration camps. As has been seen already, their administration was attacked even in quarters friendly to the Government's policy. It was vastly improved from the date when it was transferred from the control of the War Office to that of the Colonial Office. For this Mr. Chamberlain deserves the greatest credit, and it was accorded him by the Radical opponents of the war. But what verdict could posterity have passed upon an Opposition which had so far abdicated its functions of criticism as to shut its eyes to the deplorable and largely preventible loss of human life in the camps during the period of less efficient administration ? The fact that reforms were subsequently effected does not condemn the criticisms : it is rather, to some extent, their justification.

The war brought him into collision not only with those whom he was accustomed to regard as political foes, but with political friends as well. Without forming anything in the shape of a definite alliance, he was drawn more and more close to Sir Henry Campbell-Bannerman.   It would not be true to say that he looked to him for inspiration : inspiration came from within.   Rather he saw in him the leader whose ideals were nearest to his own. Similarly he was brought into close contact with Mr. Morley, from whom he received much appreciative criticism.   On the other hand, the war sundered him for the time being from the political fellowship of Mr. Asquith, Sir Edward Grey, and the other " Liberal leaguers," and, but for the Tory Government's haste to cement Liberalism by embarking on a strikingly re-actionary policy, might have made future co-operation with them impossible.   As it turned out, co-operation became an easy matter, even with Lord Rosebery, and the ease with which he again joined forces with Liberals from whom he had profoundly differed, was due in part at least to the genuine respect which, in the main, each section had felt for the other's sincerity.   His was not doubted even by opponents, and more than once Conservatives had crossed the floor to join in the congratula-tions which Radical friends showered upon him after some of his speeches in the House.   Above all other associations that he formed or antagonisms he provoked, his long duel with Mr. Chamberlain was influential upon his career.   The tenacity with which he pursued the great protagonist of the drama cost him the hatred of Birmingham and much fleeting unpopularity, but in the long run it added to his prestige.

This brings us to the question of the effect of his policy upon his career.   About this, two facts seem to be clear : one, that he could not possibly have anticipated that unflagging advocacy of a cause hated as much in his own constituency as outside it could ever benefit him ; the other, that in fact it eventually did benefit him.   Call it which you will—the caprice of fortune or the reward of constancy—the fact remains that at the price of being for a time one of the most generally despised among poli-ticians, he sprang into a prominence in which he was soon enabled to exchange notoriety for fame.   As the tumult and the shout-ing died, when the price came to be reckoned up, the day of Mr. Chamberlain's ascendancy gradually faded.   We shall see later how, only a year after the war had ended, Mr. Chamberlain, by that time almost a pathetic, instead of a triumphant figure, sat down under the lash of his young antagonist's invective, when, with bitter sarcasm, he accused him of having stolen the votes of the poor by the promise of Old Age Pensions, to reward them only with the contemplation of " the illimitable veldt."

Was, then, the appreciation quoted above right after all, when

it declared there to be but a step for a politician from unpopularity to popularity, if only he stood out boldly enough in the
blaze of publicity ?   If the writer meant that, the public memory
being notoriously short and vague, the all-important thing was
to make some kind of name and reputation, good or evil, then
certainly that is not the lesson enforced by Mr. Lloyd George's
career.   It was not that the majority of the people forgot, but
that they were converted.   Statesmen who inflame the passions
of a people into a frenzy of enthusiasm for war must expect to
pay a heavy price when the frenzy subsides, and it is then that
the counsellors of peace may gain their reward.   In the case of
the South African war, every action of the Conservative Government—its snatching of a renewed term in 1900—its subsequent
reactionary legislation—its self-righteous complacency throughout—served to make both the penalty and the rewards more
certain.

For all that, a political opportunist seeking to rise to power
would be shockingly unwise if he thought to profit by the example
of Mr. Lloyd George in opposing a popular war.   It is often a
thankless task, and its performance is only possible to men of
more than ordinary courage and a sincerity that is not too common.   " The next time this country goes into a war," Mr. Cobden said after the Crimean war, " after the first gunshot has been
fired, I will not lift up my voice and say a word against it.   You
might just as well talk to two rabid dogs fighting in the street."
Such a resolution may seem wise, statesmanlike, and politic, but
such a policy of silence as it enjoins would have been little to the
taste of one who united with fervent sympathies a real delight in
difficulties and obstacles.

CHAPTER V

I

IT is often a matter for speculation how far a statesman's rise to eminence is due to good fortune, how far to characteristics that would have triumphed over every obstacle. Nobody would argue that greatness thrust itself upon Mr. Lloyd George. He of all men has had to make his own opportunities : his quick advancement cannot be attributed merely to a felicitous knack of taking at the flood the tides in his affairs. But at this point in his career he had good reason to be grateful for the chance with which Mr. Balfour's zeal for education, and the zeal of the bishops for proselytism, served to provide him. Of all subjects there was none which would have been more likely to give scope to his energies and his abilities than the controversy which the Education Bill of 1902 stirred up anew round the pathetic figure of the elementary-school child. He had already cut a good figure in debates upon education in the House, but in the larger conflicts in which he had been engaged the cause he had championed had been the cause of Nationality. These conflicts had made him a national hero. The last of them, without in the long run shaking the allegiance of his own countrymen, had made his name known in the recesses of every English hamlet, in circumstances that did not endear it to the minds of the many. So far as England was concerned, he had not yet become known as the champion of any popular cause.

The controversy roused by the Education Bill made him the acknowledged head, in Parliament and out of it, of Nonconformity as a political force. It gave him just the opportunity he required for the display of his gifts, and still more of the knowledge and skill he had acquired laboriously in a cause than which none that was not purely national could have appealed to him with greater force. In making that reservation we have the support of his own dictum that Race is a more potent influence even than Religion. But the education fight, though it was religious rather than racial, still centred for him round the village schools of Wales. "I am a specimen of what your Church schools turn out," he said to the Tories in the House when they smarted under his attacks. He had gone perforce to a Church school and had rebelled against the formularies of the Church. For the pupil of the Llanystumdwy Church school the question of the education of village children was not, as it was for the average member of Parliament, an abstract question, remote from his personal experience. Now that he was grown to man's estate, and equipped at every point for political warfare, he was called upon to renew upon a larger battlefield conflicts to which from boyhood he had grown accustomed. The religious ascendancy of the Church had been a vital problem to him ever since the days when he held lengthy disputations upon it with the pupil teachers in David Evans's school. He knew that, however much he owed to his old pedagogue in the matter of secular instruction, he owed nothing to the Church school so far as the spiritual side of his education was concerned. All that the teaching of its own dogma by the Church could do for a Nonconformist boy was to imprint upon his mind a memory of small tyrannies that would remain with him throughout his life. His religious instruction came from the chapel and the Sunday school : the religious teaching of the Church school had served, at best, as a test of the faith that was in him. It was towards the despised " little Bethel " that he felt the emotions of gratitude and affectionate reminiscence that most of his colleagues felt towards the University and the public school. At a gathering of his fellow-countrymen at Liverpool, when the chairman had suggested " a little less attention to meetings in the little Bethel every night of the week, and more of a grappling with the great problems of life," he was quick to give an answer : [1]

Personally, I should be ungrateful if I did not say that I owe nothing to the University—I speak in all modesty and humility—I owe nothing to secondary schools. Whatever I do owe, it is to the little Bethel. Unless we utilise our educational machinery for the purpose—I will not say of improving our little Bethels—but of bringing out the best that is in them, we shall make a mistake.

But pride in the Nonconformist traditions of Wales, and memories of the little tyrannies of parsons, would have been a

[1] The occasion was the annual dinner of the " Young Wales " Society, Liverpool, St. David's Day, 1902.

poor foundation upon which alone to build a reputation in England. Oratory needs intense feeling, but great speeches cannot be made out of passion alone. This is the lesson that has to be learned by everybody with the talent of fluent and picturesque speech, and there is no better school than the House of Commons. A speech made in committee of the House of Commons, if it is to command attention, can no more be made without figures and facts, than bricks without straw. In other words, success involves drudgery, and Mr. Lloyd George, however distasteful drudgery may be to his temperament, has always known how to school himself to face it. During 1902 he lived and talked Education. No Blue book was issued on the subject that he did not diligently master. He knew the Bill from beginning to end. During its discussions he was hardly ever out of the House. He intervened often in the debates, but never too often, or only for the purposes of obstruction. He won the respect and the goodwill of his opponents, and gained concessions from them that surprised his own side. When fire and impetuosity were needed, he had enough and to spare, but no hard-headed Northerner could have brought greater application to bear upon the problem than did this ardent Celt. He had reason to be grateful for the opportunity given him, but he certainly made the most of it.

It is necessary to emphasise this, because in such a book as this it is impossible to give instances of the minutiæ of criticism. We can only deal with broad principles and controversial outlines, and in selecting typical speeches those must be chosen which deal broadly with great issues. The reason is, of course, that the expert criticisms which gave him a high place among educationists could only be quoted with long commentaries and explanations which would soon transform this book into a technical treatise. The reader must therefore be asked to remember that second-reading speeches and platform speeches did not represent the whole of his activities, or even the chief part of them.

The Education Bill was introduced on March 24, a few days after the scene which ended in Mr. Dillon's suspension. The Bill was the best commentary upon the General Election of 1900. The excuse for that election was that the Government needed a "mandate" to carry on and complete the South African War. Liberals had sought to point out that Ministries in this country cannot limit an election to a single issue, and that it was too much to expect that a Tory Cabinet would consider itself in honour bound to introduce no Tory measures. Conservative candidates, taking the lead from Mr. Chamberlain, had refused altogether to discuss details or principles of domestic policy.

They had done their best, and with enormous and flattering success, to turn the General Election into a Referendum on the single question " Are you a pro-Boer ? "   Nonconformists who approved of the war had contributed in their thousands to the overwhelming victory gained at the polls.   It was one of the misfortunes of alliance with a party which had clerical friends to propitiate that Mr. Chamberlain was driven to consent to a course which was a gross repudiation of his pledges.   He at any rate saw its dangers and knew its unpopularity : many of his colleagues seem to have regarded the votes they gained in 1900 as the expression of a rapturous enthusiasm for Tory rule, which would applaud reverently any measure they might choose to introduce.   The introduction of the Bill showed quite conclusively that the Opposition had been right in warning those who gave their votes to the Government upon the faith of pledges that the war was the only issue that they were being tricked and deluded.   For the Bill was a party measure if ever there was one.

It is true, of course, that the condition of education in this country necessitated by general consent a sweeping measure of Educational Reform.   Mr. Lloyd George has described in his own way the condition of affairs which called for a remedy.   I quote from his speech at Cardiff in 1904, when he had put himself at the head of the great movement of the Welsh people against the coercive methods of the Government.

Up to the year 1902, you had a dual system of education in this country, and I believe it is about the only country in the world where it exists, a system which is responsible largely if not entirely for the educational backwardness of England and Wales compared with the countries on the continent of Europe.   You have practically an educational civil war, friends and supporters of one system waging war upon the friends of the other system.   The result is that which follows on every civil war—the country suffering as a whole.   What were these two systems ?   You had, first of all, the system, the free and popular system, of the Board schools, where the schools are established by the people, controlled by the people, maintained by the people, where there are no theological tests, where everybody met on the basis of perfect religious equality round that Board and in the schools of that Board.

You had, on the other hand, a sectarian system, a system maintained out of public funds, largely so even before the Education Act, controlled in the main by the clergy of the one sect ; theological tests imposed upon teachers, the appointment of 60,000 of the Civil Servants of this country, subject to the test which had been abolished with regard to every other branch of the Civil Service.   Not only that, you had the children of this country, divided into two independent, almost hostile camps, trained at the public expense to think and act independently and even antagonistic-

ally, as citizens.   A more pernicious system of education was never devised.
You had half the children of the country trained in these sectarian schools,
taught doctrines which pretty well half the community repudiated, taught
at the public expense.

To another Government, the policy which might have commended itself would have been to encourage the growth of schools
under popular control, and, in so far as it assisted the denominational schools, to insist upon obtaining in return for public money
a share for the public in the administration of the schools.   But
the Conservative administration was prohibited from such a course
by its care for, or fear of, the Church.   The Government, to quote
Mr. Lloyd George again, found the sectarian system tottering :

Without consulting the people, without giving them the slightest hint
at the moment when the people could have expressed their opinions effectively, they called for a mandate from the people on other issues, when
they expressly said they were not going to deal with questions of this
character.   In defiance of their pledges, they introduced a measure which
called upon the municipalities of this kingdom to levy a contribution upon
their free constituents for the purpose of buttressing up this tottering
sectarian system, which was a rival to the popular one.

The Bill in effect put the denominational schools on the rates.
It gave the control of education to a committee of the County
Council, not directly elected, and the denominational schools
themselves were to be managed by a committee upon which the
ratepayers, who provided the funds, were only indirectly represented at all, while their representatives were to be in a minority,
so that they might be constantly outvoted by the representatives of the religious denomination.   It was upon this main issue
that the Bill was most strongly fought by Liberals and by Nonconformists.   The Bill was a direct challenge to the Liberal axiom
that public control must follow the expenditure of public money.
What was much more serious, it opened, as any one could have
prophesied that it certainly must do, the floodgates of sectarian
bitterness.   We have got beyond the stage of burning those
whom we regard as heretics, but it is too much to be asked to
subsidise the teaching of their heresies.   It was hardly concealed
by Churchmen that the object of the Bill was to gain proselytes.
The history of the religious aspect of the Education Bill
divides itself into three stages.   The first begins with the opening of the nineteenth century, when unsectarian enthusiasts
founded the " British schools."   They succeeded so well that the
Church, in self-defence, founded the National Society and opened

A NONCONFORMIST GENIUS.

(By courtesy of " Vanity Fair.")

schools in which its own doctrines were to be propagated side by side with the simple rules of reading, writing, and arithmetic.

Very often the only school in a district was a Church school, and this fact was due, not to any lack of zeal on the part of Nonconformists for education, but partly to their lack of funds, chiefly to the difficulty they found in obtaining land. I quote Mr. Lloyd George's picturesque account of what happened in too many villages.

When the Nonconformist wanted a piece of land they had to go to the squire, who was a Churchman, and he said, " No, we are going to build a nice little school ourselves." So the Nonconformists were ruled out. How were the Church schools built ? The squire gave a bit of land and a contribution, and the State sent a little subsidy. Then the villagers were summoned and asked to help, and they were told that the parson was going to get a grant of three or four thousand pounds from a society in London over which he had a good deal of influence. And so they passed a vote of thanks to the parson for being such a nice man and so useful to the parish. But not a word was said about the exclusion of Nonconformists from the management or the teaching staff. . . . After the squire had built the school the parson approached. Ah ! the tempter. He suggested what the squire had not the intellectual subtlety to conceive—the insertion in the deeds of conditions excluding from management the people who attended Nonconformist conventicles, which were robbing the parson of his congregation. If the squire had been chivalrous he would have said : " These people have done well by me, and when I dedicate a school to their children I am not going to give it with an insult to their chapels. I will defy all the parsons in Christendom before I do that." That is what he ought to have done—but he did not. You will find in all those deeds those words of offence to Nonconformity.[1]

These two sets of schools long divided primary education between them, relying almost entirely upon voluntary subscriptions. " In 1842 " (the words I quote are Mr. Birrell's) " a scheme of National Education was wholly wrecked by sectarian jealousies, and generations of children—particularly in our large towns—were allowed to grow up unable to read the Four Gospels, because Christians could not agree who was to teach them the love of God." In its next stage the controversy raged round the Act of 1870, which had the effect of handing over the old British schools to the School Boards, aided by the rates, but left the National schools in the hands of their managers, subsidised out of the taxes, but unassisted by the rates.

Where no school was provided voluntarily, Board schools in which the teaching was undenominational had to be built.

[1] Speech at Liverpool, July 6, 1905.

The Act of 1870 recognised the duty of property to provide for education. How did they face that? The importance of this is that most of the money which has been spent on these denominational schools has been spent since 1870. It is a most interesting and instructive story. In 1870 Mr. Gladstone said, " You must build schools to provide sufficient accommodation for all the children of the land, and they must be undenominational." But an enemy set tares among the wheat. They said, " If you provide voluntarily sufficient accommodation in the parish, compulsion won't come in." They started. The parsons went to the landlord, whom they influenced through his purse. They told him that if a School Board was started in his district, he would have to pay rates. " Therefore," said they, " let us build a sort of little shanty of our own here. The Board of Education will pass anything so long as it is anointed by the clergy." Thus the parson found the Act of 1870 more effective in getting money than a pocketful of the most expensive sermons. The result is that they have got twice as much money since the Act of 1870 as they got before. If compulsion had come into operation the squire would have had to pay more, the school would have been better, the staff would have been better, the equipment would have been better, and the education of the children would have been better. That is how the landlord got credit for zeal, for religious instruction, and he parades it, and the parson talks about it with his tongue in his cheek. They put down to piety what is due to parsimony.

As time went on the Board schools, aided by the rates, did a great deal better than the National schools, aided by the offerings of the pious. The zeal of the English Churchman for the religious education of the children of the poor often stopped short of paying for it. The result was that the Church had the school buildings and only lacked the money to carry them on ; if it could keep these schools and run them largely at the public expense, it was obvious that it would be in a strong position to convert to its own views the many children of Nonconformist or indifferent parents whom necessity in a great number of cases sent to the Church school. Churchmen are not to be blamed if the hope of such conversion seemed to them quite a worthy motive. Lord Hugh Cecil, whose exposition of the political aims of his Church is always on the highest level, put very plainly in the House of Commons the case for the Voluntary schools, and against the simple Bible teaching of the Board schools, upon which, in his view, it was impossible for Christians to unite. He quoted an allegorical dictum that " a Board school was a school with only one door." The child, he said, went in and learned a great deal that was valuable and went out again into the street. The denominational school was a school with two doors, and the other door led into the church or chapel, and brought the child into contact with, and under the influence of, this or that denomination. Nobody need throw any doubt upon the sincerity of such sentiments; the worst that need be said of the ecclesiastical conscience is that the Church has never been above driving a hard bargain with the State. The answer most frequently made to the Nonconformist grievance was that the operation of what was called the Conscience Clause permitted children to be withdrawn from school during the hours of religious instruction; but that answer failed entirely to satisfy Nonconformists, and for this reason, that there was no principle contended for more strongly by Churchmen than that teachers in Denominational schools should be subject to religious tests, so that the whole work of the school should be carried on in the appropriate religious atmosphere. If once this theory was admitted, if denominationalists were to succeed in their contention that their dogmas must colour every lesson that was taught to the child, and every moment of its school life, then it was obvious that a conscience clause, which at best acted as an unpleasant and invidious distinction, became a delusion and a sham.

It has been said that the Bill was a party measure, and it is right to add by way of qualification that there were in the Liberal party a few men who thought that educational advantages would be gained by the transference of the control of education from the School Board to a committee of the County Council, which would outweigh the evils of the Bill. The most prominent of these was Mr. Haldane, who, seeing the opportunity of a real administrative advance, was perhaps inclined to minimise the Nonconformist grievance. On the other hand, there were some Conservatives and very many Liberal Unionists who opposed the Bill, and in Birmingham Mr. Chamberlain had his work cut out to preserve a semblance of unity upon the subject among his followers. The position of the Irish Nationalist members was dictated largely by their zeal in the interests of the Roman Catholic schools. These were in a position a little different from that of the Church schools, because it was obvious that for a Roman Catholic the Bible teaching of the Board school was something to be avoided at all costs. The Roman Catholic school existed at least as much to defend the faith of Roman Catholic children as for aggressive proselytism. The Irishmen joined forces with the Government, and Ministers, in spite of all the hard things they had said of the Nationalists a few months before, were glad enough to avail themselves of their assistance, which enabled them, whenever the unpopularity of the Bill was urged, to point to their large majorities in the House of Commons. At the same time, the Nationalists, while they remained obdurate in their opposition to the claims of the Nonconformists, showed some desire for conciliation, and Mr. Dillon and Mr. T. P. O'Connor were conspicuous for attempts to mitigate the Protestant grievance.

Mr. Lloyd George took part in the debate on the second reading on May 8. No better statement of the Nonconformist position towards the Bill was ever made in Parliament than in this speech. It was delivered in the afternoon of the fourth day's debate, in a well-filled House. His speech, Mr. Massingham wrote in the " Daily News " " had the high interest of being a complete and sincere self-revelation."

Until Mr. Lloyd George spoke to-night Nonconformity, its intellectual attitude to education, its historical associations with the settlement of 1870, now being torn up, and its contribution to the religious problem, has gone without a recorder and a champion. Mr. Lloyd George took the vacant place to-night. . . . Here was the Nonconformist attitude in its strength and its weakness. . . . A comparison with Bright's method and style—of course, with real differences—often rose to my mind as I listened to Mr. Lloyd George, for here was Bright's simplicity of thought, directness of expression, and vivid, instinctive fighting quality.

The principle of Mr. Lloyd George's opposition to the Bill was summed up in one sentence in the speech : You cannot base any good system of education on an injustice to a large section of the community. There were Liberals who made the destruction of the School Boards their chief grievance against the measure. To him this seemed a minor consideration. So long as the source of the authority was in the electorate, it mattered little what the authority was. On the other hand, he had some words of witty criticism for Mr. Haldane, who had declined to vote against the Bill because of the importance he attached to the administrative reform it effected, and was inclined to belittle the religious grievance. He described the great Scottish lawyer as being, politically speaking, " always above the snow-line." His counsel was " very serene in its purity, but rather sterile."

The Nonconformist case was a strong one. It was computed that of the two million school children in Anglican schools, half were Nonconformists. Mr. Lloyd George was able to quote a diocesan inspector of twenty years' experience who had stated with pride, in the columns of the " Guardian," that by giving distinctly denominational instruction the schools he inspected had " trained the children of Nonconformists to be children of the Church." Now the laity were getting tired of supporting these Church schools, and public money was to pay, under the Bill, for everything except the repairs. But the repairs would cost £60,000 a year, one-tenth of a farthing per week for every adult adherent of the Church of England—" one-fifth of the widow's mite "—and a Duke had written to complain that this expense should fall upon Churchmen.

From his statement of the Nonconformist grievance he turned to deal with Lord Hugh Cecil's plea for the unity of Nonconformity and Anglicanism in face of growing unbelief. His answer was that the perpetuation of a system which broke up the country into hostile religious camps was an injury to the cause of unity. Then, turning to the Nationalists of Ireland, the Nationalist of Wales spoke " a candid word " to them. He reminded them of all that Liberals, and especially Welsh Liberals, had sacrificed for the cause of justice to Ireland. How would Ireland repay Wales ? In a lofty peroration, the more impressive by reason of its simplicity, he implored them not to join forces with the oppressors of their friends.[1]

II

The Committee stage of the Bill—Months of drudgery—Mr. Lloyd George and Lord Hugh Cecil—Two friendly antagonists—Mr. Lloyd George's suggestions for compromise—Mr. Chamberlain and his Birmingham supporters—The pledges of the 1900 election—The Kenyon-Slaney clause—" The pagans are with us "—Mr. Lloyd George's speech on the third reading—Mr. Balfour's generous tribute.

In Committee he surprised his own friends by the grasp he had obtained of the subject. It was said with a great deal of truth by some of the newspapers that he was leading the Opposition on the Bill. Mr. Balfour came more and more obviously to respect his opposition, and even endeavoured to conciliate him. Once when, to the horror of Lord Hugh Cecil, Mr. Lloyd George had screwed some concession out of the Prime Minister, Mr. Dillon said to him in the lobbies, " If this goes on, we shall soon have Cecil leading the Opposition, and you will be defending the Government." In a letter written at the end of October he mentions that he has had a very friendly conversation with Mr. Balfour, and made the acquaintance for the first time of the Bishop of St. Asaph.

He was soon one of the most formidable opponents of the Bill, because one of the best informed. In the country and in the House too, when he chose, he could enliven the dry bones of the controversy with burning eloquence or scathing satire, but

[1] See Appendix I.

his real triumph in Parliament was won by his carefully fostered capacity for taking pains. He did not set out to make striking speeches in Committee, but to win concessions and to improve the Bill. Still, there are striking phrases and sparkling passages to be found among his contributions even to those dry discussions. At one time there were rumours that, to avoid the imposition of a rate for the maintenance of denominational education, the Government was going to use the newly imposed corn tax for the purpose. "So we are to have dear food and cheap catechisms," he exclaimed.[1] On the Government's failure to do anything in the Bill for secondary education, he made a comment which was illuminating, and should serve to remind politicians that great political problems (education and the land, for instance) do not stand alone, each in splendid isolation, but are interrelated and interdependent. "Secondary education in the rural districts would do more to solve the problem of agricultural distress than anything else."[2] He put the same view more epigrammatically in a public speech: "After all, the best manure you can give the land is brains."[3]

The crux of the Bill was raised in Committee by the debate on Clause 7, which dealt with the question of managers. Now was the time, as an observer in the gallery truly said, for broadsword practice, and Mr. Lloyd George made exactly the right kind of speech for a fighting occasion. "How was it," he asked, "that the Imperialist party were founding in England and Wales a system of education which would not be tolerated anywhere else in all our Imperial Dominions? Everywhere, except in Great Britain, the effects of undenominationalism were to be seen. New Zealand, where was obtained the purest diamond of the Imperialist spirit, was reared on the secular system: so it was with Canada. The great example of denominationalism was Ireland. It really looked as if denominationalism had tended to produce pro-Boerism. In a more serious vein he insisted upon the immense importance of education to the country. Menacing rivals stood in our industrial path, and education was the best means of keeping abreast or of getting ahead of them. The ship of State was making its way through the midst of rocks, and what was the Government's proposal? "To put the chaplain on the bridge."

It was said by an astute political observer that, upon the question of education, Mr. Lloyd George and Lord Hugh Cecil were nearer to one another than Mr. Balfour was to either. Just as we have seen that Mr. Chamberlain's plain bluntness could

---

[1] June 17.   [2] June 30.
[3] At Lincoln, December 12.

understand the direct and outspoken opposition of his most ardent opponent, so the two strong denominationalists appreciated each other's attitude, because each saw that here was no case of splitting straws or of factious opposition, since vital differences of principle and aim separated them. The first step towards bridging a gulf is to admit that the gulf exists. That was just the admission that Mr. Balfour could not be induced to make.

Mr. Balfour refused to believe that there was any religious difficulty. Philosophers find it so easy to reconcile apparently inconsistent propositions that the tendency of humbler minds to divide into camps over small differences of dogma always seems to them a piece of human perversity which cannot be explained and had better be disregarded. It was much more convenient for the Government to support the clerical party than any other, but it is only doing justice to Mr. Balfour to say that if it had been necessary for him to advocate simple Bible teaching in all schools, or even the teaching of Wesleyanism in all schools, he could have found plenty of excellent arguments to show that such a policy would make very little difference in the end either to the future of education or the future of the children. What he cared about was the establishment of a single authority as a contribution to educational reform. What Lord Hugh Cecil and Mr. Lloyd George cared about was the safeguarding of the rights of conscience. To Lord Hugh Cecil it seemed most vital to secure that no Dissenter or Agnostic should be given the opportunity of corrupting the minds of the young in schools which the Church had built : to Mr. Lloyd George, that the money of Nonconformists should not be taken to pay for the endowment of High Anglican " atmospheres " or of schools with a " back door " leading to the Church. The two men were the leading figures in many debates within the House, and had much conversation outside it. On one occasion, as the Welsh member told the House, Lord Hugh Cecil lent him a treatise by Canon Moberly in the hope of converting him, but Mr. Lloyd George complained that although he had received his education at a Church school, he had found it quite impossible to understand the metaphysical subtleties which Canon Moberly and Lord Hugh Cecil seemed to think suitable for the minds of small children. He had retaliated by lending Lord Hugh Cecil a pamphlet by Dr. Clifford, and he thought that his High Church friend had the better of the bargain.

It seems hardly too much to say, though it may seem to be a paradox, that if these two antagonists could have been left to settle the denominational problem between them, they would have arrived at a solution. Once indeed, during a discussion in

Committee (July 22) they very nearly came to a complete agreement across the floor of the House. A discussion was proceeding upon the question of Church schools in " single school areas," in other words, those districts where only the Church school was available for the children of Nonconformists. There was no case upon which Dissenters had a more real grievance. Mr. Balfour, baffled in his efforts to deal with it, fell back on Dr. Johnson and quoted :—

> "How small of all that human hearts endure
> That part which laws or kings can cause or cure!"

" Even Christians," Mr. Balfour added, on his own account, " are not always talking about their differences." "That does not come very well," Mr. Lloyd George said, " from the leader of the party that is always insisting on the differences of Christians. It is because he and his followers cannot or will not come to an agreement with their fellow Christians or their fellow Protestants that this difficulty has arisen." Lord Hugh Cecil spoke next, and frankly acknowledged the existence of the grievance. "Will you help us to do something to redress it ? " asked Mr. Lloyd George. The answer was emphatic and was in the affirmative. "What will you do ? " was the next question asked. Lord Hugh Cecil's answer was that he would allow the teachers of different denominations to visit schools and to give religious instruction to the children of their own faith. Mr. Lloyd George at once closed with the offer, but this excellent chance of a settlement by consent was not seized upon by Mr. Balfour, who, on the contrary, seemed to be rather embarrassed by it. " These observations," he said, " are very interesting, but for some of us they constitute a rather trying pleasure." He warned the Committee not to allow itself to be dragged into a second-reading debate by these " two redoubtable champions." Even when Mr. Dillon, Mr. T. P. O'Connor, Mr. Redmond, and among English members, Sir Michael Foster, had urged upon the Government the desirability of remedying the grievance they admitted, Mr. Balfour refused to make any concessions. It must be added, however, that Mr. Lloyd George would not at that time have accepted such an offer as was made by Lord Hugh Cecil except on the condition that the schools were to be under public control. Otherwise he believed that a war of the sects would be introduced over the unfortunate bodies of the children who were not attached to any religious denomination. A few sentences from a speech on this point may serve to show how his gift for apt and amusing illustration could brighten the paths of dull discussion,

We should have hundreds of little theological Fashodas all over the country, one theological sect saying, "That boy belongs to us," and another saying, "He belongs to us." At one time a child would belong to one sect and in a week or a fortnight there would be a successful Jameson Raid, or there would be some local Major Marchand, who would have the child taken away. It is not a question of superior dogmas, it is a question of superior buns. The noble Lord (Lord Hugh Cecil) talks as if all the children were thirsting for Church dogma, but they are simply ravenously hungry for buns, and it is a question of blankets with the parents.

People who thought that children should be trained in the functions of citizenship might suggest, he argued, that there should be facilities for the different political schools of thought. They then might see Mr. Chaplin taking the children into a class-room and teaching them the virtues of his favourite dogma of pure beer.

The basis upon which Mr. Lloyd George believed a compromise to be possible was made clear by him in a letter published in the "Times" on October 13. He wanted his Irish Catholic friends to realise, he said, that whatever might be the opinions of those who thought with him as British Dissenters, they did not in Parliament insist on a rigid application of those views in the settlement of the educational problem. On the contrary, they went a long way towards meeting denominational scruples. Cardinal Vaughan had written that the Parliamentary contention in its ultimate analysis had resolved itself into this—whether or not there should be national liberty in any public elementary schools in England to teach dogmatic Christianity—in other words, whether dogmatic Christianity should be finally banished from all the public elementary schools in the country. He had further stated that the object of the Nonconformists was "to deny to the County Councils every vestige of discretion or liberty to permit a definite Christian creed to be taught in any of their schools under any circumstances whatever."

"Let us," Mr. Lloyd George now wrote, "examine those statements," and he went on :

What was it that really happened in Parliament ? The Nonconformist members repeatedly pressed upon the Government as a compromise the acceptance of one of the two following suggestions :

1. That the managers of the denominational schools should be elected one-third as at present, one-third by parents of the children in the schools, and only the remaining one-third by the ratepayers, who henceforth under the Bill will have to provide practically all the fund for the maintenance of these schools. If this amendment had been accepted, two-thirds at

least of the managers of every Catholic school throughout England and Wales would have been Catholics themselves, and could have ordered such religious instruction as they thought fit for the children in the schools under their control.

The same observation applies to all Anglican schools where the majority of the parents desired Church of England doctrines taught to their children. If the majority of the parents, however, happened to be Nonconformists, why should Church of England dogmas be taught to their children against their wish at the public expense? Surely all Irish Catholics can possibly require is that children shall be brought up in the faith of their fathers. This amendment would completely safeguard their position, and therefore it is not a true account of the Nonconformist attitude in Parliament to state that it implied " the final banishment of all dogmatic Christianity from all the public elementary schools in this country."

2. The Nonconformist members suggested as an alternative that, provided full control of all the schools were given to the ratepayers' representatives, every facility should be accorded to the ministers of the various Churches to teach their children the dogmas of their respective faiths. This compromise has been accepted by the Catholic Church in Manitoba, Holland, and Ontario. It is therefore not correct to say, as Cardinal Vaughan does in his letter, that the Nonconformists wish to " deny to the County Council every vestige of discretion or liberty to permit a definite Christian creed to be taught in any of their schools under any circumstances whatever."

Under the former arrangement every Catholic school in England and Wales would receive all the benefits of the Bill, and so would every Anglican school where the children were really Anglican. Under the second arrangement suggested millions of Catholic children all over the world are being taught in State schools the doctrines of their faith. We have repeatedly made these proposals both inside and outside of the House, and I think it but fair that all our Irish friends should be informed of it, so that, whatever decision they may arrive at on the Education Bill, they should not come to it under a misconception as to the Nonconformist attitude towards their schools.

I would appeal to Irishmen whether they have not found less racial and religious bigotry amongst Nonconformists than amongst the classes who are promoting the Education Bill. Welsh Nonconformists have since 1886 returned steadily to Parliament a larger proportion of members to support the claims of Ireland than Irishmen themselves sent there to demand them. It is also true that the demands of Ireland for self-government were supported at the last four general elections by a much larger proportion of English Nonconformists than of English Catholics. I would not, therefore, have Irishmen believe that Nonconformists, at any rate, would treat ruthlessly and harshly the conscientious convictions of the Irish Catholics who dwell amongst them in England and Wales.

But the concluding paragraph of his letter sounded a note of warning. By their stubborn refusal even to consider moderate suggestions of compromise Ministers had raised up an agitation which made it increasingly difficult for Nonconformist members to repeat the liberal proposals made by them in the interest of concord. If, therefore, in the sequel, Catholic schools' were to suffer, Cardinal Vaughan should not blame the Nonconformists, who advanced more than half-way to meet them, but the Government, and, above all, their ecclesiastical counsellors, who had rejected every reasonable proffer made to accommodate the difficulty.

The suggestion for compromise contained in this letter may be supplemented from his speeches ; for, although he was always in good fighting trim when the occasion demanded it, his tone was at bottom conciliatory, and he lost no opportunity of pleading for a settlement by consent. Personally, he agreed with Mr. Chamberlain in thinking that probably the best system would be one in which the control was in the hands of the people and the education given in the schools was absolutely unsectarian. He also agreed with Mr. Chamberlain that such a system would not be acceptable to the people.[1] But he believed a working compromise would have been found, either in the device of "right of entry" adumbrated in his letter to the "Times," or in the adoption of the Scottish system. The latter, he pointed out in his speech on the third reading, obtained already in some of the most important centres in Wales. In the Rhondda Valley, for instance, every denomination had agreed to develop a syllabus of religious instruction, drafted by the vicar of the parish, and there was perfect peace.[2]

Mr. Chamberlain was no longer the central figure of the political stage, but he was not out of the reach of Mr. Lloyd George's attacks. His position had become one of such embarrassment that he was peculiarly exposed to his opponent's satire, and on the whole perhaps Mr. Lloyd George let him off rather lightly. Mr. Chamberlain's efforts at uniting his rebellious Nonconformist supporters provided him with the material for one amusing speech in the House. The reference was to a conference held in October with local Unionist leaders at Birmingham, from which,

---

[1] Hansard, vol. 115, p. 1113.

[2] It is fair to quote the substance of Mr. Balfour's reply on this point. The "right of entry" or "facilities" scheme he dismissed as unpractical. As to the Scottish system he confidently challenged any one who had looked through all the controversial speeches and pamphlets issued against the Bill by the Nonconformist militant bodies to find a sentence in them hinting that those bodies would accept the abolition of the Cowper-Temple clause. A further objection was that, far more than the Bill itself, the adoption of the Scottish system would have made religion a subject for discussion in the Councils.

after an hour's speech by Mr. Chamberlain, the reporters were excluded.

There have been private meetings in support of the Bill, but even in Birmingham they could not hold a public meeting in support, not even when the Colonial Secretary addressed it himself. That is a remarkable indication in itself, but the arguments used by the Colonial Secretary with regard to the Bill showed that he clearly recognised that his own supporters were against it. He did not say " This Bill is a good one," but " If you do not carry this Bill I shall resign, and then," he said, " mark the consequences. There shall be neither dew nor rain in the British Empire for seven long years," [1] and a shudder passed over the Birmingham Liberal Unionists which lasted for four resolutions. They then recovered themselves, and another resolution was passed, which resulted in a terrible threat being used.[2]

He dealt even more caustically with Mr. Chamberlain's election speeches of 1900 :

The Colonial Secretary at the last election took the ratepayer by the hand and said to him, " Fix your eyes on South Africa. Wicked Radical politicians will tell you to look around at your own affairs, but keep your eyes on that golden shore six thousand miles away." The ratepayer followed his advice, and while the poor man was looking ahead the Government robbed his orchard, destroyed some of his best fruit trees, and now they are distributing the fruit among the clergy, at whose dictation this measure was introduced.[3]

Mr. Chamberlain, following him in the debate, said that it was perfectly absurd to complain that the Government had no right to deal with education—" because I, who was not the Prime Minister, but speaking in my individual capacity, in a single speech out of twenty, said that the principal issue was the war." A complete and crushing retort came the next morning. A letter from Mr. Lloyd George was published in the " Times " which showed that Mr. Chamberlain had delivered twelve speeches during the war, that they were nearly all exclusively concerned with the subject of the war, and that in eight instances which Mr. Lloyd George was able to give, they had contained specific and unambiguous statements that the issue upon which the votes of

[1] What Mr. Chamberlain actually said was hardly more relevant to the Education Bill than Mr. Lloyd George's parody : " Let us never consent to do anything that would assist the intrigues of those who, if they were successful, would hand over Ireland to the Home Rulers, would transfer the settlement of the great and important problems arising in South Africa to the discretion and patriotism of the pro-Boers," etc., etc.

[2] The fifth resolution was in favour of the proposal that a majority of the managers of voluntary schools should be popularly elected.   [3] November 11.

the people were being taken was the war, and the justice of the war.[1]

[1] Mr. Lloyd George's answer to Mr. Chamberlain was so conclusive that the letter may perhaps usefully be reproduced :

"Mr. Chamberlain, in seeking to explain away the extract from his Lichfield speech in 1900, which I, amongst others, quoted in the debate last night, said :

"'It is perfectly absurd . . . now to complain that we have no right to deal with education, because I, who was not the Prime Minister, but speaking in my individual capacity, in a single speech out of twenty, said that the principal issue was the war.'

"1. The first of the four statements contained in this passage is perfectly true. Mr. Chamberlain was not, and is not, Prime Minister.

"2. Mr. Chamberlain says that he spoke in his 'individual capacity.' He was, however, at the time (as he is now) Colonial Secretary, and throughout his speeches spoke as a prominent representative of the Government and its policy.

"3. Mr. Chamberlain says he made twenty speeches during the General Election. I can, however, only find twelve reported in your columns.

"4. These twelve speeches are nearly all of them exclusively concerned with the question of the war, with the exception of one speech in Birmingham, in which Mr. Chamberlain's theme was that the social programme had been carried out with the exception of old-age pensions, whilst as to that he (Mr. Chamberlain) 'was not dead yet.'

"I hope you will allow me to trespass on your space to give at all events sufficient extracts to show that, so far from the Lichfield quotation being unrepresentative of the speeches as a whole, the entire series is based upon the proposition that the one issue upon which the electors had to decide was the war, and that they could vote Unionist without prejudice to their views on domestic legislation.

"'Now we have come practically to the end of the war ; there is nothing going on now but a guerilla business which is encouraged by these men ; I was going to say these traitors, but I will say instead, these misguided individuals. The new chapter has begun ; we have now to make a settlement which is worthy of the sacrifices which you have made ; we have to quench the embers of the war, which has, I say, degenerated into guerilla tactics. We have to bring together two races in South Africa ; we have to secure that the guilty shall be punished, that the loyal shall be rewarded, and in order to do that—and remember that it is a difficult task during the present situation—in order to do that we must be able to say that we have the people of England and of Scotland behind us, and that we are strong in the expressed will of the nation to carry out the policy which we have outlined faithfully. And this is the issue at this election. If, then, you think the war a just war, if you think that the settlement we propose is a satisfactory settlement, you must give us not merely an ordinary majority, you must give us an overwhelming majority, so that we may in the future, and not as in the past, be able to present a united front to the enemies of this country. Now, was this war just ?' (Birmingham, September 22.)

"'The question which every honest man should ask himself before he gives his vote was whether the war was righteous, whether it was inevitable, and whether it could have been avoided without the sacrifice of the honour and interests of the country.' (Bilston, September 28.)

"'I go to a question which, after all, dominates all others, and that is the issue of this war in which we are engaged.' (East Birmingham, September 29.)

"'This was no ordinary election. It was an election not to decide the social and domestic issues generally before them ; at such a period they had to deal with the greatest national and imperial questions.' (Coventry, October 1.)

"'He met cries about "old-age pensions" and other social questions by saying these did not form the issue at present. . . . The special issue the electors were asked to vote upon was the war.' (Warwick, October 2.)

"'It was only by having a united nation behind them that the nation could

Those who preserve a recollection of the Education debates of 1902 will remember that no part of the Bill aroused livelier discussion than the clause which made the name of Kenyon-Slaney as famous as that of Cowper-Temple. Colonel Kenyon-Slaney, a Conservative member for one of the Shropshire divisions, moved this clause as an addition to the Bill, and by doing so brought down upon himself the fury of the high ecclesiastics and entangled the Government in a series of difficulties and complications. His proposal was intended to keep the religious instruction in denominational schools in the hands of the managers and out of the hands of the parson, and, in spite of many vicissitudes, the clause survived, in an amended but reasonably effective form, in the finished statute. Lord Hugh Cecil and his friends saw in the clause an insult to the clergy; Mr. Balfour, however, said that it carried out what had always been the intention of the Government, and refused to yield to his noble kinsman's entreaties to abandon it. Mr. Lloyd George took no part in the discussions of the clause, for reasons he explained in the third-reading debate.

I watched it as an impartial observer. . . . I took no part in the action —I thought it was better to keep out of it—that it was dangerous. There were the High and Low Churches firing at close quarters; there was crossfiring by Nonconformists and Roman Catholics, and for a timorous noncombatant I thought it looked too dangerous, and I took cover.

He had followed the discussion closely enough, although he took no part in it, and a letter from him dated November 19 refers to " a very interesting speech " by Mr. Austin Taylor, then newly elected for Liverpool, in which the Kenyon-Slaney clause had been ably supported. There was much speculation as to whether the House of Lords would throw out the clause. Somebody

secure the pacification of Africa. He asked for the support of not only those electors who were ordinarily with the Government for personal or party reasons, but of Radicals who in a time of national danger and crisis put their patriotism before their party.' (Burton-on-Trent, October 5.)

" ' A great many of the elections had already been held, and the most extraordinary feature of them was the great turnover of the mining vote. In the North of England thousands and thousands of miners who had never voted Unionist before, who still called themselves Liberals and Radicals, had on this occasion—even if it were only to be for this occasion—supported the Unionist candidates. He did not say they had changed their views. They were probably Liberal and Radical as before, and they would probably vote for Liberals and Radicals at the next election; but at this election they had voted for the Unionist candidates. Why had they done that ? . . . Because they saw that the issue at the present time was not a question of domestic policy, such as Church disestablishment or liquor prohibition, but a question of the existence of the Empire.' (Lichfield, October 8.)

" ' He urged the electors not to think of persons or parties, but only to think of Imperial interests.' (Stourbridge, October 9.)"

asked Mr. Lloyd George in the lobby what he thought about it. "They won't throw it out," he said; "people forget that many of the Lords are pagans—and in this matter the pagans are with us."

"I was not sorry when this day came—last in Committee," he writes on November 20. His devotion to the work of the House of Commons had been a severe physical strain. With the added tax of public meetings, many of which he found time to address upon the Bill, the burden upon him became one which a man of less resilient temperament could hardly have borne. But it was a fine, exciting fight, and one may well believe that he would not have missed a day of it. The campaign was a very different one from that in which he had been engaged during the preceding year. Now the flowing tide was with him. The English people had no enthusiasm for the Education Bill (it may be doubted perhaps whether they ever will feel enthusiastic about any Education Bill), and the great public who had bitterly resented expressions of sympathy with the Boers had not the least objection to trenchant criticism of the bishops. In the House of Commons he had won an acknowledged position. Men were beginning to talk of the advent of a Liberal Government as inevitable in a not very remote future, and he was already, by the consent of all, included in its ranks.

His contribution to the third-reading debate was a vigorous condemnation of the Bill in its final form. It had not, he said, even the merit of being popular. There had been a meeting at the Albert Hall in favour of it, for which the clergy had acted as recruiting sergeants, but that was not a public meeting. He had searched the newspapers and only found one instance of really enthusiastic popular support for the Bill:

There was a smoking concert held in support of the Bill somewhere in the South of England. So little confidence had those who organised it in the Bill that they appealed with influences spirituous rather than spiritual in their nature, and thought it best to pass the resolution and say as little as possible about it. "Captain Cook kindly gave a number of selections on his fine double-trumpet instrument," and he sang to this great meeting in support of the Bill, "Wait till the clouds roll by," and by way of referring to the Kenyon-Slaney amendment he sang, "The Happy Family," and ended up with "Good old Joe." It was a little irrelevant to the Education Bill, but the effect was good, because I see it ended in a "unanimous and enthusiastic" resolution in favour of the Bill.

He pointed to the effect upon the debates of the House of Commons of the religious aspects of education. "It was like a whirlpool—for hours the House swirled round and round in the vortex of a mad frenzy of theological controversy." That frenzy, he prophesied, would be reproduced in the County Councils through-out the land. The Councils would be debating the question of the repression of popery in the village schools, when they ought to be discussing the suppression of swine fever. The Thirty-nine Articles would become part of the standing orders of every Town Council ; Kenyon-Slaneys would arise in every county to keep watch and ward over village Cecils.

The formula of " the right of the parent," which was to be-come the watchword of clericalism at a later stage in the history of the controversy, had already been invented. What right, Mr. Lloyd George asked, had the parent to dictate to the State that the State should at its own expense teach any theology ?

It is not a question of the right of the parent, but of the interest of the community. Is it in the interest of the community that it should inter-vene in these squabbles between forty or fifty different sects ? You can-not say the Church has a right and the Primitive Methodists have not. If all these exercise their rights you split up education and shatter it to atoms. Lord Salisbury said with regard to India that the Government had a great horror of using its authority as a partisan of one religion more than another. Those were wise words, and I wish the statesmanship which is good enough to be applied to the people of India could be applied to the people of England and Wales. It is altogether a question of the interest of the community. I do not know that the community has a right to teach theology, but hon. members opposite ought to be logical. If it is the business of the community to teach theology it should not confine the theology to one kind. . . . Honourable members opposite say dogma is essential. Who at the present moment is their ideal of a great British patriot ? The member for West Birmingham—the right honourable gentleman who belongs to the least orthodox of the Churches. He is not a believer in the dogmatic religion of the noble lord the member for Greenwich,[1] and yet nobody doubts the genuineness of his patriotism. Dogma, therefore, even from the point of view of honourable gentlemen opposite, is not essential to British statesmanship. I am not sure that the Prime Minister is not a schismatic, according to the notions of the noble lord. Even he is not safe, if it depends upon dogma. He is the sort of man that the noble lord prays the Good Lord to deliver us from on Sundays and feast days.

He proceeded to pour scorn upon the interpretation placed by some Anglican exponents upon the injunction of the Catechism that we should " order ourselves lowly and reverently before our betters." He quoted from a handbook in use in one of the train-

[1] Lord Hugh Cecil.

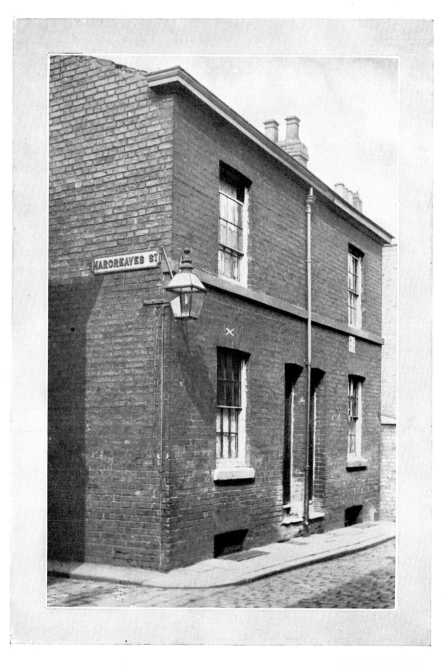

BIRTHPLACE OF DAVID LLOYD GEORGE

No. 5, New York Place, Chorlton-on-Medlock, Manchester.

ing colleges : "Who are our betters ?—Those in a higher position than ourselves, either by birth, wealth, or office." That was
taught in colleges maintained at the public expense. He called
it "repulsive snobbery "—"it was from such snobbery that the
carpenter's Son suffered."

I have seen columns of the "Times" filled with this : "Undenominational teaching in the Board schools is obnoxious to Churchmen." To
teach kindness, goodness, honesty, purity, temperance, chastity—this is
undenominational, obnoxious to all good Churchmen ! To teach them to
cringe before wealth ; yes, this is pure religion and undefiled, and therefore
you ought to endow it. And you are to order yourselves humbly and
lowly to wealth. That is not the teaching I would have. I would rather
have the words which the American schools teach : "If any man be great
among you, let him be a servant." All the great Presidents of America
have been poor men without a pedigree.

I have only one word to add. There is a clear issue before the country.
Public control—yes ; and if you are going to teach religion in the schools,
teach it from the Book which is acceptable to all Christians. Give the Bible
to the children. It is done by the Board schools, and I have seen even
bishops commend the way it is explained. There is one thing that always
struck me about these tenets of the Church catechism—how irrelevant they
are to the real perils that children have to encounter in life. Give the
children the Bible if you want to teach them the Christian faith. Let it
be expounded to them by its Founder. Stop this brawling of priests in
and around the schools, so that the children may hear Him speak to them
in His own words. I appeal to the House of Commons now, at the eleventh
hour, to use its great influence and lift its commanding voice and say,
"Pray, silence for the Master."

Mr. Balfour, speaking later in the debate, paid a striking tribute
to the work of his opponent upon the Bill :

There is the hon. member for the Carnarvon Boroughs, who through
these debates has played, in my judgment, a most distinguished part,
though, I confess, I wish he had left unsaid, even from his own point of
view, a great many things which he sometimes said. If he had omitted a
certain class of observations I think he would have greatly gained in
authority inside and outside the House. I believe that in the opinion of
both sides of the House and of the country the hon. gentleman has shown
himself to be an eminent Parliamentarian.

Those were generous words, and marked the Prime Minister's
appreciation of the fact that Mr. Lloyd George's opposition to
the Bill had not been factious or obstructive. But his opposition
did not end with the passing of the Bill into law. The placing of

the Education Act upon the statute-book opened a new and remarkable chapter in the history of Wales, in which Mr. Lloyd
George, whom English Nonconformists had been happy to
acclaim as their champion, reverted to his old allegiance and
became once more, and with higher authority and enhanced
prestige, the national leader of Wales.

III

His " first set-to " with Mr. Austen Chamberlain—Public meetings of the year—With Lord
Rosebery and Mr. Asquith at the Queen's Hall—With Mr. Perks at Lincoln.

The national struggle which he led is the next phase in his
career to be considered.   Meanwhile, to complete the chronicle
of his activities in 1902, there are one or two outstanding events
to be recorded.   It is worth noting that, in August, he had what
he describes as his " first set-to " with Mr. Austen Chamberlain.
The occasion of it was a discussion of the expenditure on the
Navy and Army which need not concern us except as a land-
mark in the relations of two politicians.   It is unnecessary to
do much more than barely chronicle some of the great meetings
which he addressed, since to detail their incidents would be to
repeat a monotonous tale of enthusiastic gatherings.
    For the Liberal Party the Education Bill came like an in-
credible elixir of new life.   Differences were forgotten, men who
had come to calling one another names during the war met upon
the platform as staunch friends.   Lord Rosebery was as strong
as any one in his opposition to the Bill.   Political life is often
kaleidoscopic in its sudden turns and changes, and men have
grown used to its quick transformations, but even so it seemed
a marvel to many when it was announced in June that Mr.
Asquith and Mr. Lloyd George were to speak at a Queen's Hall
meeting over which Lord Rosebery was to preside.   It gave a
touch of additional interest to the incident that the invitation
to attend had come to Mr. Lloyd George through Mr. Perks, for
the " pro-Boer " Lloyd George and " Imperial Perks " had said
some hard things of one another while the war continued.
Liberalism was profiting, not for the first or last time, by the
arrogance and the blunders of its foes, and Liberals were beginning to seek unity and ensure it by exercising, in Lord Rosebery's
phrase, " the habit of common action."   That habit will unify
a party much more quickly than a formula or a clean slate.
    It was a very different Queen's Hall meeting from that which
Mr. Lloyd George addressed in June 1901.   Twelve months had

worked wonders.   The great audience, in which Nonconformity was, of course, largely represented, gave an equally cordial greeting to Lord Rosebery and to the reading of a letter from Sir Henry Campbell-Bannerman.   When Mr. Lloyd George rose to speak he had perhaps the most remarkable ovation of the evening.   Applause rang out again and again from every part of the crowded building, hats and handkerchiefs were waved, and the meeting seemed carried beyond itself with enthusiasm.   Mr. Lloyd George did not presume upon his reception : his speech was short and trenchant.   They had been taunted, he said, with presenting a united front that evening.   If it was the first time, it certainly would not be the last.   They were united in opposition to a thoroughly bad Bill.   Who originated it ?   Cardinal Vaughan.   Who pressed it upon the Ministry ?   Convocation. He dealt with Mr. Chamberlain in one stinging sentence : " The advocacy of this Bill is the last act of treachery in the career of one who has sold many of his convictions."

Rather happily, he suggested an analogy between the administration of Education and of the Navy.   What would happen if the latter were placed under sectarian control, and we had a Roman Catholic battleship, a Methodist torpedo-boat, an Anglican torpedo-catcher, a Congregationalist cruiser, and a Baptist submarine ?   The enemy would be sacking Buckingham Palace, while our ships were firing at each other.

The observant among the audience noticed that when he sat down he was beckoned to a chair near Lord Rosebery, who seemed to have much to say to him.

In October he addressed a mass meeting at Leicester ; in November, at a demonstration of London Welshmen in the St. James's Hall, he had another of the oratorical triumphs that were becoming a commonplace with him.   One of his public speeches, which may be taken as typical of those he delivered upon the platform on this question, is appended to this volume.[1]   It was delivered at Lincoln, on December 12, under the presidency of Mr. Perks.   From being boycotted and distrusted, Mr. Lloyd George had become, in a few months, the most popular platform speaker that any Liberal Association could invite to address a meeting.   But duty and inclination united to turn his attention and his activities to Wales.

[1] Appendix II.

CHAPTER VI

I

Wales and the Education Act—Mr. Lloyd George on Passive Resistance—His manifesto to the people of Wales.

"AMONG the Welsh members," a Welsh correspondent wrote in the "Times" in an article on "Wales in 1902," which reviewed the history of the Principality during the year, "Mr. Lloyd George alone has succeeded in making any considerable reputation in the House of Commons, and his personal friends already confidently speak of him as the next Liberal Home Secretary. His success is due to something more than mere cleverness in debate—to confidence in himself, political consistency, and sheer hard work and application—qualities by no means typically Celtic. It is noteworthy, too, that Mr. Lloyd George, ardent Welshman as he is, has won his place as the spokesman, not of Welsh causes, but of militant English Nonconformity; and he seems likely to become another Henry Richard rather than a second Tom Ellis." The coming of 1903, however, found Mr. Lloyd George at the head of a national movement, powerful beyond the dreams of any of the political prophets. It was a movement which he was peculiarly fitted to inaugurate by the genius for organisation which he combined with daring and imagination. The Revolt, as it was called, although he always denied that a movement which he asserted to be perfectly law-abiding deserved to be styled rebellious, was an event of such importance in his history that it is proposed to proceed at once with some account of it. The dying years of the Tory Government saw the beginning of other struggles which were no doubt of greater moment to the kingdom and the Empire than this fierce fight in Wales. In all these struggles Mr. Lloyd George bore a part which must be related, but it seems proper to postpone their consideration until the story of his campaign in Wales has been told in some detail.

In England the Education Act was resented as an injustice by Nonconformists. In Wales it was regarded as an insult by almost the whole nation. Welshmen of every party were proud, and properly so, of the national achievements in the sphere of education. They could point to them as being both a practical expression of the Welsh zeal for the acquisition of knowledge, and an illustration of the success which Wales had obtained in a sphere of activity where she was sufficiently autonomous to be able to work out her own destiny. One of the direct results of the Liberal and Nonconformist revival of 1868 which followed the Reform Bill of 1867 was the appointment of a departmental committee to inquire into the condition of intermediate and higher education in Wales. Difficulties relating to rating and local government kept the question in abeyance until the creation of County Councils in 1888. The Welsh Education Act, which became law a year later, empowered the newly constituted Councils to levy a county rate for education, and brought into existence a Central Welsh Board, with partial control over the county authorities. The results abundantly justified the pride which Mr. Lloyd George showed in the achievements of his country. " I am going to swagger now," he told his audience jestingly at Lincoln,[1] when he compared the educational progress of Wales with that of England. There was every excuse for it. Englishmen are apt to grumble at the disproportionate part played in the life of England by the Welshman and the Scot. They ought to blame the schoolmaster over the border, unless indeed they can be persuaded, for their own good, to blame themselves.

It is a sad illustration of our propensity to find the cause of our failures in the injustice of others rather than in any shortcomings of our own that so many Englishmen, at the beginning of the twentieth century, were ready to attend greedily to a preacher who told them that if their businesses were not flourishing the unfair competition of Germans was to blame, while they could never be much stirred by warnings that they would never compete on terms of equality with Germans, or even with their Celtic fellow-subjects, unless they took the trouble to educate themselves and their children up to a standard of efficiency equal to that of their rivals.

By the scanty provision made in the Act of 1902 for higher education, Englishmen stood convicted of an indifference to its value which made it ludicrous that England should seek to teach lessons to Wales and force upon her legislation she disliked. In England it might be urged with some degree of plausibility that Noncon-

[1] See Appendix II.

formists were in a minority, and minorities must suffer. In Wales there were few parents who desired their children to be educated in the tenets of the Church, and for their benefit a Nonconformist country was to be compelled to pay rates for the propagation of dogmas it disbelieved and the preservation in the schools of an atmosphere which it deemed stifling and oppressive.

Where Wales had been allowed to look after her own affairs, the religious difficulty had disappeared. In the sphere of intermediate education the schools had been placed outside the area of denominational strife, and Wales had become practically a national entity. It was small wonder that Welshmen of all schools regarded as a tragic blunder the application to Wales of a measure which took no account of Welsh national needs or feelings and made her primary schools a cockpit of sectarian strife. In England Nonconformist opponents of the Act determined to refuse payment of the education rate on conscientious grounds, to allow their goods to be sold up and themselves to be imprisoned. It was no secret that Mr. Lloyd George was not very greatly enamoured of this policy of " passive resistance," in so far as it was to be regarded as a matter of tactics, although he thought it not merely justifiable, but a necessary consequence of conscientious convictions.

It is perhaps unprofitable to discuss how far resistance to a law constitutionally enacted can ever be justified. Undoubtedly the Conservative Government had a constitutional " right " to introduce the Education Act and to pass it, if they could, through both Houses. For that purpose they were using the general authority which had been given them at the election of 1900, and it is quite certain that there is no place in the British Constitution for any theory of " mandate." It is equally clear that the Government had obtained its authority by a deliberate concealment of its designs. Such a concealment did not affect constitutional " right," but an Executive which chose to abuse the rights obtained by its means was not likely to escape retribution. It is too much to expect loyal obedience from an electorate of angry and resentful dupes.

Mr. Lloyd George had defended the passive resisters in the House of Commons with some apt references to the attitude of Conservatives upon the Irish question. In the summer of 1902 [1] he reminded the Government that the whole body of Welsh Congregationalists, responsible men, with trusted and trusty leaders, had passed a resolution declaring that if the Bill were passed without drastic amendment they would deem it their bounden duty to resist the payment of rates for the

[1] July 9.

voluntary schools. Mr. Balfour had said that to resist the payment of rates would be an immoral proceeding. Why? he asked. If a man had a conscientious objection to obeying the law, was it an immoral act for him to defy it? When the Government had been challenged to take steps to preserve liberty of speech for opponents of the Boer War, Mr. Balfour had pleaded that there were " limits to human endurance " and that our weak nature could not be expected to tolerate the extreme expression of unpopular opinions. Mr. Balfour held, then, that a mob was justified, under the influence of passion and excitement, in smashing property and endangering life, while he refused to recognise in the dictates of conscience any justification for a peaceable refusal to comply except under compulsion with the requirements of law. If Mr. Gladstone's Home Rule Bill had been enacted, not only would Mr. Balfour have condoned violent resistance in Ulster, but he had openly preached the doctrine, " Ulster will fight, and Ulster will be right." It did not lie in his mouth to reproach with immorality Nonconformists who refused to pay the rates demanded of them by a law which had no moral sanction behind it.

Those who sought to show that the Nonconformist grievance against the Act was hollow and insincere made much of the fact that Nonconformists had for years suffered in silence, if they had suffered at all, under a system which subsidised denominationalism. What, it was asked, was the magic which made the imposition of a rate intolerable when the imposition of a tax had been imperceptible or innocuous? The criticism was a fair one, and needed an answer, and Mr. Lloyd George did not shirk it. Characteristically, he did not make his argument depend upon any subtle distinctions between rates and taxes. He recognised frankly enough that the Nonconformist attitude was not logical. It was illogical in the sense that a man is illogical who says nothing if you steal his matches and shouts if you steal his purse :

Why are we now objecting to pay rates, whereas we have been paying taxes all these years? Well, I think that is a very fair question ; and my first answer is that the people did not realise that they were paying taxes towards denominational schools. I doubt very much whether people realised, until the Act was carried through the House of Commons, that they had been contributing something like five millions of money every year towards sectarian education from the privileges of which Nonconformists were excluded. The thing had been done quietly and stealthily—one of the tricks of darkness—and therefore people did not realise what had been done. It was only when the Government began to tackle the rates that people thought about it. The people did not think taxes came from their own pockets. There was an institution in a district, and when any one asked who maintained it, the reply was " Oh, it is the Government." The Government was something outside the individual. It was a sort of providence to which the people felt they contributed nothing and over which they had no control. Taxation is something that droppeth like the gentle dew from heaven. People do not realise, when a thing comes from the Government, that the Government is simply another name for themselves. I do not want to flatter you, but that is what it is. But when you come to the ratepayer, the ratepayer is an individual. Look at him at an election. He comes and asks questions of his representative. No doubt he belongs to a ratepayers' association. The taxpayer is like a corporation, with no body to be kicked or soul to be damned, as the lawyers say. The ratepayer is alive—a person whom you can pinch with a heavy rate. The Government did not realise that elementary fact of political philosophy, or perhaps they would not have interfered with the rates. That is the first reason. I will give you another reason. The thing was done so stealthily. Prior to the Act of 1870 the sectarian schools of this country got something like £500,000 a year. That was all. From £500,000 it had grown to pretty nearly five millions before this Act was passed. That sum was given to sectarian institutions, managed by sects and the nominees of sects, and the special privileges of which went exclusively to sects. The only thing for the general body of taxpayers to do was to pay the five millions. How had that been altered? It had been altered gradually. There was a little bit of an Act giving free education. A few millions went to the Church schools by that Act. There was an act of the Council for another purpose, giving a few hundred thousands to the Church schools. Gradually, without the nation realising it, the sum given to Church schools has risen from £500,000 to five millions in the course of a generation. But at last the Government have made a mistake, and I am glad they have done it. They made the mistake a burglar sometimes makes. When a burglar sticks to one drawer, the moment it is open he makes no noise and he can scoop it clean. But if he opens a fresh drawer, he awakens the inmates and is liable to be arrested. That is exactly what the Government and the clergy have done. As long as the taxpayer's drawer was open there was no noise, no fuss, no friction, and they gathered in the shekels year after year. But they were like all foolish people are—and who so greedy as the clergy when it comes to a question of power for their own order? They started opening a fresh drawer—the ratepayer's drawer—and the ratepayer's drawer is very near his pillow, and he wakes up. What is the difference now between our attitude towards the taxes and our attitude towards the rates? Formerly Governments were dealing with a nation that was asleep. They are now dealing with a nation that is awake. It is very easy to rob a sleeping nation.[1]

Mr. Lloyd George accepted " passive resistance," then, as a principle, if not as a policy. Considered as a means of em-

[1] Aberystwyth, October 1903.

barrassing the Government, it was likely to be ineffective ; but that did not affect the question of its ethical justification. For Wales, however, he had a much bolder scheme, which in England would have been impossible. It was a scheme to which only a strong national feeling could have given any hope of success. Party feeling would have been worse than useless : resistance to an Act of Parliament by a mere faction only serves to rally to its support the habitual opponents of that faction. In Wales the ordinary party divisions were ready to be broken down. On every side there was resentment against the Act which only needed leadership to swell it into revolt.

The unanimity with which Wales looked to Mr. Lloyd George for that leadership was a remarkable tribute to the place he had gained in public life. Some hoped that he would declare for the heroic course of refusing to administer the Act at all, others that he would find a way of compromise. But, for the most part, men to whom different courses recommended themselves were content to look to the member for the Carnarvon Boroughs, a man just forty years of age, for guidance in the struggle and to accept whatever policy his sagacity might dictate.

On January 17, 1903, he issued an address to the people of Wales.[1] He declared definitely against a general refusal by the County Councils of Wales to administer the Act. He knew a better way : " Let us capture the enemy's artillery and turn his guns against him." In other words, his plan was to work the Act, to work it thoroughly and systematically, not indeed according to the intention of its authors, but by so taking advantage of the letter of the law as to convert a measure of oppression into a means of regeneration.

" Our object ought to be," he declared, " to labour for complete educational autonomy for Wales." Tom Ellis had hoped to obtain autonomy for his country by using and developing the power of working in combination which the Act of 1888 conferred upon the County Councils it created. He had seen that it was not impossible to make such co-operation the germ of Welsh Home Rule. Similarly, Mr. Lloyd George now proposed to use the powers granted to the Councils by the Education Act to bring into being a National Council of Education. That was his ultimate constructive aim ; meanwhile it was necessary to thwart the scheme for subsidising denominational teaching. He had managed to get an amendment accepted which relieved a local authority from undertaking the upkeep of a school unless it was in proper repair. It was notorious that the fabric of many

[1] Appendix III.

of the Church schools in Wales had been sadly neglected. He advised that a survey should be made, impartially, of all the elementary schools in each county, and that none should be taken over until the building had been put into good and tenant-able repair. " The sectarian schools should be properly cleansed and clothed before they are allowed to associate on equal terms with more decently clad institutions."

For the rest, his plan, as he now propounded it, was one which he summarised later in the phrase " No control, no cash." He advised that only the Parliamentary grant should be transmitted to the schools, and that no rate aid should be afforded them, unless the trustees consented to public control of the funds voted and to the abandonment of all religious tests for the teachers engaged. But the Councils, while declaring war, should proclaim their readiness to make peace. The basis for compromise should be an offer of the " Colonial " system of " facilities " for teaching the doctrines of the parent. If that offer was refused, Liberals and Nonconformists would have escaped the responsibility for whatever mischief followed.

If the Councils adopted this policy, there would be no occasion for individuals to refuse rates. If any of the Councils enforced the collection of a rate for the purposes of the Act, then it would be the duty of Liberals and Nonconformists to make the collection of the rate as difficult as possible. But if, after the County Council elections, to be held in 1904, the electors chose to return denomina-tionalists to the Councils, they must accept the judgment of the electors unless they were prepared to say that under no conditions would they contribute towards the support of denominational schools, even though the nation after due deliberation resolved upon it. For a democratic community such a proposition seemed, he said, untenable.

At first sight Mr. Lloyd George's advice to refuse rate aid looked like flat rebellion. But, as we shall see presently, he was able to justify even that part of his plan according to the letter of a law which no one had studied more carefully than himself. His scheme was as ingenious as it was daring, and perhaps its greatest merit lay in the fact that while it was militant enough to satisfy a nation now thoroughly aroused, it was yet not so rebellious as to alarm an essentially law-abiding people. It embodied, as Mr. Lloyd George himself put it, Portia's principle of the pound of flesh and no more, and the Welsh acclaimed a Daniel come to judgment.

II

The first Cardiff Conference—A demand for equality—The plan of campaign.

Mr. Gladstone once said to the Welsh people : " Your sub-missiveness is sheep-like." " We are going to substitute for the sheep on our national flag the dragon," said Mr. Lloyd George. The response to his appeal was immediate.

A great national gathering at Cardiff was convened by the Welsh National Liberal Council, of which Mr. Lloyd George was now President. There were present representatives of County Councils, School Boards, religious bodies, and political institutions, met to consider the new demand made upon the local authorities by the Government.

The Government came to the County Councils—Nonconformist County Councils—to say, " The Church schools are being starved out of existence gradually, and we call upon you Nonconformist County Councils to levy a rate, which will be paid in the main by Nonconformist ratepayers, for the purpose of preventing this system—which is an injury and an injustice to your faith—of preventing it from going out of existence and being substituted by a free, a popular, and a fair system." That is practically what they asked us to do. It is exactly as if the Boers in the late war had come to us and said, " Gentlemen, we are not fighting on equal terms ; you have captured all our ammunition, you have deprived us of food. We really can't keep up the fighting on these terms ; in fact, it is an intolerable strain on our resources, and unless you help us we shall have to surrender. We observe you are voting large sums of money to your own army in South Africa ; be fair, vote a few hundreds of thousands to us, so that we can fight on equal terms." Now, that is practically the demand which has been made upon us by this Act of Parliament : we are to vote the supplies for the purpose of keeping up a hostile army ; we are to fill their war-chests, their ammunition boxes. What for ? In order to enable them to fight the only educational system which gives a scintilla of fair play to men of our own faith.

A self-respecting nation has only one answer to give to that, and that is " No, thank you." [1]

At the Cardiff Conference of 1903 the question was what form the negative should take. Resolutions were carried based upon the address to the Welsh people which Mr. Lloyd George had issued. He persuaded the fiercer spirits that the policy of refusing to work the Act at all would be a misguided one. Let them work it for all it was worth—they would find it had been so

[1] Speech at the second Cardiff Conference, October 6, 1904.

badly drafted that there were things in it worth working. Where they found provisions in the Act which they thought unsuitable to the needs of the locality, let them work it in the good old spirit of the British Constitution, which was never in a hurry about anything.

He founded his policy upon four main principles. The first was " equality of citizenship." There was no equality of citizenship if the parishioners had no voice in the management of the parish school. One man gave an acre of land out of five thousand acres on which to build a school, or perhaps his father gave it before him. He had a voice by right in the management of the school, to which he never sent a child. The parson had a voice in the management. The carpenter, the farmer, the farm labourer, the grocer—men as necessary to the village as the parson (a parish might prosper even spiritually without a parson)—had no voice. It was true they had no acres to give away, and they were not in Holy Orders, but they made a larger contribution than any one—they contributed the children, and contributed to the children's welfare.

The three other principles were equality of creed, equality of opportunity for the children, and equality of nationality. Religious tests for teachers infringed the principle of equality of creed. The children had not equality of opportunity while posts as teachers were reserved for a select few, and " they must ascend by the Anglican ladder if they wished to reach to the top." There was not equality between the nations : England, Scotland, and Ireland had systems which suited them ; Wales, who had done so well with her own system of secondary education, was expected to submit to a system of primary education forced upon her by an outside nationality.

Scotland has her own system of education. It may be good or it may be bad—it just depends upon taste. Some like Scotch broth, some do not. I think the Scottish system admirable, and I would recommend it for Wales. Scotchmen, with that natural intelligence which they have developed, have got hold of the right idea. They have their own system. Ireland has her own system. Her schools are managed by the priests, but she has the system because she wants it. England has her own system, if system it can be called. It is everything, higgledy-piggledy : partly sectarian, partly School Board, party County Council, but above all thoroughly English.

These words show a very sound tendency to make the democratic principle the keystone of policy. The theorist and doctrinaire looks for an ideal system of education and seeks to impose it universally. There is no ideal system of education : there may be ideal systems. Democracy means government by consent of the governed. Nationalists recognise that the consent of the governed is not obtained unless and until the units of responsible government are coincident, as far as may be, with areas of common language, common habits of thought, and common aspirations. The Government's educational policy towards Wales was ultimately based upon a denial of her nationality. Such a denial made government by consent impossible, and, with the best intentions, substituted a half-hearted absolutism for a generous democratic rule. If the County Councils had tamely acquiesced, and levied a rate for the assistance of the voluntary schools at a time when feeling ran so high, they would have had to face a much more serious and widespread " Passive Resistance " movement than ever existed in England. As it was, by Mr. Lloyd George's persuasion, they adopted a policy for which he claimed that, when it was pursued in its integrity, as it was by the majority of the Councils, it kept within the four corners of the written law in every particular.

In his speech at Cardiff, and again a few days later at Pwllheli and Carnarvon, he amplified the details of the policy he recommended. He built largely on the fact that the denominational schools had been treated with great leniency by the Board of Education. In fact, many of them were not efficient, according to the most modern tests. But Government inspectors, looking with a favourable eye upon voluntary schools, had been charitable enough to represent them as efficient. The Act placed upon the Councils the duty of " keeping " these schools efficient. It was possible, Mr. Lloyd George argued, to keep them in the condition which, previously to the passing of the Act, had been accepted as efficiency, without having resort to the rates at all. The Act had increased the Parliamentary grant which the denominational schools had enjoyed since 1870. This grant would, he contended, be found to be amply sufficient to keep them in a condition not less efficient than that which had satisfied the Board of Education. " No doubt the Board strained the law and the truth in calling them so. But they are estopped now by their own conduct from prosecuting county councillors as law-breakers for the mere offence of imitating the Board's own example." [1] It was indeed open to the County Councils to take a more extreme course and to refuse even the Parliamentary grant to schools which were not in good order and repair. This was another reason of his advice to Councils to make a careful

[1] See " Westminster Gazette," May 14, 1904.

survey of the schools within their control. If they exercised
their powers to the full, they could, he held, refuse to transmit
even the Parliamentary grant to schools which were found to
be inadequate, unsuitable, and insanitary. Unfortunately such
schools existed in large numbers. " Up to the present," he said
a year later, " we have not exercised our full powers. This is
the only point in which it can be fairly said that we have not
carried out the law."

He would not admit that it was a policy of defiance. It was
intended to be a policy of administering the strict letter of the
law—" the letter that killeth."

We decided that if they were going to insist on their Act of Parliament,
or, in Shakespearean language, if they were going to insist upon redeeming
this bond obtained through the House of Commons by a species of Parliamentary fraud, we would give them the bond, but only " just a pound
of flesh "—not more or less than just one pound—not " so much as makes
it light or heavy in the substance, or the division of the twentieth part
of one poor scruple, nay, that it should not turn the scale even in the
estimation of a hair." We said, "We will deal with these ecclesiastical
Shylocks upon that footing. We will give them just one pound of flesh,
but no blood except what we have drawn." [1]

III

The attempt at a Concordat—The Bishop of St. Asaph—A Conference at Llandrindod—
Sir Henry Campbell-Bannerman on " the Revolt."

Mr. Lloyd George, as an Alderman of the Carnarvon County
Council, had an opportunity of directing the campaign in his own
constituency. He was appointed a member of the Education Committee, and at its first meeting he proposed a resolution urging the
Council to approach the authorities of the denominational schools
with a view to compromise. The suggestion made was that the
voluntary schools should accept the Colonial plan of facilities,
outside school hours, for special religious instruction, and content
themselves otherwise with a measure of unsectarian teaching on
the generous lines adopted under the Cowper-Temple clause by
some of the leading School Boards. The committee was constituted of members of both political parties, and the resolution
was seconded by Mr. Greaves, the lord-lieutenant of the county
and its most influential Unionist. It was not Liberals and Nonconformists alone who were bent upon making public control
effective in Wales, and giving their country a system which
could be called national.

[1] Cardiff, October 6, 1904.

Among the clergy, unfortunately, there was no general willingness for compromise. There was one notable exception. One Welsh bishop stood alone among his colleagues in his readiness to make peace and pave the way to a national system. This was Mr. Lloyd George's old opponent, Bishop Edwards of St. Asaph. The three other Welsh bishops refused even to meet the County Councils. There were negotiations between the Councils and the St. Asaph Diocesan Association which for a time promised well to lead to a "concordat." A conference at Llandrindod was followed by round-table discussions in London. We have Mr. Lloyd George's testimony to the fact that "the meetings were of the most friendly and pleasant character."[1] Among the representatives of the Church was the distinguished novelist, Mr. Stanley Weyman, "who was most reasonable and helpful." These moderate champions of Anglicanism asked that a syllabus of religious instruction should be drawn up, modelled on that of the London School Board, and should be adopted for all the schools impartially, while for the children of parents who desired it there should be definite denominational instruction at least four times a week, given outside school hours, in every school. It was conceded by the Churchmen that there should be no compulsion upon any child to attend during this religious teaching. The negotiations were broken off upon the question of the appointment of teachers, owing, it was suspected, to the fact that the Bishop could not carry the clergy of his diocese with him. The County Council representatives were not prepared to give the clergy the right to teach not their own children only, but all the children attending elementary schools, and refused to give up the control of the schools.

The breakdown of the negotiations, Mr. Lloyd George said, had nothing to do with the purely spiritual side of the Church demands.

The Welsh people have good ground for believing that a section of the clergy overruled the wiser heads among their leaders. The Bishop of St. Asaph, in order to shield this section of his clergy, chivalrously ascribes their action to other motives, but the laity—Church and Nonconformist— will continue to believe that it was attributable to their reluctance to surrender the practical monopoly of power and patronage in the voluntary schools conferred upon them by the various Education Acts. As long as this attitude is maintained by the clergy anything in the nature of a friendly arrangement of the difficulties is out of the question.

The Welsh County Councils can consent to no terms which will not include the appointment of the teachers whose entire salaries they will be

[1] "Westminster Gazette," May 14, 1904.

now called upon to pay—neither can they accept any proposals which
involve the imposition of any sectarian or theological tests in the selection
of any of the members of the school staff, or which will confer any privileges upon the clergy of one denomination which they are not prepared
to extend to the ministers of all denominations. Subject to these general
limitations, they are willing to meet the sincere wishes of Church parents
as to the training of their children. They are also prepared to give practical recognition to the fact that the Church has invested enormous sums
of money in the erection of their schools. Intolerance and confiscation
are alike averse to the policy of the Welsh Progressives. They can appeal
confidently to their record on the Welsh School Boards and the county
governing bodies and the County Councils in support of this contention.
Churchmen have secured positions under these various bodies in numbers
which are largely in excess of any proportionate claim they could set up.

Now that the moderate proposals of the Councils have been rejected
by the clergy, nothing remains to be done but to fight out the issues
between the parties. When the next Parliament comes to deal with the
question the clergy will have good cause to regret the stubbornness which
prompted them, in spite of all counsel given them by the best friends in
their own household, to refuse to agree with their adversary in the way.[1]

The failure of the Llandrindod Conference was followed by a
further conference, this time at Swansea, of representatives of
local authorities.[2] At this conference Mr. Lloyd George still
maintained that the Councils could destroy the purpose of the
Act by administering its letter. He was anxious to make clear
what risk was run, and he admitted the possibility that the local
authorities might be brought into conflict with the Courts and
the dread weapon of "mandamus." The granting of a mandamus
is, as he reminded his audience, a matter of discretion, and even
if judges were inclined, in the exercise of their discretion, to grant
it, they could not do so until all the facts—facts, as he believed,
conclusive of the justice of their case—had been elicited, not
before that court alone, but before the tribunal of the public
conscience. "It was their business to bring out the facts from
the obscure little parishes of Wales and plant them on pinnacles
where all could see them."

A resolution was carried at his instance, which declared it
to be unjustifiable to provide money for the voluntary schools
out of the rates unless and until the whole management of the
schools was vested in the body levying the rate, and recommended
the Councils to refrain from applying rates to the support of such
schools.

So successful was his policy that in July he was able to tell

[1] From an article by Mr. Lloyd George in "The Pilot," June 1, 1903.
[2] May 19, 1903.

MR. LLOYD GEORGE AT PLAY.

The upper photograph shows Mr. Lloyd George with his brother. The figure in the lower
is Mr. G. P. Williams, his first Sunday-school teacher, and an old supporter.

(Photographs by Ernest Mills.)

an enthusiastic audience of Nonconformists, assembled at the Albert Hall, that up to that time not a single one of the Welsh County Councils had levied the rate. The occasion was a meeting, one of the greatest which even the Albert Hall had ever held, called to protest against the London Education Bill, by which the Government was abolishing the London School Board and extending to the metropolis the principles of the Education Act. Mr. Lloyd George counselled passive resistance to the seventeen or eighteen thousand Free Churchmen who had assembled. In Wales he said there was no passive resistance, because there was nothing to resist. Let London follow the Welsh example.

At a Welsh Liberal Conference held at Bangor in September, and attended by Welsh members of Parliament and representatives of the County Councils and the educational institutions of Wales, a resolution which declared that no system of education would satisfy Wales unless it were national and unsectarian, with safeguards against dogma and religious tests, was carried by an overwhelming majority. The discussion was notable for a declaration which it drew from Mr. Lloyd George upon the so-called " secular " solution. An amendment to the resolution was proposed in favour of the abolition of all Bible teaching in the schools supported by public money. Mr. Lloyd George opposed it in a speech which was received with acclamation. In effect, he said, the amendment asked the Government to place the Bible upon an Index Expurgatorius, and he would vote for no such proposition.

At the end of 1903 Sir Henry Campbell-Bannerman gave his benediction to Mr. Lloyd George's campaign in a speech he delivered at Tredegar :

How magnificent is the attitude of Wales ! The spirit of religious liberty has been kept alive in the recesses of your mountains, and you are resolved that a measure which is repugnant to the moral feelings of the community shall not be forced upon you. Oh, but they say you are only a set of narrow-minded Nonconformists, caring about your little sect, but caring but little for the education of your children. This is the taunt constantly hurled at Mr. Lloyd George and his friends—Mr. Lloyd George, your foremost champion—yes, and the champion of us all—against clerical pretensions and political injustice. This is the taunt levelled against them again and again by the Prime Minister—that they have thought and spoken of the religious difficulty, and not of education. All this is said to Welshmen, who have shown a devotion to higher education, whether intermediate or university, and an ability to organise it, and an interest in its progress, second to nothing south of the Tweed.

CHAPTER VII

I

The County Council elections, 1904—A great triumph—The Government's difficulty—
The "Coercion of Wales" Bill.

IT was due to the foresight of Mr. Lloyd George that the administration of the Act in Wales had been given to the County Councils. At his instigation Sir Alfred Thomas had moved an amendment, which the Government in its innocence accepted, abolishing the county governing bodies and making the County Councils the supreme authorities in Wales as in England. By many, that amendment had been regarded as a leap in the dark. It had, however, a very real purpose behind it, and was in reality a brilliant stroke of generalship. The hope of Mr. Lloyd George's plan for removing the sting from the Act lay in the unity and solidity of the County Councils. They were elected bodies, and Mr. Lloyd George had counted upon the fact that the County Council elections were to be held in 1904. In 1903 the personality of Mr. Lloyd George had done much, and the activity of the Free Church Councils hardly less, to keep the County Councils up to the necessary pitch. Only two Councils, those of Radnor and Brecon, had consented at this date to give rate aid to schools refusing to admit popular control and maintaining religious tests for teachers. At the beginning of the first Session of 1904 the air was full of rumours as to the intentions of the Government towards recalcitrant Wales. Some prophesied that they would introduce a pacificatory measure which, if it offended the more extreme clerics, would at least satisfy the great majority of laymen, whose views the Bishop of St. Asaph was felt to represent with greater accuracy than his three colleagues. Others believed that some kind of coercive legislation would be introduced, replacing by shorter and sharper methods the cumbrous and ineffective weapon of the mandamus. The latter course seemed the more probable except to the most optimistic, since it needed more courage than the senescent Cabinet possessed to make a wise and timely surrender.   Now was the time, then, for the County Councils to be marshalled in even closer formation. Mr. Lloyd George bent all his energies to the task of ensuring the most complete unanimity possible in the new bodies.   Under his advice Welsh Nonconformists throughout the land took steps to make the administration of the Act the single issue of the elections.   Every old member, and every new candidate, Liberal or Conservative, Nonconformist or Churchman, was put to a rigid test.   Three questions, substantially the same in every district, were submitted to each of them.   Every candidate was asked to pledge himself—

(1) To the policy of full public control of all schools supported from public funds.

(2) To the abolition of all religious tests in the appointment of teachers.

(3) To the support of the declared "no-rate" policy of the Councils.

Nonconformist, Liberal, and Progressive organisations, on their side, pledged themselves not to support any candidate, even if on other questions he were a Liberal, who did not give his adherence to this threefold policy; not to oppose any Conservative or Churchman who did subscribe to its terms; and, finally, to nominate a new Progressive candidate in every constituency where the sitting member would not support their programme. These Progressive associations had the will of the people behind them, and all over the country members who had doubted the expediency of Mr. Lloyd George's plan of campaign hastened to give him their allegiance.   "Throughout the length and breadth of the land," Mr. Lloyd George proudly declared, "there was such an uprising of the people as had not been seen in Wales since the days of Llewellyn." [1]   The only fear was, according to the Welsh correspondent of one of the organs of Nonconformity, [2] that Mr. Lloyd George himself might once more be involved in the meshes of a "concordat."

They [the rank and file] have more faith in his fighting powers than in his diplomatic skill, and they would regard with very considerable apprehension any re-opening of negotiations in which their honestly daring leader would have to encounter the wily diplomacy of the Bishop of St. Asaph.

However unwise the apprehensions of the writer may have been, his belief in Mr. Lloyd George's conciliatory disposition was

[1] Carnarvon, January 5, 1904.   [2] "Christian World."

not unfounded. In February the member for Carnarvon unanimously carried a resolution, at a meeting of the Welsh members of Parliament, which expressed a hope that the voluntary-school authorities of Wales would be approached with a view to a friendly settlement on the basis of the "Colonial" plan. Meanwhile he did not relax his efforts in the organisation of a sweeping victory in the elections. At Llandrindod he encouraged the warriors of Radnorshire with a fiery oration. If Nonconformists were to take their part as citizens of the Empire, then they insisted on enjoying the full privileges of citizenship. No self-respecting citizens could tolerate the degradation of inferiority in their own land, the badge of inferiority because of the faith they loved, in which their fathers died. And this was the answer of Nonconformists to this Tory Government : "We are British citizens." If Radnorshire had courage, had manliness—if the Nonconformists of Radnorshire had a spark of the spirit of their fathers—they would emphasize this answer at the polls.

Wherever he went he found, he said afterwards, "a spirit of fierce determination animating all classes of the people." A few days before the elections the Government threatened the Carmarthenshire Council with a mandamus—"evidently," Mr. Lloyd George said, "with a view to influencing the result of the elections." If that was indeed the object of the threat, it failed ignominiously.

The result of the elections exceeded the wildest hopes of the Progressives. In every one of the twenty-eight counties, including Brecon and Radnor, the pledged supporters of the "no-rate" policy were in a strong majority. So strong were they that there were only three counties in which it would conceivably be possible to form a quorum if all the Progressive members resigned. In most cases the supporters of the policy of the Act were in a contemptible minority. In Carnarvonshire there were only six opponents of Mr. Lloyd George's policy in a council of sixty-five. In Merionethshire the figures were fifty-two to three. In Brecon, where the Progressive cause was weakest, thirty-nine members of a council of sixty members had taken the pledge imposed by Liberal and Free Church bodies in pursuance of the "Welsh national policy."

"It is an inspiring victory," Mr. Lloyd George said to an interviewer. "Wales for the first time in anything like recent history is united in its stand for freedom. Even in the great year of 1868 there were a few constituencies that stood outside the national movement. To-day Wales is one and undivided. There is something quite thrilling in the quiet but firm note of defiance issued by the Welsh people through the ballot-box in reply to the menace of this Tory Government." [1]

He gave a piece of advice to the Councils which went further to increase the strength of their resistance. It was the fair and salutary habit of the Liberal County Councils of Wales to treat their opponents generously in the way of giving them a proportion of the Aldermen. Under ordinary conditions it would have been wise and equitable, he said, to continue that generous policy, but unfortunately the Government had issued a declaration of war, and their friends must accept martial law. It was of primary importance that where the Tory councillors did not constitute a quorum, their numbers should not be so increased as to enable them to make a quorum by themselves without the presence of the Liberals. He therefore urged the Councils, as a temporary measure, to hold the advantage gained at the polls and cut down the number of Conservative Aldermen.

After this, Mr. Lloyd George was able to face the Government with calm confidence. On March 14 he moved to reduce the vote on the Estimates by £500 in order to call attention to the administration of the Education Act. His speech was agreed on all sides to be temperate and restrained : in the circumstances he could afford to dispense with rhetoric, and it was said that he quite disappointed Sir William Anson, who had expected a violent onslaught and nerved himself to meet it. He urged the Government to " prevent the worst features of the Act from being rigidly carried out " pending the settlement, which, as everybody was beginning to believe, must come. He warned the Cabinet, with incisive sarcasm, that it was as difficult to persuade a man with strong convictions to abandon his position as it was to persuade the members of a Government with no convictions to abandon their posts—an unpleasantly apposite allusion to the unsettled convictions of the Cabinet upon the topic of Free Trade. He quoted the precedent of that " sound constitutional authority," Mr. Walter Long, who had said of the statutes relating to the driving of motor-cars that the law had been defied and—there must be amendment. He quoted some remarkable instances of the way in which the Act was working. In one case (Pantglas) the parishioners were almost exclusively Nonconformist. Everybody in the place had contributed to the building of the school. But the site for it was given by a member of the Church of England, and so it came about that the trust-deeds of the school were so framed as to make it a " Church " school. In course of time it had become necessary to repair and enlarge the school,

[1] " Manchester Guardian," March 12, 1904.

and the parishioners had been called upon for further subscriptions. They made it a condition of their offerings that the school should be managed, in a real sense, as a parochial school. The vicar bowed to the inevitable, and a committee of management was appointed which represented the parishioners. Upon this state of things the Education Act supervened. The clergyman, allured by the dazzling prospect of enforced contributions from the bottomless purse of the ratepayer, at once threw over the parishioners and obtained an order from the Board of Education for new managers. In the result a school, built and maintained largely by Nonconformists, which had not a single child of Anglican parents in it, was being managed by a board on which no Nonconformist sat.

Sir William Anson's reply was to attribute to his Welsh opponents the motives of political animosity, religious bigotry, and even personal ambition. Mr. Balfour threatened vaguely that, if illegality were persisted in, " some remedy must be devised." He might well hesitate to prescribe. An ingenious collector of the unconsidered trifles of debate was not slow to remind him of some words he had used in 1900 when the Housing question was before Parliament.

How is it to be remedied ? According to the leader of the Opposition it is to be remedied by giving greater powers to the local authorities. . . . But if the local authorities do not use the powers placed in their hands, then they are to be compelled to do so. How are you going to compel the Corporation of Manchester, let us say, for the sake of example, to do something which the central authority thinks it ought to do, but which the Corporation, freely elected, thinks it ought not to do ? Are you going to put them in prison ? Are you going to execute the law over their heads ? A wilder scheme than that of having a central governing authority which is to compel great municipalities like Manchester, Liverpool, and Leeds to do what they do not wish to carry out—a wilder scheme never seems to have entered into the head of a practical statesman.

It was left for Mr. Balfour to conceive the scheme of compelling not a municipality, but a nation, to carry out a scheme against its will.

Mr. Lloyd George had advised that a further conference of delegates from the Welsh educational authorities should be held after the County Council elections. This took place on April 5. Nonconformists were triumphant, but triumph did not turn their heads. There was a sober and serious desire for peace, which Mr. Lloyd George studiously fostered. The best chance of compromise still seemed to be the scheme of facilities for all denominations, and to this he lent the weight of his authority, with the proviso that denominational instruction should be given only outside the ordinary school hours. He gave an answer to the argument which the clergy were in the habit of advancing against this modification of a proposal which in principle appealed to many of them. The clergy said that the right of entry was valueless to them if they could only give religious teaching outside school hours. Why? Because they thought there would not be a very large attendance. But if the parents of the children did not wish them to attend, why should they be forced to attend?

On April 26 the Government did their worst. Their plan to bring the County Councils of Wales into subjection was styled officially the Education (Local Authority Default) Bill, but as it was aimed solely at Wales it was soon known in the common parlance of politicians as the Coercion of Wales Bill. It was a simple and ingenious measure. Where any local authority made default in the performance of its duties, the Bill proposed to empower the Board of Education to expend over the heads of the Council the money required by the managers, and to treat the money so expended as a debt due from the Council to the Crown. There would be no difficulty about collecting the money, as it might be deducted from the Parliamentary grant. Thus a Council which refused to provide money out of rates for the denominational schools would find the Parliamentary grant correspondingly reduced, and would have to levy a heavier rate in order to meet the liabilities of the Council schools. Mr. Lloyd George made a short speech in which he promised a strenuous resistance to the Bill.

If all the County Councils had followed the example of that of which Mr. Lloyd George was Alderman, there would have been no shadow of excuse for the Coercion Bill. As a matter of fact, his plan of campaign had been adopted almost universally. In Carmarthenshire, however, the Council refused to touch the accursed Act at all, and at the end of March the Government sent Mr. A. T. Lawrence, K.C. (afterwards Mr. Justice Lawrence), to inquire as Commissioner into the default of the Council. That authority had plenty to say as to the merits of the case, but this was a topic into which the learned Commissioner was not authorised to inquire. As to the Council's failure to administer the Act, the facts were not disputed. But Carmarthenshire was not a typical case. It had, Mr. Lloyd George said, occupied a more advanced position in the fighting-line than other counties, and that had been a source of weakness and even danger to the national policy. Carnarvonshire had instructed its surveyors to report impartially upon the condition of all schools, board or voluntary. Its refusal to take over the working of the schools had been confined to those which were not in proper repair, and in refusing to administer them it was acting within powers conferred upon it by the Act.

The counties of Carnarvon and Glamorgan, he said at Bangor in the first week of May, had not broken a single letter of the law. Even the Board of Education admitted that. But if the Board insisted upon tightening the screw, Wales would have to consider seriously whether the demands of conscience were not paramount. If the Government did not think the Act sufficiently stringent, despotic, and unfair, and insisted upon strengthening the most obnoxious clauses and oppressing the consciences of Nonconformists, there was but one course—as a nation they would fling back the Act in their teeth, and tell the Government to administer it themselves.

II

The Bishop of St. Asaph's proposals—Mr. Lloyd George's speech on the second reading of the Defaulting Authorities Bill—"The Goths" of Lambeth—The Committee—The guillotine closure—Mr. Lloyd George's protest—Mr. Asquith leads out the Opposition.

The Bishop of St. Asaph and Mr. Lloyd George, those old antagonists, were gradually drawn closer as the controversy proceeded. Here again, as in the case of Mr. Lloyd George's relations with Lord Hugh Cecil, one may notice that the best hope of the ultimate solution of the problems of religious education seems to lie in compromise between men of really strong convictions on either side. At the end of 1903 the leader of the Welsh " Revolt " and the Bishop had met upon a common platform to urge the cause of higher education. In 1904 Mr. Lloyd George was the Bishop's guest at the episcopal palace, and a story went the rounds which told how the layman, anxious to accept his host's invitation to golf with him, and finding himself without a coat suitable for the purpose, had been arrayed in a garment of ecclesiastical design from the Bishop's wardrobe. In May the Bishop made his first attempt to embody a possible concordat in a Bill. He proposed to apply to education the principle of " local option," and to permit the Councils to agree with the Church upon a general system of religious education. So far Mr. Lloyd George was in agreement with his proposals. But he would not accept the further option in the Bill by which facilities for religious instruction might be given during school hours. He had no great love for the " right of entry " proposals except as a compromise, and he felt, with many of his compatriots, that the utmost point of concession to which it was proper to go was the grant of "facilities" outside school hours. On those terms he believed the Welsh people would still be ready to compromise, although now that "feelings had been embittered by the inevitable incidents of a great campaign, the temper essential to discussion and compromise was for the moment absent." [1] Against what was known as " inside facilities," he said, there was a growing feeling all round.

It would dislocate the arrangements of the schools and perpetuate the worst evils of sectarian intrusion into the domain of school life. I trust that the Bishop, who has shown conspicuous moderation and foresight throughout this troublesome controversy, will be sufficiently well advised to modify his demands in this respect. [2]

The second reading of the Defaulting Authorities Bill was taken on July 15. In his speech on that occasion Mr. Lloyd George made great play with the alternating devotion of the Government to the claims of the Church and the liquor trade. The Licensing Bill was now one of the leading points of controversy between the parties, and Mr. Lloyd George represented the new Education Bill as a compensatory sop to the clerics whose timid souls had revolted at the Ministry's generosity to Bung. The Government, he said, found their Empire tottering, and, like the Roman Empire of old, they had to buy off the Goths. One day the Goths came from Burton-on-Trent : the next from Lambeth. They threatened to sack the city. For a year or two the Education Act satisfied them, but the brewers' Endowment Bill brought the hordes back. " Our consciences will not stand this," they said. " I'll square that for you," said the Prime Minister, and he put matters right with the Bill for the coercion of Wales. " It is like compounding a spree on a Saturday night by putting a threepenny bit in the plate on Sunday."

The Committee stage of the Bill was reached at the close of a Session remarkable for legislative barrenness. The Government, embarrassed by Mr. Chamberlain's independent campaign for the reversal of the fiscal policy of the country, and divided in its counsels, was marking time with one paramount object—to remain in office. If they went forward, they died : if they went backward, they died : it was better to remain as nearly motionless as possible, if only they might so preserve their existence, even in

[1] " Westminster Gazette," May 14, 1904.
[2] " Manchester Guardian," May 11, 1904.

a state of suspended animation. The Local Authority Default Bill was not introduced, as has been seen, until the end of April, after the Eastertide recess. The result of the delay in this and other matters was, as a Ministerial journal admitted, " that important measures were being rushed through at a pace, and with an absence of facilities for reasonable examination, to which only the exigencies of a desperate situation could give any colour of justification." [1] Like all who procrastinate, the Government was in a desperate hurry to finish its work at the eleventh hour. The Bill was drawn in such a way that the matters contained in it, although distinct, were combined in one clause. Efforts were made to obtain a separate discussion of the several questions at issue, which only led to the closure being moved thrice by Mr. Balfour during the afternoon. Mr. Lloyd George accused the Prime Minister of " dragooning the House," and asserted that the Bill had been drafted in a single clause with the deliberate object of curtailing discussion. Mr. Balfour, he said, relied on his authority and influence with the Chair to effect his purpose. The supporters of the Ministry saw in this observation a reflection upon the impartiality of the Chairman of Committees, and there were cries of " Withdraw." The Chairman was Mr. Lowther (afterward, Speaker), and he dealt with the situation in that vein of combined dignity and humour for which he afterwards became so justly celebrated. " If the insinuation is against the Prime Minister," he said, " it is in order : if it is against me, it is out of order." Mr. Lloyd George promptly explained that his strictures were upon the Prime Minister alone.

After a scanty and by no means obstructive discussion, Mr. Balfour proposed to closure the first five lines of the clause. There seemed to be no justification at all for the motion, as there had not so far been any waste of time, and it had the effect of shutting out numerous amendments, many of them most substantial, including one which aimed at ensuring that Councils should not be called upon to work schools which were insanitary and ill ventilated. Mr. Lowther, however, accepted Mr. Balfour's motion, which the rules of the House of course gave him a discretion to refuse. When the Chairman ordered that the House should be cleared for a division, Mr. Lloyd George, on a point of order, submitted that it was disgraceful that the closure should be applied in this way, and urged the importance of the amendments passed over, especially that with regard to the sanitation of the schools. Mr. Lowther's answer was that, as the law stood, it was the duty of the Board of Education to see that schools

[1] " Standard," August 6, 1904.

were efficient. "But they do not do their duty," Mr. Lloyd George answered.

"You must not blame me for it," the Chairman replied.

"I am blaming you for not giving us an opportunity of discussing a question of this sort."

Feeling on the Liberal, and especially the Welsh benches, was running high. The Chairman, in response to questions from other members, said that in deciding whether he should accept the closure it was his duty to have regard to the substantiality of amendments "and also to other circumstances." "What circumstances?" Mr. Lloyd George asked him—"the exigencies of the Government? The exigencies of the Cecil family?"

"I do not see any object," he added, a few moments later, "in taking part in a farce of this kind—absolutely none. It is a perfect farce that we should not be allowed to discuss a question of light and air for the children. I think it is monstrous."

Mr. Lowther begged the Welsh members who were refusing to obey the rules of the House, and leave its precincts for a division, to bow to his ruling. He recognised, he said, that they had made a "dignified protest," and asked them to be content to go no further in their resistance. Finding they would not be moved, he reluctantly "named" first three Welsh members, including Mr. Lloyd George, and afterwards a number of others. Mr. Lowther was in a position of some difficulty. The Speaker was absent through illness, so that it fell to him to play the double part of Chairman and Speaker, and this necessitated his taking the chair as Deputy-Speaker and reporting to the House his own ruling as Chairman of Committees.

Mr. Lloyd George addressed him with respectful firmness. They were exceedingly sorry, he said, to disobey the rulings of the Chair, but they were doing it from a keen sense of public obligation.

We must make a most emphatic protest against the action which you, Mr. Deputy-Speaker, have taken at the instigation of the Prime Minister. We consider that you ruled out questions of vital importance to our constituents, and we cannot, consistently with our sense of duty, take any further part in this farce of a Parliamentary Session.

Mr. William Jones and Mr. William Abraham (Mabon) joined in the protest. When the latter began by an expression of his sorrow, "in the interests of education," at the course they were compelled to take, there was some scornful laughter. "If hon. members had come here without having been educated, they would not laugh," the old miner replied. "If they had known what it was to start work in a colliery at ten years of age without education, they would not laugh. I am now becoming one of the oldest members of the House, but I will protest even though I have to be carried out."

Mr. Lowther was not unmoved by the dignity of these appeals, and could hardly help feeling some sympathy with the grievance of the minority. Honourable members, he said in a conciliatory tone, had always treated him with the greatest courtesy, and he felt that they were deeply moved in the action they were taking. They had made a protest, and (as he had already said) it was a dignified protest, and worthy of them in the difficult circumstances in which they were placed. But he appealed to them not to compel him to have recourse to the enforcement of the rules of the House.

Mr. Asquith, who was leading the Opposition, left the front bench to confer with Mr. Lloyd George. After a hurried colloquy, the latter announced that while he and his friends felt they could take no further part in the discussion, they had no wish to appear to defy the ruling of the Chair. They would walk out and wash their hands of the whole business. He was followed by Mr. Asquith, whose intervention marked his sense of the grave injustice of the course taken by the Ministry. He was quite certain, he said, that they all felt it would be desirable to avoid any of the unseemly scenes which they had witnessed in the past. He was glad, therefore, to hear what Mr. Lloyd George had said. He entirely sympathised with him, and with those associated with him in the protest he had made, and if Mr. Lloyd George took the course he had suggested, the rest of the Liberal Party would leave the House with him and take no further part in the debate.

It was a dramatic ending to a " scene " which the restraint of the insurgents never allowed to degenerate into unseemliness. With Mr. Asquith, Mr. Lloyd George, and Mr. Bryce at their head, all the Liberals in the House rose and walked out. In two minutes not a single member was left above the gangway on the left of the Chair. Below the gangway Mr. Crooks, of Woolwich, and one other member had the front bench to themselves. A few Irish Nationalists sat behind them. The only other occupant of those benches was Mr. Winston Churchill, who had not long since crossed over. In a few minutes the Bill was passed through Committee, and the House adjourned.

A few days later the "Times" published an unauthorised but well-informed article upon the new campaign which Mr. Lloyd George was to inaugurate against Sir William Anson's coercive measure. In a leading article, published at the same time, it admonished him in a paternal manner to forsake the paths of revolt, suggesting to him that " his present rebellious outbreaks " were " something of an anachronism."

Five or six years ago, in his callow Parliamentary youth, these schemes might have been regarded as promising methods of self-advertisement adopted by a young politician who must at any cost attract notice. But that time is long gone by. Mr. Lloyd George should no longer adopt tactics worthy only of his own distant past and of Mr. Winston Churchill's present. He has become a serious politician, and a serious claimant for high office.

If the " flowing tide " flows further, and brings the Opposition fleet into the harbour that it longs for, Mr. Lloyd George will be there among the foremost. He is to be, they say, President of the Board of Trade, or perhaps of the Board of Education, with a seat in the strange new Cabinet. He must recollect that a Minister is a member of a Government, and a Government, it is understood, is a body which governs. How will Mr. Lloyd George proceed to govern if any section of the future Opposition that feels itself aggrieved by his measures sets itself to organise a general strike ?

Perhaps, in that event, he will sometimes be heard to lament that he himself set so evil an example ; that he condescended to become the chorus-leader of rebellion ; that, knowing better all the time, he consented to purchase a little notoriety and a little temporary influence with the more fanatical of his countrymen by pandering to their political passions, and by consciously helping them forward on a course which tends to bring law into contempt and to destroy all respect for Parliament.[1]

The flowing tide had far to flow to the day in 1912 when the " Times," in Mr. Lloyd George's phrase, " gasped out sedition " against the author of the Insurance Act.

III

The second Cardiff Conference—The policy of a nation—" Freedom of conscience "—The fight with the Board of Education—Failure of the scheme for a National Council.

The manner in which the Act for the coercion of the Councils had been forced through the House of Commons served to increase the acerbity of feeling in Wales, where a signal from Mr. Lloyd George was eagerly awaited.

After a meeting of the executive of Welsh County Councils at Shrewsbury (September 14), a second National Convention was summoned again at Cardiff. Between five and six hundred delegates were present. An observer said that the tone of the meeting was remarkable—" enthusiastic, and yet full of good-humoured confidence." Resolutions were carried which outlined

[1] " Times," August 11, 1904.

the plan by which the " Coercion " Act was to be met. First, it was decided that if the powers given to the Board by the Act were exercised in any Welsh area, the education authority for that area should forthwith take all such legal steps as might be necessary to relieve themselves from further responsibility for the maintenance or control of all schools, denominational and undenominational alike, within their jurisdiction. Next, it was resolved that in any area where the new Act was put into operation, the parents of children attending denominational schools should withdraw them. Finally, that County Councils should decline any longer to maintain schools declared to be in default in respect of structural arrangements. These resolutions meant that if the Board tried to make use of the new Act, it would find itself faced with the necessity of taking over the administration of the whole of Welsh education from London.

"Those who are assembled here," Mr. Lloyd George said, addressing them, " are the members of local education authorities of Wales."

It is not a political gathering in any sense of the term. It is a gathering of those who are responsible for the local government of Wales. We invited men of all sections, of all creeds, and of all parties, and if any parties are unrepresented it is because they have deliberately chosen not to come here to represent their views. Now, what is it we are met for ? We are met to take part in probably one of the greatest struggles for religious equality which this generation has seen.

In words which have already been quoted[1] he outlined the history of the struggle down to the first conference at Cardiff in 1903.

We met here at Cardiff. It is where we have decided all great questions in recent years. And provided Cardiff takes the resolution to really lead, we shall very likely meet here again to settle equally important questions affecting Wales in the years to come. But unless Cardiff really means to throw in its lot, for better or for worse, with Welsh nationality, then I would personally rather see the capital of Wales planted on the heights of Plinlimmon.

"I have never seen anything to equal it," Mr. Lloyd George said afterwards. "It was an indubitable proof that Wales is one, united as it has not been for centuries." His speech was worthy of a great occasion. "Wales has entered the lists," he said, " to champion the most sacred cause that was ever entrusted to the charge of a people."

[1] See p. 363.

What is that ? The great cause of Freedom of Conscience. Gentlemen, you hear sneers and gibes at conscience. Take this warning. Never trust an individual, never trust a party, whose stock jest is a gibe at conscience.

I say it in all solemnity, it is God's greatest gift to the human mind, the propeller and the rudder of human progress. And it is for the freedom of that in this land, in the schools where our citizens are brought up—it is for this freedom of conscience that we have entered the lists to fight as a people. We have staked our reputation by the result. By our demeanour in the contest shall we be judged for all ages. I know the history of my country pretty well. I think I know its present temper as well as most people, and I venture to say that although we have been charged with almost every vice and defect in the whole category of human flaws as a race, not even our worst defamers have ever accused us of cowardice.

If we run away now, we shall not merely be taunted, but we shall deserve the taunt. It is a great struggle, and there are great sacrifices. Great sacrifices we must make—close our schools if necessary. Yes, but we will see our children do not suffer. We have buildings where we can teach them. " Ah ! " say our enemies, " teach them ! It will be inferior education." Inferior ? Why inferior ? I say that the children will be trained in these circumstances in such a way that they will receive an education higher than any Welsh child has ever received in his daily training. What will it be ? Every child will be taught at the outset of his career, he will have it engraved upon his young heart, so deeply that the impression will not be worn away till it crumbles in the dust, this great lesson of the Master, that man shall not live by bread alone. We shall teach the children that there are principles eternal, outside, beyond, above the limited atmosphere of their daily lives, like a firmament to which they must lift up their eyes, if they would not be as the beasts of the fields. These are the lessons that we will teach them during the year we shall be exiled from our schools. And when the contest is over Wales will have the proud satisfaction of knowing that she has been in the forefront of the battle that has established for ever in the British Constitution this principle, that no man on British soil shall suffer any proscription at the hands of the State for any belief he honestly holds as to matters that pertain to his own soul.

At the Cardiff Convention there was not a dissentient voice. Bold as was the course proposed, the County Councils were quite ready to adopt it. Nothing can unite more surely than a common resentment of oppression. It is the sense that the Anglican Church is the oppressor which, for generations, has welded into a compact political party in Wales the most diverse temperaments and minds the least likely to agree. The Education Act seemed to Welshmen to be the culminating point of the arrogance of a minority hedged round by privilege, and resistance to it gave a great opportunity to Wales to speak with one voice. Even on such a subject one may doubt whether many leaders would have obtained such strikingly loyal support. During the struggle two County Councils, those of Carmarthenshire and Merionethshire, had failed to adopt the policy Mr. Lloyd George proposed, but their only fault was that in their zeal they had marched in advance of the main army, and by his persuasion they fell back. By the end of 1904 only two of the local educational authorities shrank from refusing rate aid to denominational schools—the town councils of Carmarthen and Wrexham. It can seldom have been said with more truth of any policy than of that recommended to Wales by Mr. Lloyd George that it was " the policy of a nation."

In the Liberal camp there were some voices of protest, but they were drowned in the general chorus of acclamation. Mr. Lloyd George's old ally, Mr. Bryn Roberts, opposed the scheme, with its ultimate plan for the closing of the schools, as unworkable and disastrous. He said as much in October to the Eivion Liberal Association. They heard his speech with the respectful silence which was his due, and at its close passed with acclamation and with unanimity a resolution in favour of Mr. Lloyd George's policy.

The stage seemed to be set for an epoch-making struggle. Yet, as it turned out, no exciting drama was to be played. The Board of Education was not anxious to provoke a conflict, and the County Councils were pursuing Mr. Lloyd George's policy too carefully to give the Board a strong case against them. During 1904 the provisions of the Defaulting Authorities Act were never enforced. In 1905 the Government lived under the cloud of impending dissolution, and was in too weak a position to allow the struggle to become acute. With the advent of a Liberal Government the whole situation changed. True, the no-rate policy did not die, and for years after the General Election of 1906 one or two of the Councils regularly compelled the Board under a Liberal regime to use the powers of the Act of 1904. But the fight became less and less serious, just as " passive resistance " in England became less and less a factor to be considered, and the foundation in 1907 of a Welsh Department of the Board of Education, responsible directly to the President, did a good deal to satisfy Welsh feeling.

The national council of education, which Mr. Lloyd George had hoped might come into being as a result of the Act of 1902, is still a dream. This was not the fault of Mr. Lloyd George, nor, let it be said in fairness, of the Board of Education. It says something for the British genius for administration that in the midst of all the wrangles of 1904 the Board, pursuing (in Mr. Lloyd George's own words) " a very liberal and sympathetic policy," succeeded in agreeing with him and other representatives

MR. AND MRS. LLOYD GEORGE AND MEGAN.

(An at-home portrait by Ernest Mills.)

of the Welsh County Councils upon a scheme for the creation of such a council for Wales. Differences between North and South as to their representation in the constitution of the new body ended for the time being a proposal full of promise for the future autonomy of Wales.

But the "Revolt" had emphasized, as weaker measures could not have done, the case for Welsh autonomy. It is significant that, towards the end of 1904, Mr. Winston Churchill, then in his novitiate as a Liberal, and surveying the world of politics from a new vantage-ground and with a fresh outlook, recognised that the chief importance of the fight over the schools was the new stress it gave to the demand for a grant of self-government to Wales in her domestic affairs. He drew this moral from the contest at a demonstration which he addressed, together with Mr. Lloyd George, at Carnarvon : [1]

We hear a great deal about the Irish question, but is there no Welsh question, too ? We have seen and heard enough in the last few months, and we are likely to hear and see more in the next few months, to convince us that the Welsh aspect of devolution is not one which can well be over-looked. I observe that Scotland is a country which enjoys complete educational peace, yet the history of Scotland is marked by sectarian struggles whose bitterness and whose cruelty and whose prolonged and ferocious aggravation have not been surpassed, or have hardly been sur-passed, in any part of the United Kingdom. And yet to-day, so far as education is concerned, she has settled her differences. The people are contented. And, while religion is not banished from the schools, Scotsmen are able to unite upon what is, after all, the principal object of education, the furtherance of secular efficiency. What is the reason ? It is because the Scotch have got the educational system which they like, which the good sense of the Scotch people desires, and which national requirements dictate. Why cannot we achieve the same result in Ireland and in Wales ? Why can we not allow them to have the educational liberty which they desire ?

I put this question plainly to my Conservative friends, across what is, I fear, an ever-widening gulf. Why, if Scotland has the educational system which she chooses, should not Ireland and Wales have the educational systems which they respectively want too ? The more you can interest localities in education, the more generous will be the provision which they will make for it, the more effective will be the control which they will exert over the spending of the money they have themselves provided. It seems to me that the Irish demand for self-government and the Welsh demand for devolution ought not to go forward separately. They should go forward together, hand-in-hand, strengthening each other and also limiting each other.

[1] October 18, 1904.

It is in the fresh illustration it provides of Mr. Lloyd George's zeal for the unity of Wales and the preservation of her nationality, and of his capacity for the leadership of men, that the " Revolt " has a biographical interest. Whether the fight would have succeeded if it had been more prolonged and fought against a less enfeebled foe, it is impossible to say with any certainty.   That it was a great achievement to rally Wales, almost without distinction of parties, to a standard of something not unlike rebellion, is a matter about which no doubt can exist.

CHAPTER VIII

I

WE have already noted, in dealing with the two great conflicts which it has been the purpose of this volume to describe, that, diverse as they were in scope and object, at bottom Mr. Lloyd George's adherence in each case was to the cause of nationality. There are some historians who clothe with sanctity the accomplished fact, who see a mistake in every failure and deride every lost cause. These will find nothing in the story of Mr. Lloyd George's " pro-Boer " campaign except a record of wasted endeavour. Others, who are willing to believe that in the field of politics, as in the field of war, the big battalions are not always fighting for a just cause, may see in his campaign a splendid failure, and it may be doubted whether upon a broad view it was a failure at all. It may be, after all, that the insistent protests of the small and neglected peace party were in the long run no more futile than are the protests, equally insistent and not less irritating, of an honest man's conscience when he hardens his heart against it. Conscience keeps the honest man awake, for all his willingness to neglect it, and the " pro-Boers " kept England awake. A nation which is conducting a great war need not congratulate itself if it has no peace party, any more than a man who is killing his fellow ought to congratulate himself if he feels no qualms about the business. There are occasions where hardly anybody doubts a man's right to kill or the corporate right of a nation to slay and despoil. But it is not well to kill without scruple or compunction, even in the best cause—for instance, under the most urgent compulsion of self-defence. If that is true of a man it is not less true of a nation. The nation that is wildly and unanimously enthusiastic about the righteousness of its cause in a war is probably on the wrong side : it is certainly in the wrong frame of mind.   We ought to hear and appreciate our enemies' case.   We ought to know the worst that can be said about us by critics, even by critics of (if you will) biassed and prejudiced minds.   Monks in their debates allow an advocate even to the devil : a nation in arms should not refuse a hearing to those who plead its adversary's cause.

The " pro-Boers," if they did not wholly succeed, at any rate did not wholly fail in teaching England that the South African dispute had two sides.   There is, however, a much wider sense in which it can be said of them that they succeeded.   For when a later chapter in South African history opened with the grant to a united South Africa of the status of a self-governing colony, the Prime Minister of England was a "pro-Boer," Mr. Lloyd George was in the Cabinet, and the fiercest among our Imperialists were uttering futile prophecies of woe and desolation from the Opposition benches.

The fight for the control of the schools was a drawn battle, or, more truly, an unfinished battle.   The election of 1906 would have finally settled the issue in the sense Mr. Lloyd George and his followers desired, if the Constitution had not been so adjusted as to weigh down the scales in favour of reaction.   As it was, the perpetuation of the endowment provided in 1902 for denominational schools became a count in the indictment against the House of Lords.   The educational controversy was to merge in the larger constitutional issue.

In all great struggles there are thrown together men of very different temperaments, influenced by widely diverse motives, and with ideals distant as the poles.   One need only bracket together the names of two such opponents of the war as Mr. Lloyd George and Mr. Labouchere in order to exemplify this truth, and the comment would apply with hardly less force to the educational controversy.   There, as has been suggested already, Mr. Lloyd George's policy was dictated by a sentiment in part racial, in part religious.   It would be a bold man who would deny that the stern religious convictions which upheld many a fighter in the ranks on either side had in them a strong element of bigotry, and many critics laid bigotry to the charge of Mr. Lloyd George.   But to be tenacious of belief is not to be bigoted.   Could a bigoted Nonconformist use words like these of the Roman Catholic Church ?

Sometimes we criticise the Roman Catholic Church very severely, but there is no Church that has made a surer and deeper search into human nature.   The Roman Catholic Church, the greatest religious organisation in the whole world, conducts its worship in a common tongue. The Roman Catholics conduct their worship in the language of worship. Their Church utilises every means of taking people outside everyday interests, and seeks to induce them to forget what is outside. Thus the language of commerce and of everyday occupations is left outside, and the people are taught the language of worship. That shows a shrewd, deep insight into the human mind.

Mr. Lloyd George spoke these words at the opening of a Welsh Calvinistic chapel at Altrincham.[1] He saw an analogy in the use of the Welsh tongue by Welshmen throughout the kingdom in their own chapels. The Welsh, he said, preserved their language for the hearth and for worship. English would become the language of commerce, the language of the professions, even, he feared, the language of the street, but the Welsh language, when it died, would die at the steps of the altar.

But indeed it hardly needs such a quotation to show that his attitude towards the Church of Rome had more of sympathy and less of prejudice than is consistent with bigotry. His quarrel was never with the Roman Catholics. They had a special claim, which he readily recognised—the claim of a minority to be protected. His real antagonism was towards those Churchmen who would not admit that England was a Protestant country. He was ready to compromise even with them, but his fighting speeches did rest upon the assumption that a refusal by Churchmen of " simple Bible teaching " as sufficient for the schools was tantamount to a confession that they wished to teach a bowdlerised code of Christian ethics. The answer of High Churchmen was that the teaching of the Bible without the exegesis of the Church upon it amounted to no more and no less than Nonconformist instruction. That answer he claimed as an admission in favour of Nonconformity.

It was partly his tenderness towards Roman Catholicism, partly his sense of justice, which saved him from seeking revenge upon the Irish for their support, not merely of the Education Bill (which was to be expected), but of the " Welsh Coercion Bill " as well. He was asked early in 1903 what his views were upon the proposal of a redistribution of seats which should cut down the Irish representation to a level commensurate with the population of Ireland. He would oppose it, he said, on the ground of its injustice, because the depopulation of Ireland was due to British administration. Apart from that, he would have nothing to say against it. " We on our side of the House would rather deal with a large British

---

[1] July 25, 1903.

representation than an Irish one. The Education Bill showed once more that the Irish members never consider us, and from their point of view they are right. The smaller that body is, the better for any British party."

One other instance may be given of a breadth of mind which was growing with the years. Lord Salisbury, of whose policy, as has been seen, he had on occasion made strong and incisive criticism, passed out of politics during the period with which we are dealing, and not long afterwards died. Mr. Lloyd George pronounced a fervent eulogy upon him, of which a narrow-minded opponent of his general policy would have been incapable. He was, he said, a counsellor whose honour was above reproach. Britain had been peculiarly fortunate in securing the services of such men for her governors, and nothing gave greater confidence for the future of her people.

He won the reputation of a great statesman in an age of great statesmen, a generation that knew Gladstone, Bismarck, Disraeli, and Gambetta. He rendered the greatest service a ruler can give to his race, for it may be said of him that on more than one occasion he alone preserved the peace of the world. When the last years of the nineteenth century were drenched in British blood, it was not Lord Salisbury who was mainly responsible for that tragedy. He has now passed away, and with him seems to have vanished the potency of the great political combination which placed him in power, and the dominance of which in the counsels of the nation his great sagacity and stately character so long maintained.

When the aftermath of the Transvaal war was making the War Office the butt of popular criticism, Mr. Lloyd George was more indulgent to Mr. Brodrick than many of his own nominal supporters. The War Office, he held, had always been inefficient, especially at the commencement of a campaign.

I regard Mr. Brodrick as the victim of a policy which was not his own, and I object very strongly to see the way in which he is baited in the House and out of it. The one man of all responsible for this extravagant expenditure, by rushing us into war when we were not prepared, is Mr. Chamberlain ; yet he is the only man of the whole Cabinet who has acquired any popularity out of it, and all the others are paying the penalty of Mr. Chamberlain's sins.

II

Looking forward—Ireland—Army Reform—The Navy—Taxation of ground values.

It is interesting to see how, at the close of 1902, Mr. Lloyd George faced the political future. In Ireland, he was ready to look favourably upon Mr. Wyndham's forthcoming land-purchase legislation. He thought, he said, that the Government were going to make " a big effort " with regard to Ireland. " I think they do mean to make a real attempt to satisfy both landlord and tenant."

He was asked if they would meet with his support.

In the main, yes. This question has got to be settled somehow. I daresay I shall not agree with the Government upon the amount of compensation which has to be paid to the landlords : they will probably want to give them too much. But it is we who put those men there hundreds of years ago to look after our interests, and, even though they have taken more care of their own interests than of ours, I think it is we who must get them out once again, even at some considerable sacrifice, if needs be.[1]

His views upon the Army and Navy, as they stood at the end of the war, justify the assertion that he was not temperamentally a " little Englander."

I believe in Army Reform, but I do not believe in increasing our Army. We do not want a big Army, and we have no need to imitate our Continental neighbours. Please make no mistake. I do believe in a strong Navy. We have a vast Empire beyond the seas : it has got to be defended. We have an unparalleled commerce ; our food-stuffs nearly all come from abroad. And, moreover, a large Navy has another good side ; it prevents any possibility of panic. But a large " Continental Army "—no, we do not want that.

" Is there any other matter," he was asked, " which you think will come into prominence next Session ? "

Yes, we Progressive members are going to make a big bid for taxation of ground values. This is only one of many social reforms for which we intend to press. But it is the most obvious and the most urgent. It includes, of course, the taxation of unoccupied land at its true value. It contains no new principle ; it only sets right an inequality between land and other species of property, and, moreover, the principle which we wish to see adopted is admitted in several other countries. It lies at the back of the Housing Problem and other pressing evils.

For the present let us content ourselves with noting that at the beginning of 1903 he already regarded the taxation of land values as the most obvious and urgent of reforms.

[1] See the London " Echo," February 20, 1903.

III

It has been found necessary in this volume to continue the account of the educational controversy in Wales down to 1904 in order to present a consecutive and comprehensible narrative. So far as the general events of Mr. Lloyd George's life are concerned, we have only dealt with the years of the war and of the education fight in the House of Commons. They were anxious years, and above all very busy years, and when the tale of their political activities has been told there is not very much else to be recorded. Mr. Lloyd George and his family had now moved to Wandsworth Common. The domestic history of the period is notable for one event of first-class importance—the birth on April 22, 1902, of a daughter, Megan Arvon, Mr. Lloyd George's fifth child.

He had added to his activities an interest in the " Daily News," which, from being an Imperialist organ at the beginning of the war, had, by a change of Editors, become the mouthpiece of the " pro-Boers." He was still practising as a solicitor, although the time he was able to give to his profession grew gradually less. One episode of his legal life at this time is noteworthy. In 1900 the long drawn out struggle between Lord Penrhyn and his men at Bethesda was at its height. It was a struggle in which from 1897 onwards Mr. Lloyd George played an active part. The men, he said, addressing the Trade Union Congress in 1902,[1] were fighting for the elementary right claimed by every workman in the country and by the capitalist—the right of organisation and representation. With a courage, devotion, and sacrifice which had given the men a place in the annals of the great struggle for the emancipation of labour, they had stood firm. How they had done it Heaven alone knew : no one who knew their circumstances would have predicted that they could have gone on more than a few months. Still they stood firm, with the firmness of the rock they had hewn for so many years for Lord Penrhyn. If he were a Bethesda quarryman, he said on another occasion, rather than yield he would break stones on the road.

In November 1900 a prosecution was instituted on behalf of Lord Penrhyn against a large number of the strikers for riot and disorder. The case was to be heard at the Bangor Petty Sessions,

[1] September 2.

and the happy idea occurred to the strikers' representatives of securing Mr. Lloyd George as advocate for the men. Mr. D. R. Daniel, of whom mention has been made in the first volume, was the men's secretary, and it fell to him to come to London and give his old friend instructions as to the case. Mr. Daniel arrived at Wandsworth Common to spend a week-end with Mr. Lloyd George before taking him back with him to Wales. He had provided himself with a carefully-drawn statement of the case, and had expected to spend at least some hours in consultation with his advocate. But Mr. Lloyd George seemed ready to talk on every subject except the case. At last Mr. Daniel brought him to bay in the study, and definitely broached the subject. " Let us go for a walk," said Mr. Lloyd George, " and talk afterwards." They took their walk, and there was no more conversation that day about the Penrhyn quarries. Mr. Daniel contented himself with the prospect of the long train journey, which would give plenty of time and opportunity for a consultation. Even that hope was vain, and when Bangor was reached the " brief " was not yet opened. Mr. Daniel confesses that he was a little alarmed, and began to feel his journey had been made in vain. But when the Court opened the next morning he found to his relief that Mr. Lloyd George had the case at his fingers' ends.

On this occasion it was Mr. Lloyd George's fortune to be pitted against one of the greatest advocates known in our time in the criminal courts of the country, Mr. Charles Mathews, or, as he afterwards became, Sir Charles Mathews. Sir Charles Mathews has been kind enough to tell me his recollections of the case and of his first meeting with Mr. Lloyd George. Of his skill and ability as an advocate, Sir Charles says, there can be no doubt. His cross-examination was in the highest degree successful, not less successful, perhaps, because, with the consent of his opponent and of the Bench, he cross-examined, in several instances, in Welsh. His efforts were in most cases rewarded with an acquittal; in no case was a sentence of imprisonment passed.

Sir Charles Mathews takes pleasure in recalling one incident, which, as he says, showed him that Mr. Lloyd George knew how to do a kindly act in a graceful way. The quarrymen of Bethesda, anxious that their view of the prosecution should be manifest, had marched in almost military order to Bangor. Some hundreds of them were assembled outside the Court-house, and a very formidable body they looked. Mr. Mathews, who was of course not known by sight to the quarrymen, entered the Court unobserved, but Mr. Lloyd George's arrival was greeted with a tumultuous ovation. After the trial had begun, Mr. Mathews had no longer the security which the crowd's ignorance of his identity had given him previously.   At the mid-day adjournment he was walking out a few paces behind his opponent.   Suddenly Mr. Lloyd George turned round to him and said, with a twinkle in his eye, "I think, Mr. Mathews, that my reception will be more enthusiastic if you walk down the street with me."   "Mr. Mathews" was glad to accept the invitation, and so, says Sir Charles, "instead of being booed and execrated, I participated in an ovation."

There has been more than one reference in this volume to the late W. T. Stead, whose sympathy with the Boers made him take a lively interest in Mr. Lloyd George's doings during the war. In a letter which Mr. Lloyd George wrote at the end of 1902—on Christmas Eve—there is an amusing account of a conversation between the two men.   Mr. Lloyd George had been lunching with Stead.   "He is now full of a scheme," he writes, "to destroy the Church by giving the appointment of the clergy to the Parish Councils, with no religious tests at all.   He would make each clergyman responsible legally for the moral condition of the parishioners.   If there was drunkenness and immorality in a parish he would court-martial the rector!"

APPENDIX

I.—MR. LLOYD GEORGE'S SPEECH ON THE SECOND READING OF THE EDUCATION BILL, MAY 8, 1902

Sir,—I do not propose, in the course of my observations, to criticise the machinery of the Bill, but I shall simply endeavour to present, as shortly as I can, the Nonconformist case against the principle of the measure. Those who heard the speech of my hon. friend the Member for East Mayo [1] must have felt that the case for the denominational schools had been presented with great ability and moderation, and, as a Nonconformist, I thank him for the very sympathetic treatment he accorded to our case. I believe it would have been more sympathetic had he known more about it. The representatives of the denominational schools have given frequent assurances that they are prepared to consider the grievances of Nonconformists in Committee. I do not feel very convinced that those assurances will bear much fruit when the time comes, but still I feel confident that the hon. Member for East Mayo will fulfil his pledge and will vote for such amendments as will enable us to make the best of a very bad Bill. All he desires, as I understand, is to protect the Catholic schools, and he is not anxious to rivet the old clericalism on Nonconformists in the rural districts of England and Wales.

Now I come to the speech of the Attorney-General. [2] It struck me that it was based on a very badly-drawn brief. He quoted in support of the Bill a resolution passed by the County Councils Association, and asserted that the County Councils had met in conclave in London and passed a resolution in favour of the Bill. I should like the House to hear the first few lines of that resolution, which the hon. and learned Gentleman claims to be in favour of the Bill. It says :

Without expressing any opinion on the controversial questions raised by the Education Bill, etc.

Can the hon. and learned Gentleman point to a single clause in the Bill which is not controversial ? If he can, then he may claim the resolution as being in favour of it ; but I submit that he cannot. The Attorney-General also

[1] Mr. Dillon.   [2] Sir Robert Finlay.

said that there was no proselytism in Church schools. That shows how he was instructed. The hon. and learned Gentleman cannot possibly have known what is going on in the rural districts of England and Wales, or he would not have made that statement. This is what a diocesan inspector of the Church schools wrote to the chief organ of the Church, the " Guardian " :

Our syllabus is arranged so as to give distinctive denominational instruction. I always saw it was given, and always asked the children, chiefly the children of Nonconformists, questions bearing upon it. Thus, in fact, we trained the children of the Nonconformists to be the children of the Church.

That was Canon Pennington, a diocesan inspector for twenty years. It is obvious that to say there is no proselytism is absurd.

Mr. A. J. Balfour : When was that written ?

Mr. Lloyd George : On August 4, 1897. The hon. and learned Gentleman rather indicated who instructed him when he came to analyse his ideas on definite religious teaching. The only illustration which he gave of dogmatic teaching given in Anglican schools which Nonconformists could not support, and which could not be given in Board schools, was the historical view of the Reformation. But, as I understand it, the view accepted by all Protestants, whether Anglicans or Nonconformists, of what took place at the Reformation was the same up till recently. There is, of course, a fundamental difference between the Roman Catholic and the Protestant view, and I can quite understand it is absolutely impossible to teach that history in such a way as not to be unfair to the Catholics. The view of the Reformation accepted by Nonconformists was that accepted by Anglicans until recently. But if it is wanted to have a new view of the Reformation taught in rate-aided schools, a view which is not acceptable to Protestants, if the managers of Church schools want that, then let them frankly throw in their lot with the Catholics. We shall then know how to deal with them. They have no right to pose as members of the Protestant Church and to proceed to create dissension and strife with regard to dogmatic teaching, purely in order to teach views of the Reformation which, by their own oath of office, they are bound not to take. It is very significant, and I hope the Protestant Church of England will take note of it, that the Attorney-General has said that a new view of the Reformation is to be taught.

Mr. A. J. Balfour : He never said that.

Mr. Lloyd George : " A different view from that taken by Nonconformists and Protestants "—what does that mean, then ? What did the hon. and learned Gentleman mean when he said there was nothing which could not be taught in Board schools by common acceptance of all Protestants, but not of Catholics ? He said you want something different, that you want something definite which belongs to Anglicans ; and I say that everything that belongs to Anglican Protestants equally belongs to Nonconformist Protestants. What becomes of his contention that that is the one thing which divides him from the Nonconformists ? Yet it was the only illustration he gave of the different kind of teaching that was required. If he simply wanted to make a case for the Catholic schools, I should agree with him.

But where is the case for the Anglican schools, which is a far more important matter ? I agree with the hon. Member for East Mayo that the question of the authority is really not the important point of the Bill. There is only one important question that divides us—that of rate aid for teaching religion of which a large section of the ratepayers do not approve. That is the whole question, so far as we are concerned. Speaking from observation and experience in Wales, I say that if the people are in earnest about education, and if the source, at any rate, of the authority is the electorate, it does not much matter what the authority is. I cannot comprehend why my hon. friend the Member for Haddington [1] said that the authority was everything, and advised Nonconformists not to mind these religious squabbles. You cannot base any system of education on an injustice to a large section of the community. What is the injustice, and where does it come in in this case ? If you are perpetuating an injustice you are doing the greatest harm in the world to the cause of education. Politically speaking, my hon. friend seems always to be above the snow-line. His counsel was very serene in its purity, but rather sterile. Let him descend from the region of eternal snow and come down to bare facts, and he will find that things are not so easy to settle as they seem. The religious difficulty is the one we have got to settle before we can get a good system of education in this country. The Government are going to get rid of the School Boards. (*An Hon. Member :* No, no.) The hon. Gentleman opposite says No, but the Government are simply going to put an end to their corporate existence and financial capacity, and that is what you do to a criminal when you execute him. You are setting up another authority. Personally, I do not mind that, so long as it is a representative authority, so long as you give real control to the people of the country—for then you will have a watch-dog on the Committee. He will, I know, be only one watch-dog, as against two parsons, and that is unfair odds. But the great evil is that the popular representative will be in a permanent statutory minority. He will know that, and so, too, will the others. It is not like the case put by the right hon. Gentleman the Member for West Monmouthshire,[2] where the man in a minority has a chance of converting the others. He will never be able to do that. I agree in one respect with the Member for Tonbridge——

Mr. Griffith Boscawen (Kent, Tonbridge) : I have not spoken as yet.

Mr. Lloyd George : The hon. Member cheered a sentence and thus showed that he agreed with me when I said you cannot build any good system of education upon injustice. Perhaps he meant by his cheer that the injustice was on the Church side. I maintain it is on the Nonconformist side. Every hon. Member who has spoken on that side of the House has admitted there is a Nonconformist grievance—every one except the hon. Member for Cockermouth.

Mr. Randles (Cumberland, Cockermouth) : I do.

Mr. Lloyd George : I am glad to hear that. The hon. Member belongs to the Nonconformist National Scouts.[3] He has won his commission by

---

[1] Mr. R. B. Haldane (Viscount Haldane of Cloan).   [2] Sir William Harcourt.

[3] The reference of course is to those of the Boer nation who fought under the style of " National Scouts " for England and against their own countrymen.

fighting against his own people. But I say that, by common consent, there is a Nonconformist grievance. What is the grievance of the Church ? The Catholics I put in a different category. Special advantages and privileges are given to the Anglican denominational schools which are not given to the Nonconformists and to the Board schools. The Church have over 12,000 schools in the country, which are mission rooms to educate the children of the poor in the principles of the Church. In 8,000 parishes there are no other schools, and the whole machinery of the law is there utilised to force the Nonconformist children into them. You tell them : " You will have no religious instruction at all unless you are prepared to take the instruction of the Church of England." The total expense for the staff of these schools is £3,400,000 yearly, and the State gives £3,600,000 per annum, so that the staff engaged in teaching Church of England principles is wholly paid by the State. Another advantage possessed by the Anglican Church is the patronage of 60,000 excellent appointments in the Civil Service —exclusive patronage to 60,000 appointments to one of the best, most remunerative, and most honourable careers that a child can possibly enter upon. A Member on the other side said yesterday that the Nonconformists have a grievance there. So they have. Out of 2,000,000 children in Anglican schools, 1,000,000 are Nonconformists. Are hon. Members aware that there are 700,000 Methodist children in these Church schools ?

Mr. Talbot (Oxford University) : Will the hon. Member say on what basis those figures are calculated ? There has been no census.

Mr. Lloyd George : The right hon. Gentleman is mistaken. The Methodist Connexion have gone very closely into the matter, and it is upon their authority, which is quite good enough for me, I make the statement. In Wales, at any rate, the vast majority of the children in the Anglican schools are Nonconformists, yet they are not allowed to enter the teaching profession except on condition of their becoming members or attending the services of the Church of England. The hon. Baronet the Member for Oxford University said yesterday :

Here is a grievance from which Nonconformists are suffering ; I am prepared to redress it.

How ?

I am prepared to support any amendment, compatible with the denominational character of the schools, by which the Nonconformist children should be allowed to enter the lower grades of the teaching profession.

There are 1,000,000 of these children, containing among them probably the best suited for the teaching profession, but, however well-behaved, able, and bright they may be, all you say to them is, " We will allow you to become a lower-grade official in this school, but nothing beyond that." Where does the principle of equality come in ? All we ask is equal treatment, especially in these 8,000 parishes.

Mr. Ernest Gray (West Ham) : Entering the lower grade would give them the opportunity of advancing to the higher.

Mr. Lloyd George : Really, the hon. Gentleman might take the trouble to master the elements of the denominational case. If he had only listened to the speech to which I referred——

Mr. Ernest Gray : I did.

Mr. Lloyd George : Then perhaps he has forgotten that the hon. Baronet said he would not make them principal teachers. Does the hon. Member really mean to say that in any Anglican school in those 8,000 parishes a Nonconformist would be allowed to become a head teacher ?

Mr. Ernest Gray : The argument has been entirely misrepresented. The statement made yesterday was to the effect that under this Bill the training of teachers would occupy a totally different position. Instead of it being necessary for a pupil teacher to go into an ordinary elementary school to get his training, the Nonconformist or Anglican child would go into a proper establishment for the training of teachers and get his training there altogether apart from denominational influences. The entire argument has been that this Bill redressed the grievance of which complaint was justly made.

Mr. Lloyd George : That argument has the disadvantage of being irrelevant. I am coming to the question of training colleges, but at present I am dealing with elementary and State schools in these parishes, and I say that, even after the concession of being allowed to enter the lower grades, a Nonconformist can never hope to become the chief teacher in any one of these schools. But take the training colleges. Most of them are denominational, but built largely and maintained almost exclusively out of State funds. Only one-twentieth of the expense of maintaining the Anglican colleges is provided by the subscriptions of the Anglican Church. Take the case of the Oxford Diocesan Training College. The total expenditure was £1,300 ; the voluntary subscriptions from individuals were nil, and from the Diocesan Board £13 10s., the remainder coming out of Government grants and the pockets of the students themselves. These are denominational colleges, and the hon. Gentleman says they enjoy no advantages which Nonconformists have not at the same time.

The fourth difference is that in these parishes the prestige and influence which come from having the complete control of these communal institutions are in the hands of the Church of England.

These are the advantages—60,000 positions in the Civil Service, the control of these communal institutions, the machinery of the law to force children into the schools to be taught the doctrines of their particular faith— and what do they give for them ? They give £650,000 a year, as against £4,000,000 from the State. Taking their own claim as to the number of the adherents of the Church in this country, that is exactly a farthing per week per head for every adult adherent. This is the " intolerable strain " for all these privileges, but the maintenance of the schools is now to be thrown entirely on the rates ; they have simply to keep the schools in repair. They are grumbling even at that. The Duke of Northumberland writes to complain of it. At the very outside, the repairs will come to £60,000 a year, representing, say, one-tenth of a farthing per week for every adult adherent of the Church of England—one-fifth of the widow's mite, and Dukes grumble at it ! There is no coin of the realm sufficiently trifling and insignificant to mark the maximum of sacrifice which these fierce religious zealots are prepared to make for their faith. It is simply imposing on the credulity of the country and the House of Commons to say that it is their earnest desire to give definite dogmatic teaching to the children of the land. Let them give some proof of it. I am not so sure that this slackening in the desire for definite religious teaching is not attributable to something else. An interesting report was published a few years ago by the National Society. The Secretary wrote to the comptroller of the funds of the National School in each district for a report as to the condition of the school, and some of the replies are very interesting. Here is the reply from the Monmouth Archidiaconal Secretary :

I fear, however, that the laity are beginning to get tired of supporting Church schools. I regret to say that I know many who consider themselves to be good Church people, and yet who fail to recognise the duty of supporting religious education. There seems to be an increasing idea that the Board-school Bible reading is nearly, if not quite, as good.

That is really the explanation of the desire of the friends of religious education to throw the schools on the rates. Their own people are beginning to get the idea into their heads that the religious training given in the Board schools is quite as good, apart from the pure question of proselytism.

Then we are told there is equality at the present moment. Says the Anglican : "The Nonconformists have their schools, and we have ours. The Board schools are Nonconformist schools." Let us see how thoroughly preposterous that statement is. The control of these schools is in the hands of the ratepayers, a majority of whom, according to hon. Members opposite, are Church people. More than that : the majority of the members of these Boards throughout England and Wales are denominationalists— Catholics and Church people ; and some of the largest and most influential Boards in the Kingdom, such as in Liverpool and Manchester, are run entirely by the denominationalists. For years the London Board was run by Mr. Diggle and Mr. Riley, who are not, I believe, very fierce Nonconformists. How absurd it is to say that Board schools are Nonconformist schools ! But that is not all. There are several School Boards run in the interests of voluntary schools. Some districts are so poor that they cannot find the money for a voluntary school. The Board of Education insist on a school being set up, and in order to prevent the absolute breakdown of the denominational system, the School Board is called upon to run up a school as a supplement—that is, the School Boards are used as a means of buttressing denominational schools in several large districts in the country.

Let me give another reason to show that Board schools are not Nonconformist schools. The teacherships are open to Churchmen, Catholics, and Nonconformists. The noble Lord the Member for Greenwich admitted the other day that the majority of the teachers were Church people. Of course they are. Can it be said that they are Nonconformist schools ? Let me instance two parishes that I know, both overwhelmingly Nonconformist, the one with a School Board and the other with an Anglican school.

MR. TOM ELLIS.

(Photograph by Lafayette, Ltd.)

In the latter there has not been a Nonconformist teacher since I have known it. Every one of the Nonconformists who enter the teaching profession has to go through the portals of the Church, although five-sixths of the funds of that school are provided by the Nonconformists. Go to the next parish. The School Board is Nonconformist ; the head teacher in the school is a Churchman ; the two masters are Churchmen ; the majority of the appointments in the school are filled by Church people, although it is kept up by Nonconformists. Where is the equality of which the right hon. Gentleman speaks ? Go to the next parish : The same state of things exists there. There is never any distinction made. We are told that the religious teaching given in Board schools is Nonconformist, but why are we told this ? Is the Bible a Nonconformist book ? It is not for me to repudiate the suggestion, but we do not claim a monopoly in it. I could understand that argument from a Roman Catholic point of view, because I understand their Bible is different from ours. But why should the education be said to be Nonconformist ? Hon. Members who say that the religious teaching given in these schools is undenominational, and therefore must be Nonconformist, do not know what they are talking about. There is no such thing as undenominational education in England. The differences in dogmas between the different sects of Nonconformists are quite as great, in their own view, as the differences between Nonconformists and members of the Church of England. Some differ so much that they will not admit the others to communion. But Nonconformists recognise that they must make some sacrifices for the common good. What would have been the situation if Nonconformists had taken as greedy a view as some denominationalists, I am sorry to say, set up ? Suppose, for instance, that they had insisted on having their own schools and their own doctrines taught in every district by their own masters. The difficulty would not have been the question of providing school buildings, for in almost every case they have already school buildings, and use them on Sundays. The result would have been that, instead of there being one school in the district of a fairly good stamp, there would have been five or six miserable and ill-equipped schools, giving no such education as is given even now. Therefore, the Nonconformists say that as it is a matter of education, which is a matter of national life, they must all sacrifice some convenience for the benefit of the rest of the community. Therefore, they say, " Teach the Bible. We have such confidence in the character of our religion that we shall be able afterwards to teach our dogmas and creed." But hon. Members say, " It is an education which satisfies you, but which does not satisfy us." But does it satisfy the Nonconformists ? If by that you mean that they regard the teaching as sufficient without its being supplemented, it certainly is not satisfactory. They supplement it at their Sunday schools and their Bible classes in the evening, where they teach their own dogmas in their own way. This is the position of things in this country. This is the only country I have ever heard of where, the community being divided up between five or six powerful sects, one sect has monopolised the control of education. America is divided up among a number of powerful sects, of which the Congregationalists are the most numerous, but there is no one sect monopolising the conduct of education. Lord Salisbury, on Wednesday night, said he was full of admiration for the type of manhood turned out by our Colonies, but that type of man is not turned out by the kind of education supplied in this country. In Holland you have the same state of things ; no religious teaching is given with the other lessons which is obnoxious to anybody, but the clergymen of each particular denomination are permitted to come to the schools after school hours and teach their own doctrine to their own particular flock. This is the system which should be adopted in this country. I quite agree that if we, as a large sect, insist on denominational teaching for our children, we have no right to object to other sects insisting on it also. I was in a Church school for years, and I went through all the catechism. For better or worse, I am the sort of article that denominational schools turn out. In Church schools you have a time-table providing so much teaching which is dogmatic and so much teaching that is not dogmatic. One morning you will read the books of Kings, Judges, and Samuel—and I defy any one, however dogmatic he may be, to extract any dogma out of the operations, military or otherwise, of these monarchs. On the following morning you have the ten commandments, and the following day you have the catechism ; and what I ask hon. Gentlemen to do is to follow out in their minds this arrangement. Would it be more difficult to, say, teach the books of Kings, Judges, and Samuel and the undogmatic part of the Bible, in the early part of the day, and leave the clergyman of each denomination afterwards to give his catechism ? The present system is the worst, from the point of view of the clergyman teaching, that ever was.

The noble Lord the Member for Greenwich,[1] in his eloquent speech the other day, held that the time was coming when Nonconformity and Anglicanism would have to fight shoulder to shoulder against unbelief. Is the present system the best method of fighting ? Is not the teaching in the Church schools apostasy ? In the Church schools the majority of the children are Nonconformists (cries of dissent)—yes, certainly. What is the use of denying such a truism ? There are hundreds and hundreds of schools in which the majority of the children are Nonconformists. Take a school of that kind, if you like, with a majority of Nonconformists. The noble Lord says that the whole basis of doctrinal teaching is baptism into membership. What does that mean ? I know perfectly well that when you question a child the first thing you ask is, " What is your name, M or N ? " and so on. For every Nonconformist child in the school it is untrue ; it is false. What a training against unbelief that is ! It starts with inculcating a doctrine that every child in the school knows, so far as he is concerned, is false in fact, and which his parent teaches him is false in principle. That is not training against unbelief. It is training for scepticism in matters religious. No : whether it is for the interests of education or the interests of religion, it is better that we should agree. Let us have one school. In America what are they doing ? They have discovered what mischief there is in education in these little rural schools, and instead of taking the school to the child, they choose the reverse order, and there, now, there is a sort of State arrangement for the purpose of building one large school and carrying

[1] Lord Hugh Cecil.

the children for miles and miles to one school, in order to have them all together and to have a bigger school and a better staff. Whilst our most important rivals have learned that lesson, we are bringing in a Bill to reverse the order and to split up the rural schools into five or six. What folly, from the point of view of education to begin with, and also from the point of view of citizenship and good feeling ! It is most important that we should learn to act together in a country like this. The Premier was full, last night, of the dangers to which we are exposed—dangers internal, dangers external, dangers from foreigners, from our own Colonies, and from our own people. There is no doubt that the time will come when we will have to stand shoulder to shoulder against some of these dangers, and how are we preparing for it ? By perpetuating a system that splits up this country into an infinite number of hostile camps. I think the lesson of Ireland might very well be taken to heart. I am not sure that a great many of the evils of Ireland are not attributable to the fact that you have two bitterly hostile religious camps— people who have been trained, as it were, disciplined and taught from their childhood, not to act together but to act in hostility and bitterness towards each other. With the lesson of Ireland, the lesson of the Colonies, the lesson of Germany, the United States, and Holland before us, we are going back and teaching our people to split up, to quarrel, and to keep alive those religious dissensions among us. It is folly of the worst type, and not statesmanship.

My hon. friends from Ireland were candid with the Nonconformists, and I should like to give one candid word to them. I deeply regret that they support this Bill. If it were purely a Bill for starting Catholic schools for the teaching of their own children—not proselytism—I could not complain. But this is but a tenth part of the whole of this controversy. It is a Bill, not for starting such schools, not for teaching children in the religion of their parents. It is a Bill for riveting the clerical yoke on thousands of parishes in England. Who are the men who rejoice most at the introduction of the Bill ? The bitterest enemies of Ireland. Who are the men who will be saddened most because they have done it ? The best friends of Ireland. Let me put another consideration. We are a small minority in the House opposing the Bill ; we are impotent to stop it, whatever the force of public opinion behind us may be, if the Government force it through. Is it because the people of the country are against us on clericalism ? No ; I believe the people of England are as determined as ever that they will not have the clerical yoke. If we have a straight issue on the question of the control of our schools by the State priesthood, I venture to say that, as we beat them in 1868 with the help of the Church, and defeated them in 1885 against the Irish, we would do it again on that straight issue ; but, unfortunately, we are in a minority—for one reason and one reason only, and I am not ashamed of it. It is because we committed ourselves to the cause of Ireland. Now this is what I put to my hon. friends. It is rather hard. In 1886 we threw over our most cherished leaders in this country—Spurgeon and Bright, Dr. Allan, Dr. Dale, and even the right hon. Gentleman the Member for West Birmingham.[1] We threw them over for one reason only ; because we felt what was due to Ireland ; and it is rather hard, I think—if they will forgive

[1] Mr. Joseph Chamberlain.

me for speaking candidly—to be put in this plight of being beaten down for the cause of Ireland, and that Irishmen, of all people, should help our foes and theirs to make our defeat the more intolerable. Let them remember this. Who are the people who will benefit by this Bill? The people who benefit by it are the people who coerced Ireland, and supported every measure for throwing the leaders of the Irish people into prison, and for keeping Ireland down with soldiers and police. Who are the people who are hit by the Bill? The people of Wales. We were offered, by the right hon. Gentleman the Member for West Birmingham, Disestablishment, if we would throw over Home Rule. We did not do it, and some of the men who declined to do it will be sold up for rates under this Bill, and probably imprisoned under the mandamus of this Bill. They will remember that the instrument under which that happened was forged partly by the Irish Members. In the matter of Home Rule even the chiefs of their own Church have not been as good friends as the chiefs of Nonconformity. Cardinal Vaughan, a priest of their own Church, passes them by when they are fallen on the roadside. I am not sure that he did not join in helping their assailants.

Mr. James Hope (Sheffield, Brightside) said that Cardinal Vaughan had never expressed an opinion on Home Rule.

Mr. Lloyd George : Cardinal Vaughan did his very best to help to return hon. Members opposite. Yes, the Rev. Hugh Price Hughes, and the other Nonconformist Samaritans from the Catholic point of view, who are distant as the poles in their religious views, declined absolutely to listen to the appeals of religious bigotry, and helped them, notwithstanding all the risks which they foresaw. I do appeal to hon. Members from Ireland sincerely, for the sake of their own country—I am not merely a Nonconformist ; I believe in the sacred cause, as they do, of small nationalities, of which they have been the guardians in this House—I appeal to them not to join, in oppressing Nonconformists who have been their friends, with the enemies of their faith and their race.

II.—MR. LLOYD GEORGE'S SPEECH AT LINCOLN, DECEMBER 12, 1902

WHEN I left the House of Commons this afternoon I told a very prominent Liberal politician, " I am off to Lincoln to address a meeting under the chairmanship of Mr. Perks." His reply was, " Well, then, really Liberal unity has arrived." During the last three or four years the energies of the Liberal Party have been paralysed by that horrible war. Now it is over, and there is nothing left but the bill. We have succeeded in killing the African hedgehog. I am afraid the result has been disappointing. There is not much fat on the poor animal ; scarcely a hide. There is nothing left but bristles. However, it is over at last, and the bills are coming in, and it is not such good fun to pay.

One of the bills is called the Education Bill. That is one of the bills which is coming in to be paid. If it had not been for the mandate obtained on this war no Government would have been returned to power that would have dared to submit a Bill of this kind to the judgment of Parliament. I venture to submit to you that it is one of the worst Bills that has ever been presented to the House of Commons, and I will give you a few reasons why. It perpetuates, in its worst form, a system of education which really retards educational progress in this country.

Has it not struck you as a curious thing that here is the richest country in the world, the nation that can best afford to give a good education, the nation that can least afford to give a bad education to the people, and yet it compares unfavourably with all its great trade rivals in that respect? I heard the great speech delivered by the Bishop of Hereford in the House of Lords last night. He was pointing this fact out, how unfavourably we compare in the matter of education given to the children of the people, with, say, Germany. Absolutely true. Compare us with practically any of those great Powers, any advanced, civilised Power, and we come badly out of the comparison. I was very curious the other day to compare the state of education in this country with Switzerland. Switzerland is not a rich country. If you take the valuation per head, as it were, the aggregate riches per head of the population, it would be a poor country compared with ours. And yet, how does Switzerland come out in educational comparisons? I will tell you. Switzerland spends fifty-five times as much per head of the population as this great and wealthy Empire, whose praises we are never tired of singing on our platforms. Never was such an Empire! Great! colossal!—I have forgotten the adjectives! There was a perfect ocean of them at the last election, and this Government swam into power on them. Never was such an Empire! And yet here is this one miserable little country of Switzerland, which has no Colonies, on whose dominions the sun does set, where the tax-collector does go to bed, which has no Navy, no great wars, no Colonial Secretary!—this little miserable country spends fifty-five times as much upon the development of the brains of its people as this great Empire.

Something has been said about Wales. Well, I am going to swagger now. Here is this country, the land of wretched Nonconformists, which grows nothing but Radicals—actually sends pro-Boers to Parliament— spends on secondary education twenty times as much per head of the population as this great country of yours. Are you surprised that they send Radicals to Parliament? Why does Wales spend so much on secondary education, as compared with primary education? I will tell you why. We got an Act of Parliament, ten or fifteen years ago, to establish a system of education there—secondary education—and we introduced a clause into it which declared that no catechism and no formulary of any sect should be taught in any school. What is the result? A Welsh bishop actually got up in the House of Lords, and said, last night, that the system was a grand success, and, curiously, the reason was that catechism and formularies were kept out of the school. Let him try the same experiment with the primary schools in England. In these schools two-thirds of the children come straight from the elementary schools. I remember when I used to travel to Carnarvon, the chief town in my constituency, by the eight o'clock train in the morning—I used to get up early in those days—when we came to a little mining village of Cwmffyngg —you cannot pronounce those names—you have not got secondary education—when you spend as much as Wales, you will be able to say Pwrnynnm. When we came to this little mining village, the carriage would be inundated with little youngsters so high—quarrymen's children ! Where were they going ? To the secondary schools, having won scholarships from the Board school, which enabled them to travel every morning, and get the same education as the richest man in that constituency. I'll tell you what we want ; less catechism and more education.

Well now I went into the matter of comparing—and you will get the material in these books which the Government have provided for us, but, as the Bishop of Hereford said, never read themselves, for comparing a Swiss canton and an English county of exactly the same size and population. I took Berne and Gloucestershire. The result is very curious. The canton of Berne spends every year, out of the rates mind you, £148,000 a year upon secondary and technical education. There is a sort of prejudice against secondary education here, because they say it is the education of the children of the people who can afford to pay for education. That is not what secondary education means in Switzerland. Every peasant's child gets it exactly the same as the son of the richest man of the canton. £148,000 a year ! What do you think they spend in Gloucester ? The same area, the same population, but three times the wealth ; they spend the colossal sum of £7,000 a year. There is not a secondary school in Gloucester maintained out of the rates, no school to which the children of the artisan class can go. Look at Berne ! There are seventy-two secondary schools maintained by the canton. One School of Commerce, one University, one School of Fine Arts, one veterinary school, five training colleges for primary teachers, one training college for secondary teachers ; all maintained by a canton of the size of Gloucester. Compare the two ! Are you surprised that the Swiss lads beat your Gloucester lads when they meet them ? What advantage has Gloucester ? Oh, they say, you must sacrifice something to get a good religious education. Gloucestershire has the inestimable advantage of a superior theology. Has it ? Is the theology of Gloucester superior to that of Berne ? The best of its theology comes from that country. Like everything else that is borrowed it is rather soiled and damaged by the borrower. Are the Gloucester morals superior to those of Switzerland ? I can only look at the police rate, and I find Gloucester spends three or four times as much on its police. Is the Gloucester cheese even better ? I don't believe it is, even when it is ripe with reaction. This is what I am coming to. How is it that England, with all its wealth, with all its enterprise—for it has no lack of enterprise—with all its courage and daring whenever it undertakes any task, how is it that it is so far behind these countries in the matter of education ? There is but one answer. We are not spending money on education according to our needs. We are spending it purely and simply according to the extent to which our rulers dare go to support the sectarian system, without giving up the control. The one thing they are thinking about is the sectarian schools, and whenever there is a great educational demand, the first thing they say is, not " Is it necessary ? " not " Will it be of advantage to education ? " Not at all. The first question they ask is, " What will be the effect upon the sectarian schools ? " Well now, I say if any system makes it necessary for a big party in the State to address such a question to itself before it does what is necessary for the people, that system should be doomed.

Now I have compared these two systems and given you the reason why I think we are not making progress.

This is a very serious thing for this country. Take it if you like from the trade point of view. Purely from the industrial point of view it is a very serious matter. We need not be reminded that we are engaged in a series of wars more dangerous to our supremacy than the South African War. War with the United States. War with Germany. What kind of a war ? An industrial war, a war for commercial supremacy. Not long ago one of our biggest fleets was captured in this war. Mr. Perks is engaged with a commando up in London fighting an American army. I am very glad to say up to the present the English battalion under his command is more than holding its own. The result will be a great victory, I think, for General Perks and his army. But still it is really a serious war, and I am not sure how this country will come out of it. I am not myself a pessimist. I have always heard pessimistic prophecies ever since I was able to understand what was told me, and they never came to anything. Therefore when I am told the commercial supremacy of this country is disappearing, I say I have heard it before, and, now I am getting to be an old man, these things do not affect me. But still you must take these things into account. We can't go on for ever, unless we are prepared to meet the contingencies that arise from time to time. We ought to train our men. On the Continent they train every man to the use of arms. We ought to train every man to the use of his industrial arms. We ought to have our arms to fight in the peaceful battles, and unless we are trained we will be beaten by the better trained countries. But what happens here ? Everybody says you must train your youth ; you must develop their brains, strengthen their minds ; you must make them fit and proper men to fight the commercial battles of their country. But then the parson come in and says, " You must first of all learn my little drill-book—my halfpenny catechism first, and every little company must be under my command." Let us tell these gentlemen to clear out of the way. It is too serious a matter for this country to be bothered by the parson. He is blocking the traffic with his one-horse shay. Tell him, " My dear sir, your intentions are good, your motives first-rate, but we have got to get along, and unless you clear out of the way our motor-car will run over you." This battle is to be won by brains, and I don't think the parson can help us there.

Now let me show you what a serious difference it really makes. There was a very curious inquiry, set up by the State of Massachusetts in America, as to the effect education has upon what they call productivity. You know that we want to get an intelligent farmer. Yes, and to get that man to apply his intelligence to the land. The best manure you can give the land is brains, after all. Place him in your own district; he doubles the produce of the land, and if he doubles the produce he may double or quadruple the labour and be a benefit to the whole country around. I know a farmer; I have him in my mind now. I turn in there, and find a well-stocked library. Most of the farmers say, " Look at that man wasting his time on books. Alison's ' History of Europe,' Macaulay's ' History of England.' Good gracious! A good dung-heap would do him more good." But that farmer has put Macaulay's "History of England" into the land, and he is twice as good a farmer as any of his neighbours. This is not merely an agricultural problem. If I were to suggest to Mr. Chaplin that education had anything to do with agriculture he would be tremendously shocked. He would say it is all an affair of pure beer, and he would as soon think of educating his oxen. But it has; and what is true about the land is true about every industry. And now I am coming to Massachusetts. I started there before, but I took a cheap trip to Mr. Chaplin's constituency.

Now I will come back. What happened there? Throughout the United States the average attendance of children is four and a half years. What have they done in Massachusetts? There the compulsory average attendance is seven years per child. It means that they give a better education and a more thorough education in that State than in any other State. What is the result? They find that the average productivity—same capital, same opportunities, same labour—is 50,000,000 above that of any other State of the American Union. Do you follow it? By the same capital, by the same amount of labour, but with three years' extra accumulated brain-power, this State produces 50,000,000 a year more than any other State of the union. What would that mean in this country? Seven years, for every child, of education, from the bottom rung of the ladder to the top, helped up by the community—it would mean an increase of wealth annually of £300,000,000. With the same capital, the same people, but better brains. And how many problems would be solved! Capital might get a better remuneration without reducing wages. Wages might be increased, and still get better returns for capital. Above all, the improved condition of labour would bring the end of civil war between capital and labour, which destroys industry, creates bitterness and strife. But why Massachusetts, and not Lincoln? Same stock! This is the country they went from. It is from somewhere in the eastern counties that the New Englanders went. Why should the sons be better than their parents? I will tell you why. They will have no parsons meddling and wrangling. They say in America, " Religion, yes; but the Bible is good enough for us." We want the pure grain of the Gospel, not the husks of curates.

That is the industrial problem, but that is not all that education would do. Education is not merely useful for the purpose of grinding out mere wealth—filling the sacks more rapidly with better brains. I am not despising that.   There is too much poverty, too much misery, too much want and distress in this country for me to take a high line and say, " I won't take a material aspect of education."   I do.   You must feed these poor people.   Yes; and I wish some of these parson gentlemen, with their aristocratic friends in Parliament, would remember, when they talk about educating the masses and making them religious, that the great Founder of our faith fed the thousands first and taught them afterwards.   But that is not all.   What is the next thing you have to do ?   You want, with education to make, better citizens.   Not a thing to be despised.   Better citizens! The people reign now.   The " Government of the sovereign people " is not a mere phrase.   We say the Government is a bad one.   Heaven knows it is. But it is yours.   It is yours ; you have sent them there.   The people made them, and I hope the people are proud of their creation.   The people can unmake them.   And so they will.   If you make bad Governments they generally come from bad citizenship.   It is the people who are to blame. Don't let us flatter ourselves.   It is the people who are to blame for bad government in a democratic country.   Let us educate our sovereign.   The people are the sovereign power.   There are terrific problems in front of us. One can see them moving in the not very dim or distant future.   A little distress will bring them to the front.   A little of the storms of poverty, and the agitation which will come from it will sweep away the mists, and we shall be face to face with these terrible problems.   The hoar frost is thick on the ground.   We see these great meetings of the unemployed, and what they demand.   I don't know what the problems may be ; the future will decide in this country.   But one thing I know, I had rather trust them to settlement by an educated, thoughtful people, than I would to men who have got three years' catechism from the parsons.

That is not all.   Education does more than that.   The people, I venture to say, do not appreciate that education is more for them than for the rich.   The rich man can afford to be ignorant ; the poor man cannot. What does education do ?   It increases the power, widens the range, and improves the quality of the pleasures of life.   I had rather be a poor man with a sixpence to buy, say an " Ivanhoe," than an ignorant man who could send half-a-dozen relays to a well-stocked wine cellar any day. The greatest thing that is needed in this country is to teach the people that there are realms of unexplored delight for the educated man—the man who not merely learns to read, but who acquires the taste for it as well.   Let the people acquire the same craving for learning as they have got for drink—and the £140,000,000 drink bill, which ruins and wrecks and degrades the nation, will disappear like a morning miasma.   That is what education will do for this land, and for this Empire.   I won't say it will do everything, but it will do great things for any land; and here we are allowing a handful of selfish, greedy priests to stand at the doors of this popular paradise and to bar the entrance to the people.   Let us clear them out.

And what are they doing it for ?   They are not doing it for education. From any point of view the parson is the last man to whom I would hand over any administration.   I am not disparaging him as a parson.   He may be a most brilliant pulpit orator, and I dare say they all are. I don't know; I have never heard them. But the most brilliant pulpit orator is not the best administrator. Parsons are the men who are least acquainted with business, the men who have had the least training in business, and they should not be allowed to administer the most important branch of the communal administration. It is not their business. They are not cut out for it. It is not their calling. Let them stick to their business. There is plenty for them to do. They say, " Religion demands it ; that is the test for everything." Well now, religion is all right, and religion would be all the better if we had less of these theological squabbles about it. The best of religion is that which is common to all sects, and the most barren region of religion is that which is filled with theological controversy. We don't want to perpetuate these in the schools. You can't avoid them outside. Parsons must live, and it is quite as necessary to them as litigation is to the lawyers ; but what on earth have theological ideas to do with the qualification of a teacher ? Take a man for what he is, for what he knows, for the training he is possessed of, for his gift to impart the knowledge which is in him. And how will this bill work to select a teacher ?

Three men come, each of them having good certificates ; but every man who has got a good certificate is not a good teacher. Certificates don't decide a man's capacity, as any one will know. Well, the first man comes up. First-rate testimonials, splendid experience, all speak well of him. He has got first-class certificates from his training college, and the Board of managers say, " This is first-rate." Then the parson says, " What are your views about apostolic succession ? " The teacher says, " I have no views about it." Then the parson says, " You can go." Second man comes up. Very good testimonials, not so good as the first, still, they are good. Second-class certificates, second-class testimonials, second-class experience, and they say, " That is very good." The parson says, " Can you play the organ ? " and he says, " No, but I can play the cornet." They say, " No, thank you, I don't think that will do." Third man comes up. Third-class testimonials, third-class experience, third-class certificates. The parson says, " Can you play the harmonium ? " and he says, " Yes, like Paderewski." So Paderewski is appointed. First-class teaching testimonials don't count, even second-class don't count. The one thing which will dominate the selection of the teacher is the handiness of the man for the purpose of assisting the clergy on Sundays. He is the clerical handyman. We don't want that. The nation pays for the teaching, and the nation has a right to demand it.

Ah, but it is all religion. If there is any sort of mismanagement or tangle, it is always religion that is quoted, as if that didn't make it worse instead of better. Religion has taken care of itself for a good many years, and I think religion can do it yet. But the religion that depends upon the rate-collector, the bailiff, and the prison looming in the distance, is a failure. When religion calls in the assistance of the State, to the extent of that assistance that religion is a failure. Rate-collectors, police, bailiffs, gaol-warders, judges, all these men will bear witness to the failure of that particular religion. It is not merely an injury to the State; it is an insult to the Christian faith. "Oh ye of little faith," I would say to these parsons, "that ye should go to the rate-collector." Let them trust it. It will not benefit them—no, nor their creed—to associate force with the dire wrong to the consciences of half the people of this country.

But the bill has left the House of Commons. Sent with all its imperfections on its head, unhouseled, unanealed, to that legislative purgatory, the House of Lords. It has got worse in purgatory by now, and there is nothing we can do but send it to the other place. But we have in the next few years to fight this thing in every constituency, in every district, in every parish, fight it in the councils, fight it eventually at the polling booth. And then we will fight again on the floor of Parliament. It is to teach religion. I gave them a sample of what they were teaching in the House of Commons the other day. Would you like to have an extract? Well, now, those of you who have not had the advantage of the catechism, I will send you away with a good denominational instruction. This is the thing I was taught in one of these schools myself. I was taught to order myself lowly and reverently to my betters. With an inquisitive instinct I asked, "Who are my betters?" and they said, "The squire." Well, I had my doubts then. I have none now. But I will tell you what I did. Fifteen years after I submitted that very question to the electors of the Carnarvon Boroughs, as to whether he or I were the better man, and the majority, who knew us both, said the catechism was wrong. The squire could not believe it, said there must be a mistake, so he submitted the same question again, and they gave the same answer by an increased majority. So I believe he has given up the catechism. They say it is right that you should order yourself lowly and reverently towards men who are better than yourself. True, but that is not the interpretation. This is the interpretation given to the little children—I have got it out of a training college, for which you and I pay taxes, and it is taught to the students who are sent out as teachers. This is the explanation: "Explanatory questions and exercises. Who are our betters? Those in a higher position than ourselves, either by birth, wealth, or office." I don't say the chairman is not a better man than myself, but it is not a question of birth and wealth. You meet a man in the street, and you say, "I am not sure whether I should take my hat off to you or you to me. I am a faithful servant of the catechism. Would you, to inform me, tell me how much money you have in your pocket?" Then you count yours, and you say, "You have more—your humble servant." What is meant by being lowly? "By being lowly I understand I must know and keep my true position as being under them." You are to cringe to the rich. If you see a wealthy man crawl before him. You are to humble yourselves before the bank balances. What an unmanning faith! Do you call this Christianity? Is this what the carpenter's Son came down for? Is this what the Galilean fishermen faced the world in order to teach. Order yourselves lowly before the Roman centurions and senators, who are wealthy. That is not Christianity. And it is to keep this up, to buttress this, that you have got this educational system which is ruining

—ruining the education of millions of the children of this country. No, it is not religion. It is snobbery.

I had rather have the religion which, in America, brings the millionaire's son, side by side, to learn in the same school with the carpenter's son. Why? I will tell you why. Because the millionaire's son never knows what may happen to the artisan's boy at his side. He knows that the artisan's boy can climb up to the secondary school and to the university. And it is but a step for a capable man from there to the White House. There was once a rail-splitter who was President of the United States. No; this snobbery is out of date. Teach religion in the schools, give the children the Bible. Let Him speak to them in His own words, so simple that a child can understand them—not confused and perplexed by these theologies that priests for years and years have defined, until no man of ordinary intelligence can comprehend them. No; let all this din and clamour of priests and the schools subside. Let the children hear for themselves the voice of the best friend they ever had, and the most dangerous foe the priest could ever encounter.

III.—MR. LLOYD GEORGE'S ADDRESS TO THE PEOPLE OF WALES, ISSUED JANUARY 17, 1903

The Education Act of 1902 has brought Wales face to face with one of the most momentous practical problems it has probably ever been confronted with. Shall the Welsh Councils administer the Act at all, and if they determine upon administering it, then how and upon what lines? The decision Wales arrives at on these questions, and still more the manner in which it carries out that decision, will, in my judgment, largely determine the national position and prospects of the Welsh people for the immediate future.

It has been suggested that we should decline altogether to handle this Act administratively. It is contended that such a refusal, if backed up by the sixteen Welsh County Councils, would produce such a state of chaos and paralysis that the Government would be forced to concede complete popular control as the only alternative to educational anarchy. This proposal naturally appeals to the violent hostility which every true Liberal must have conceived against the provisions of this unrighteous measure, and equally against the methods by which the electorate was tricked into furnishing a majority for passing it.

Still, after much reflection, I have personally come to the conclusion that not only would it be unwise to pursue this course, but that by doing so we should be playing into the hands of the enemy. In the great majority of cases there is no greater tactical mistake possible than to prosecute an agitation against an injustice in such a way as to alienate a large number of men, who, whilst they resent that injustice as keenly as any one, either from tradition or timidity decline to be associated with anything savouring of revolutionary action. Such action should always be the last desperate resort of reformers. Amongst the men who will hesitate if our cause is discredited with violence will be found some of the best and most upright of our friends. We cannot afford to lose their valued aid and counsel in the great struggle before us. It behoves us also to think what the effect would be upon the education of the children. The school boards will disappear, and if the County Councils decline to carry on their work, the Education Department will set up some provisional arrangement, necessarily crude and imperfect, to fill up the gap. The interests of a whole generation of children will be sacrificed. It is not too big a price to pay for freedom, if this is the only resource available to us. But is it? I think not.

My advice is, let us capture the enemy's artillery and turn his guns against him. How is this to be done?

In considering this question, we ought to fix in our own minds what is the educational ideal we should aspire to in Wales. Having ascertained that, it remains but to consider the best and surest methods of arriving at this national objective.

When one contrasts the large measure of indifference to educational progress which unfortunately still prevails in considerable tracts of England with the undoubted educational zeal which is the most hopeful accompaniment of the national revival in Wales, it will be conceded that the Welsh people are much more likely to develop a sound and successful educational system, adapted to their genius and necessities, if left to work out their own ideas upon their own lines. Our object ought, therefore, to be to labour for complete educational autonomy for Wales. How would our purpose be best effected?

The first question the Councils will have to consider will be the formulation of a scheme under which the Act will be administered within their respective areas. It is of the utmost importance that, as far as the Welsh Councils are concerned, their schemes should, in their fundamental principles, be identical. To these cardinal points I shall now devote a few lines.

(a) The Act enables County Councils to combine for common educational purposes. At least, those who piloted the measure through the House of Commons stated that this power was conferred by the Act. The Welsh Central Board will remain in existence to control secondary education throughout the Principality; the only difference made by the Act in this respect is that under Sir Alfred Thomas's sub-clause the County Councils will appoint the representatives on that Board formerly nominated by the county governing bodies—a small but a salutary improvement. Every scheme ought therefore to provide:

1. For the appointment of representatives on the Central Board.
2. For the delegation to the Central Board of a portion, at least, of the powers given by the Act as to making provision for training of teachers and as to inspection and general supervision of elementary as well as secondary schools, and over all training colleges receiving grants from the Councils.

I attach great importance to the powers here mentioned being conferred upon a National Board. The work will be done more effectively and economically than by each county frittering away its resources in ostentatious and vain efforts to undertake tasks which it has not the means to adequately perform.

For contributions, on the basis of rateable value, to a common fund, to enable the Central Board to carry out the functions imposed upon it.

If something of this sort is done, there will come from a centra authority of this character, manned by experts and the picked business brains of the nation, an initiation and a guidance which will really co-ordinate all forms and grades of education, gradually bring up the backward counties to the level of the foremost, and build up the system of education which is best adapted to develop the intelligence of our race.

The only other suggestion I would make about the scheme is this :

(b) No schemes should contain a proviso for nomination by outside bodies which are not themselves representative of the ratepayers. The parish and district councils certainly ought to have a representation on the County Committee, and in my opinion the County Council would do well to leave the local management of the schools largely in the hands of these Councils, subject to the general control of the education authority.

Now, a few more suggestions as to what the education authorities might do towards ensuring efficiency and helping the movement for attaining complete popular control of all the schools.

1. They should forthwith instruct a competent surveyor or architect to report on the condition of all the school buildings within their area—whether, in respect of capacity, ventilation, sanitation, lighting, playground, and state of repair, they are up to the standard requirements. There should be no distinction on this score drawn either against or in favour of sectarian schools. If the report discloses deficiencies in the state of these schools, the education authority should, as a condition precedent to their taking over any responsibility for their maintenance, insist that these defects should be remedied and that the fabric should be put into good and tenantable repair. The Bishop of Manchester's amendment makes it all the more incumbent that this course should be pursued. If the Councils are to be liable for wear-and-tear, their financial responsibility should be confined to damage done after the Act came into operation. There are hundreds of the sectarian schools that have not been even painted or whitewashed for years, whereof the memory of man runneth not to the contrary. The sectarian schools should be properly cleansed and clothed before they are allowed to associate on equal terms with more decently clad institutions.

2. It is also advisable that a searching inquiry should at once be instituted into the endowments now administered by voluntary-school managers, with a view to taking action if necessary for securing them for the benefit of the parish rather than of the denomination.

3. Should the Councils give any subsidies out of the rates to the

denominational schools ? In my judgment, the education authorities should devote no portion of the public funds levied by them to any schools, unless the trustees consent (*a*) to give full and complete public control of the funds voted towards the support of these schools (this, of course, necessarily involves the appointment of the staff) ; (*b*) forego the imposition of all religious or political tests on the appointment of their teachers.

If any schools within the area decline to accept these conditions, money paid by the Treasury in respect of those schools might be transmitted to their managers, provided all the conditions as to efficiency, repair, etc., imposed by law are complied with, but no assistance should be given them out of the rates.

If, on the other hand, the managers of any denominational schools within the area exhibited any disposition to meet the educational authorities on these two vital points, for my part I would advocate the extension to such managers of ample facilities for teaching the children of their own denomination the doctrines of the Church to which the parents belonged. That is, I would in every county proffer to Churchmen the Colonial compromise. I believe it will be found that many moderate and tolerant Churchmen will deem that this concession fairly meets their views. If the majority of Churchmen are so ill-advised as to reject what their fellow-religionists in every British Colony accept as a satisfactory solution of their difficulties, the responsibility for the strife, bitterness, and consequent mischief which will inevitably ensue must rest with them. At any rate, in making them this tender we shall have done all that neighbourly good feeling can possibly demand.

What I have written above represents simply my view of the general principles which ought to be borne in mind in shaping our administrative policy under this Act. As to non-payment of rates, there will be no need for such a method of action if the Councils act on these principles. If, on the other hand, certain county, town, or urban councils decide to levy a rate towards the support of the denominational schools without securing full control of those schools, what course ought Liberals and Nonconformists then to pursue ? Personally, I have no hesitation in the matter. The Parliament which passed the Act was elected on other issues. The Councils which will administer the Act for the next twelve months were also elected on other issues. If the latter, therefore, decide, before the Council elections of 1904, to levy rates for propagating doctrines profoundly disbelieved in by the bulk of their constituents, Nonconformists should make the collection of those rates as difficult as possible. If, on the other hand, the question is left in abeyance until after the elections of 1904, and the electors then choose to return denominationalists to the Councils, we ought to accept their judgment on the point, unless we are prepared to say that under no conditions would we contribute any rates or taxes towards denominational schools, even though the nation after due deliberation resolved upon it. In a democratic community like ours such a proposition seems untenable.

The Education Act of 1902 has presented Wales with its greatest political opportunity. It is exceptionally equipped, by training, convictions, and habits of thought, to take full advantage of this opportunity. Wales presents the spectacle of a well-ordered and highly disciplined community, where intense political and religious convictions produce no excesses which repel the most sensitive friend of good order. A patriotism at once as ardent and as broad as that which inspires any nation in the world. A patriotism which has not fallen into the fatal error of confounding depth of greed with breadth of outlook, or into the equally fatal error of imagining that war and politics are the only fields where a man can exhibit his love for his native land. A patriotism which for generations was almost purely literary before it became religious, which was religious fully a century and educational at least a generation before it annexed politics, and which, in adding new interests and activities to the national life, never forsook the old. If in this great struggle we are now entering upon Wales acts with a firm courage and a dignified restraint—and I feel confident of its strength to do so—it will emerge from the conflict with a national position surpassing the dreams of the line of prophets who foretold great things for " Gwalia Wen " ere they passed to their rest under the shadow of its hills.

Printed by Hazell, Watson & Viney, Ld., London and Aylesbury.